PENGUIN BOOKS

THE PEEPSHOW

Kate Summerscale, formerly the literary editor of *The Telegraph*, is the author of *The Book of Phobias and Manias* and *The Suspicions of Mr. Whicher*, a number one bestseller in the UK, which was translated into more than a dozen languages and won the Samuel Johnson Prize for Non-Fiction and the British Book Awards Book of the Year. Her first book, *The Queen of Whale Cay*, won a Somerset Maugham Award and was shortlisted for the Whitbread Biography Award; *The Wicked Boy* won the Edgar Award for Best Fact Crime; and *The Haunting of Alma Fielding* was shortlisted for the Baillie Gifford Prize. Summerscale lives in London.

***

PRAISE FOR *THE PEEPSHOW*

A *NEW YORK TIMES* NOTABLE BOOK OF 2025 * A *NEW YORK TIMES BOOK REVIEW* EDITORS' CHOICE * NAMED A BEST BOOK OF 2024 BY *FINANCIAL TIMES* * WINNER OF THE 2025 ALCS GOLD DAGGER FOR NON-FICTION * NOMINATED FOR THE WOMEN'S PRIZE FOR NON-FICTION

"Riveting . . . Simultaneously revels in and criticizes the press's shameless bravado in shaping the Christie murder investigation . . . The author questions our own ambivalent complicity in the 'peep-show' of true-crime reportage. . . . Ms. Summerscale's evocation of Christie's purse-lipped self-satisfaction and his bossy, neurotic pride relates British repression to obsession, prudishness to prurience."

—Sara Lodge, *The Wall Street Journal*

"Summerscale, the multiple-award-winning author of six previous books, brings a novelist's eye and a sociologist's understanding to a trove of thrilling material. . . . Peppered with eccentric figures and interesting asides . . . Summerscale gives equal time to Christie's unfortunate victims, treating them as real people rather than pawns in someone else's story. And she skillfully examines the racism, sexism, economic privation, and class prejudices that permeated postwar England. . . . There's so much to admire in this engaging, deeply researched book." —Sarah Lyall, *The New York Times Book Review*

"Very good . . . Persuasive social analysis, both historical and contemporary . . . Absorbing, authoritative, and well researched."
—Chris Hewitt, *The Minnesota Star Tribune*

"A gripping true-crime tale that is an unflinching portrait of a postwar Britain riven with sexism and racism."
—*Financial Times*, Best Books of 2024

"Summerscale . . . revisits one of the most controversial murder cases in British history in this engrossing true crime page-turner. . . . She introduces a few eyebrow-raising wrinkles to the publicly accepted narrative and paints a compassionate portrait of the victims. It's a rigorous look at a still-potent tragedy." —*Publishers Weekly*

"Exhaustively researched . . . the arrest of John Reginald Halliday Christie, his trial, and his eventual execution serve as a narrative clothesline upon which hang detailed biographies of the key players, set amid a racist and misogynistic society slowly emerging from the rubble of the Blitz . . . the haunting biographies of the victims themselves, their families, and their upbringings. The true heartbreak lies in its depiction of poverty-stricken young women who were sex workers or much-less-well-paid cleaners and domestic servants, some sleeping in public lavatories. The cruelty and indifference meted out to them strikes the reader as true crime." —*Kirkus Reviews*

"Gripping, entertaining." —*BookPage*

"[An] absorbing portrait of post-WWII London." —*Booklist*

"A remarkable read, riveting without ever being salacious, this offers a fresh perspective on one of Britain's most notorious cases. Rillington

Place has often been covered but Summerscale recreates the grime, greyness, and repression of an utterly different era with a novelist's eye and an appreciation of the difficult, rootless lives of the victims."

—Judges, ALCS Gold Dagger for Non-fiction

"Summerscale captures all the horrible fascination of Christie's crimes but also expertly situates them in their troubled postwar setting. The result is a gripping account of murder, misogyny, and spectatorship that has implications well beyond the tragic orbit of the case itself. A haunting, thought-provoking, deeply unsettling book."

—Sarah Waters, author of *Tipping the Velvet*

"Once more, Kate Summerscale shatters our preconceptions of a classic crime." —Val McDermid, author of *Past Lying*

"There are few authors whose work I look forward to as much as Kate Summerscale's, and *The Peepshow* does not disappoint. It is a forensic reappraisal of a grimy episode in postwar British history; at once shocking, impeccably researched, lucidly written, and always utterly compelling." —Graeme MaCrae Burnet, author of *His Bloody Project*

"Kate Summerscale's multilayered page-turner *The Peepshow*, which inverts the classic true-crime structure, is masterful. The mystery is not who committed a series of murders in 1950s London but whether there had been a gross miscarriage of justice, as told through one tabloid reporter's attempt to redeem himself by revealing it. It's also an unflinching examination of the true-crime industry—a look at the boundary between making visible the unseen and the exploitation of tragedy—and no one, not even the reader, escapes complicity."

—Becky Cooper, author of
We Keep the Dead Close

"*The Peepshow* is a masterclass in true-crime storytelling. Stark and compulsive, it tells a story both of murder and those who write about it in a way that is as relevant now as it was in the 1950s."

—Jennie Godfrey, author of the *Sunday Times*
bestseller *The List of Suspicious Things*

"I blame *The Peepshow* for too many late nights, when I simply couldn't put it down. Horrifying, intriguing, and entertaining in equal measure."

—Becky Holmes, author of *Keanu Reeves Is Not in Love with You*

"Quite apart from its superb pacing and prose, and its deep social history, there is a brilliant strain of feminism."

—Laura Cumming, author of *Thunderclap* (via X/Twitter)

"*The Peepshow* is a savory story sure to keep readers up all night. Summerscale delivers a jewel in the true crime genre, one so thoroughly researched and deliciously British that for anyone to miss it would be to miss out on something masterful."

—Jax Miller, author of *Hell in the Heartland*

"A crystalline, compelling account of a notorious crime you think you know well . . . Seamlessly blends the pleasures of a good novel with the enlightenment of masterly reportage. A gem."

—Dominic Nolan, author of *Vine Street*

"Summerscale rebuilds the dark past with such captivating intelligence that she makes eyewitnesses of us all."

—Laurence Scott, author of *Picnic Comma Lightening*

"This intelligent and implacable account of a notorious postwar horror proves that no established memory of the past is definitive. *The Peepshow* is ruthless for truth, for previously unregarded details that expose the true horrors of a conflicted landscape, internal and external. This re-visioning of a dark London nightmare has the rigor and complexity of the best novels."

—Iain Sinclair, author of *Pariah Genius*

"Gripping as a thriller and supremely atmospheric, *The Peepshow* gazes inside the murder house of 10 Rillington Place and reveals, beyond that, the bombed-out postwar Britain that this sad, sordid, significant case both fascinated and reflected. Superb storytelling from the queen of true crime."

—Laura Thompson, author of *Take Six Girls*

"[One of] the best true crime writers working today . . . Summerscale has uncovered a wealth of information." —Meaghan Walsh Gerard

"A gripping, pacily written peek into a lost world."
—Robbie Millen, *The Times* (Books of the Year)

"A remarkable new look at the Rillington Place murders . . . In a manner reminiscent of Hallie Rubenhold in *The Five: The Untold Lives of the Women Killed by Jack the Ripper*, Summerscale restores the dignity of Christie's victims. . . . In portraying the public hunger for sensationalism, or chronicling the race riots in Notting Hill in 1958, the author draws no explicit parallels with the present day. She trusts that her readers will make their own conclusions, and her work is the more powerful for it. I hope she will forgive me if I say that—in the best sense—this is an awful book: but its shocking truths are necessary ones." —Erica Wagner, *Financial Times*

"Summons up a murky London underworld . . . *The Peepshow* examines the macabre saga with tremendous skill and verve."—*The Times*

"An inspired storyteller . . . Summerscale's greatest achievement . . . is to empathize with the victims of Christie's violence. In the 'true crime' genre there is a tendency to focus on the monstrous criminal, leaving his victims to fade into the background. The author resists this temptation, revealing the complex characters of the women who were murdered. . . . A meticulously researched and lively tale of crime, journalism, and gender roles in postwar Britain."
—Joanna Bourke, *The Times Literary Supplement*

"*The Peepshow: The Murders at Rillington Place* . . . is Kate Summerscale's most affecting historical true crime since *The Suspicions of Mr. Whicher*. . . . She pieces together Christie in the way you might try to repair a smashed mirror: no matter how well the pieces seem to fit, the overall impression is that of disturbingly multifarious personality who seemed, while on trial, 'a bemused spectator of his own atrocities.' . . . All told, it's a masterful piece of work."
—Declan Burke, *The Irish Times*

"Every bit the gripping, page-turning treat that true-crime fanatics salivate for. What sets it apart is the author's decision to use this classic murder story to expose the rotten underside of postwar Britain in the early 1950s. She paints a backdrop of grime and squalor, of flickering gas lamps, toxic smogs, and bombed-out dereliction, bringing to the fore a society that routinely demeaned women and eroticized violence against them, particularly through a flourishing tabloid press."

—Mark Bostridge, *The Spectator*

"Takes a novel approach to the retelling of the Christie murders . . . [Summerscale] skewers an era, the squalid, rackety, hand-to-mouth life of 1950s London, its pawn shops and doss houses and late-night cafes. . . . Books like *The Peepshow* invite us to look closer."

—Anthony Quinn, *The Observer*

"As one would expect from the author of *The Suspicions of Mr. Whicher*, this is a riveting read, grisly and chilling though much of the detail is. By making the figures of Harry Procter and Fryn Tennyson Jesse so prominent, Summerscale finds a new way of telling the story, and she draws on an impressive amount of research to re-create a postwar world of bombsites, squalid living conditions, prostitution, backstreet abortions and eye-wateringly blatant racism, while not neglecting the wider, happier world represented by the coronation."

—Nigel Andrew, *Literary Review*

"Journalistic hunger for lurid detail combines with intelligent consideration of the ethical implications of exploring true crime."

—Maggie Fergusson, *The Tablet*, Books of the Year 2024

"Now, we can re-examine [the murders] through the probing eyes and incisive mind of Kate Summerscale, who has a penchant for the macabre in British domestic life and a gift for conjuring the feel and smell of a time and a place. . . . Gripping . . . Summerscale has worked hard to find out as much as she can about the lives of each of Christie's victims."

—Ysenda Maxtone Graham, *London Review of Books*

"Engrossing."

—*Crime Monthly*

"Littered with delicious details of time and place . . . I don't do true crime, but this is one of the best books I've read all year."

—Declan Burke, RTÉ Radio 1 *Arena*

"The most gripping true crime story I have ever read . . . You feel, as she describes Notting Hill in 1953, and all that is going on there, that this is alien soil. Miss Marple and Hercule Poirot would have been out of their depth, though maybe Dostoyevsky would have felt at home."

—A. N. Wilson, *The Tablet*

"This gripping true-crime investigation breathes life into the women whose lives were ended there and suggests a thought-provoking new theory."

—Deirdre O'Brien, *Best* magazine

"*The Peepshow* is a compelling re-examination of this macabre saga."

—*The Week*

"Gripping, thrilling, deeply researched, *The Peepshow* sweeps you up into the world of 10 Rillington Place, the lives of the victims, and the terrifying search for the killer. Heart-stopping, unforgettable."

—Kate Williams

BY THE SAME AUTHOR

The Queen of Whale Cay
The Suspicions of Mr. Whicher
Mrs. Robinson's Disgrace
The Wicked Boy
The Haunting of Alma Fielding
The Book of Phobias and Manias

KATE SUMMERSCALE

THE PEEPSHOW

THE MURDERS AT RILLINGTON PLACE

PENGUIN BOOKS

PENGUIN BOOKS
An imprint of Penguin Random House LLC
1745 Broadway, New York, NY 10019
penguinrandomhouse.com

ISBN 9780593653654 (paperback)

THE LIBRARY OF CONGRESS HAS CATALOGED THE HARDCOVER EDITION AS FOLLOWS:
Names: Summerscale, Kate, 1965– author.
Title: The peepshow : the murders at Rillington Place / Kate Summerscale.
Description: New York : Penguin Press, 2025. |
Includes bibliographical references and index.
Identifiers: LCCN 2024050263 (print) | LCCN 2024050264 (ebook) |
ISBN 9780593653630 (hardcover) | ISBN 9780593653647 (ebook)
Subjects: LCSH: Christie, John Reginald Halliday. | Evans, Timothy John, 1924–1950. |
Serial murderers—England—London—Case studies. |
Murder—Press coverage—England—London—Case studies. |
Murder Victims—England—London—Case studies.
Classification: LCC HV6248.E75 S86 2025 (print) | LCC HV6248.E75 (ebook) |
DDC 364.152/3209421—dc23/eng/20250205
LC record available at https://lccn.loc.gov/2024050263
LC ebook record available at https://lccn.loc.gov/2024050264

First published in Great Britain by Bloomsbury Circus,
an imprint of Bloomsbury Publishing Plc, 2024
First published in the United States of America by Penguin Press,
an imprint of Penguin Random House LLC, 2025
Published in Penguin Books 2026

Printed in the United States of America
1st Printing

The authorized representative in the EU for product safety
and compliance is Penguin Random House Ireland, Morrison Chambers,
32 Nassau Street, Dublin D02 YH68, Ireland, https://eu-contact.penguin.ie.

For Sam

CONTENTS

'As for this particular key, it is the key to the small room at the end of the long passage on the lower floor. Open anything you want. Go anywhere you wish. But I absolutely forbid you to enter that little room, and if you so much as open it a crack, there will be no limit to my anger.'

Charles Perrault, 'Blue Beard' (1697), trans.
Maria Tatar in *The Classic Fairytales* (1998)

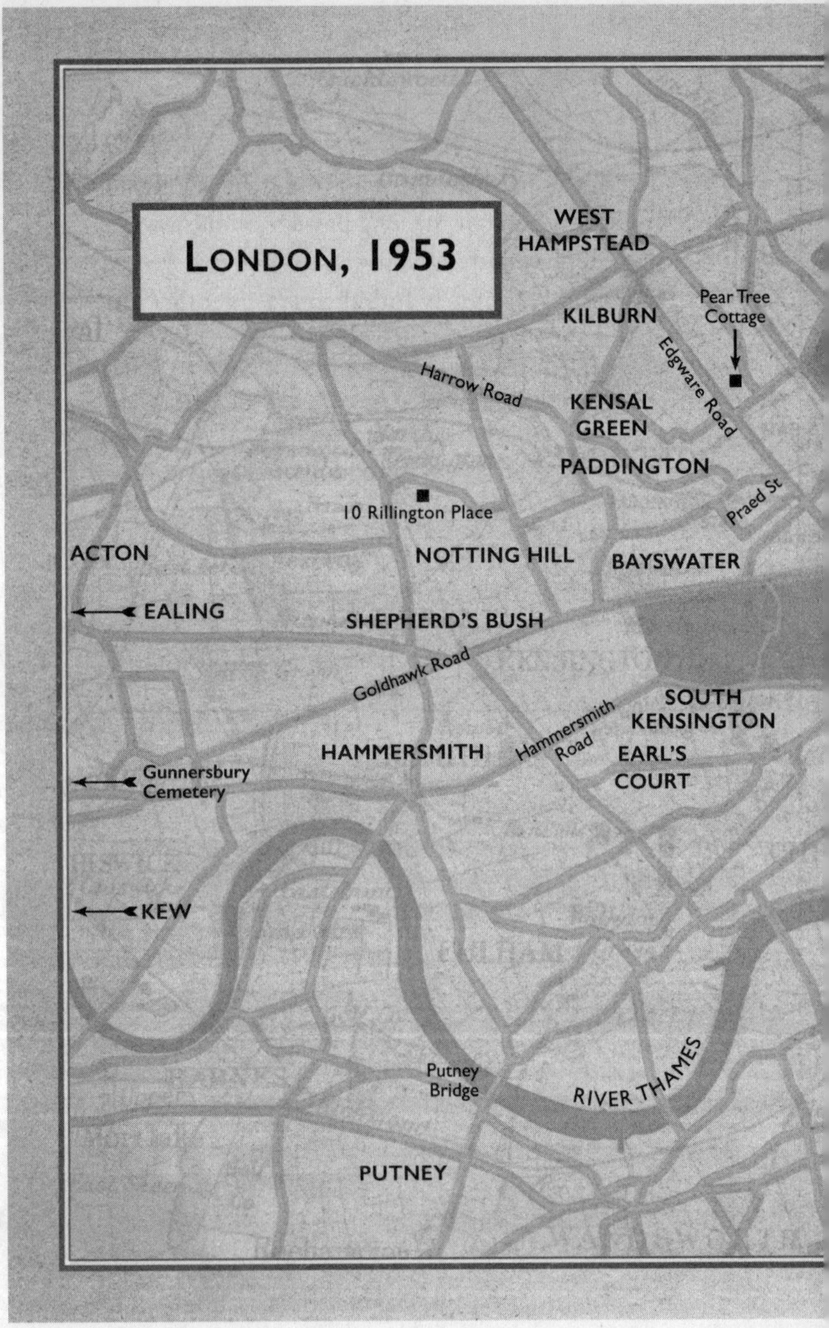

LONDON, 1953

WEST HAMPSTEAD
KILBURN
Pear Tree Cottage
Edgware Road
Harrow Road
KENSAL GREEN
PADDINGTON
Praed St
10 Rillington Place
ACTON
NOTTING HILL
BAYSWATER
EALING
SHEPHERD'S BUSH
Goldhawk Road
SOUTH KENSINGTON
Hammersmith Road
HAMMERSMITH
EARL'S COURT
Gunnersbury Cemetery
KEW
Putney Bridge
RIVER THAMES
PUTNEY

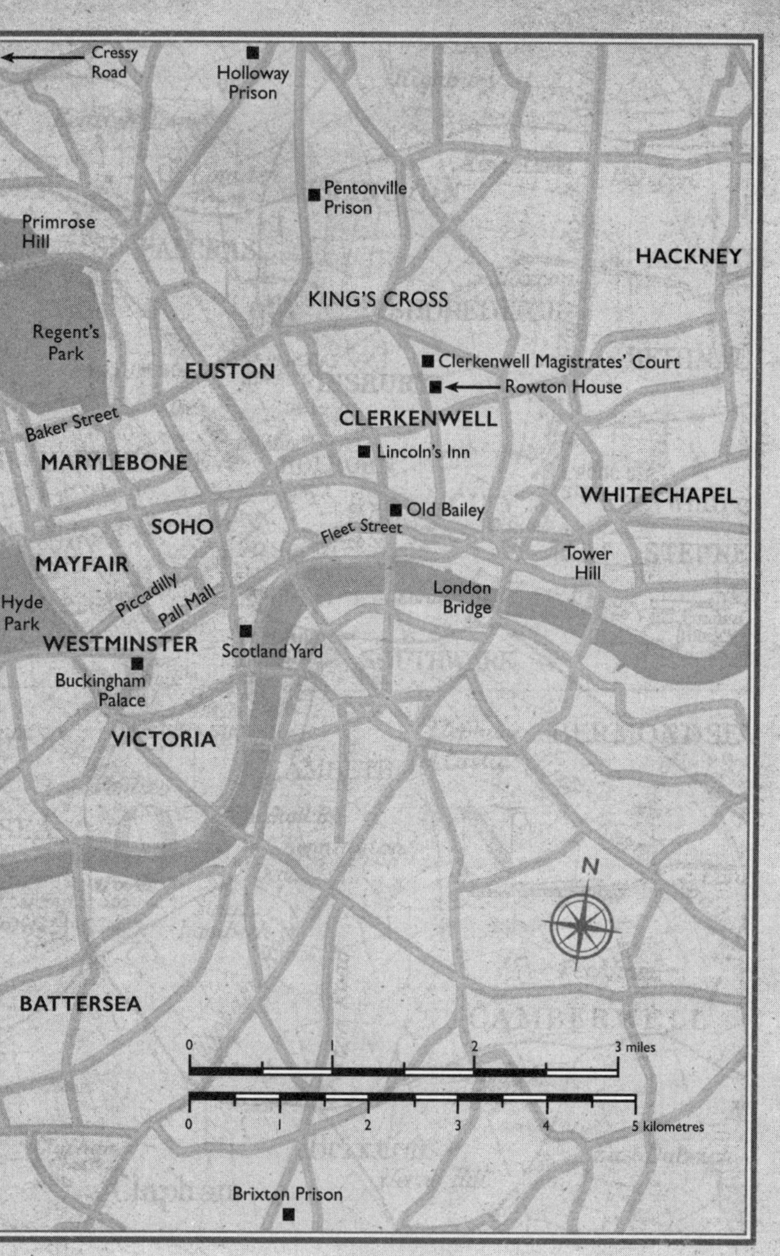

Cressy Road
Holloway Prison
Pentonville Prison
Primrose Hill
HACKNEY
KING'S CROSS
Regent's Park
EUSTON
Clerkenwell Magistrates' Court
Rowton House
CLERKENWELL
Baker Street
Lincoln's Inn
MARYLEBONE
WHITECHAPEL
Old Bailey
SOHO
Fleet Street
MAYFAIR
Tower Hill
London Bridge
Hyde Park
Piccadilly
Pall Mall
WESTMINSTER
Scotland Yard
Buckingham Palace
VICTORIA
N
BATTERSEA
0
1
2
3 miles
0
1
2
3
4
5 kilometres
Brixton Prison

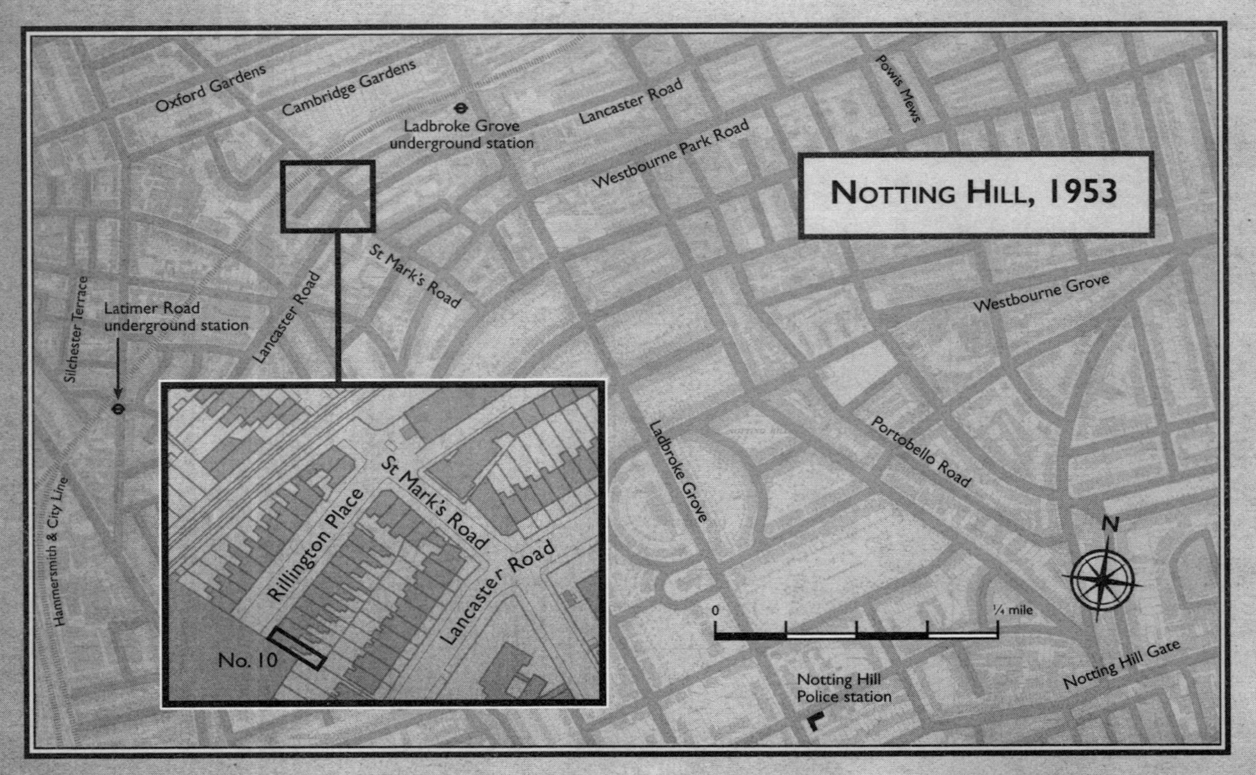

Notting Hill, 1953
Oxford Gardens
Cambridge Gardens
Ladbroke Grove underground station
Lancaster Road
Powis Mews
Westbourne Park Road
St Mark's Road
Lancaster Road
Silchester Terrace
Latimer Road underground station
Westbourne Grove
Portobello Road
Ladbroke Grove
Hammersmith & City Line
Rillington Place
St Mark's Road
Lancaster Road
No. 10
0
¼ mile
N
Notting Hill Police station
Notting Hill Gate

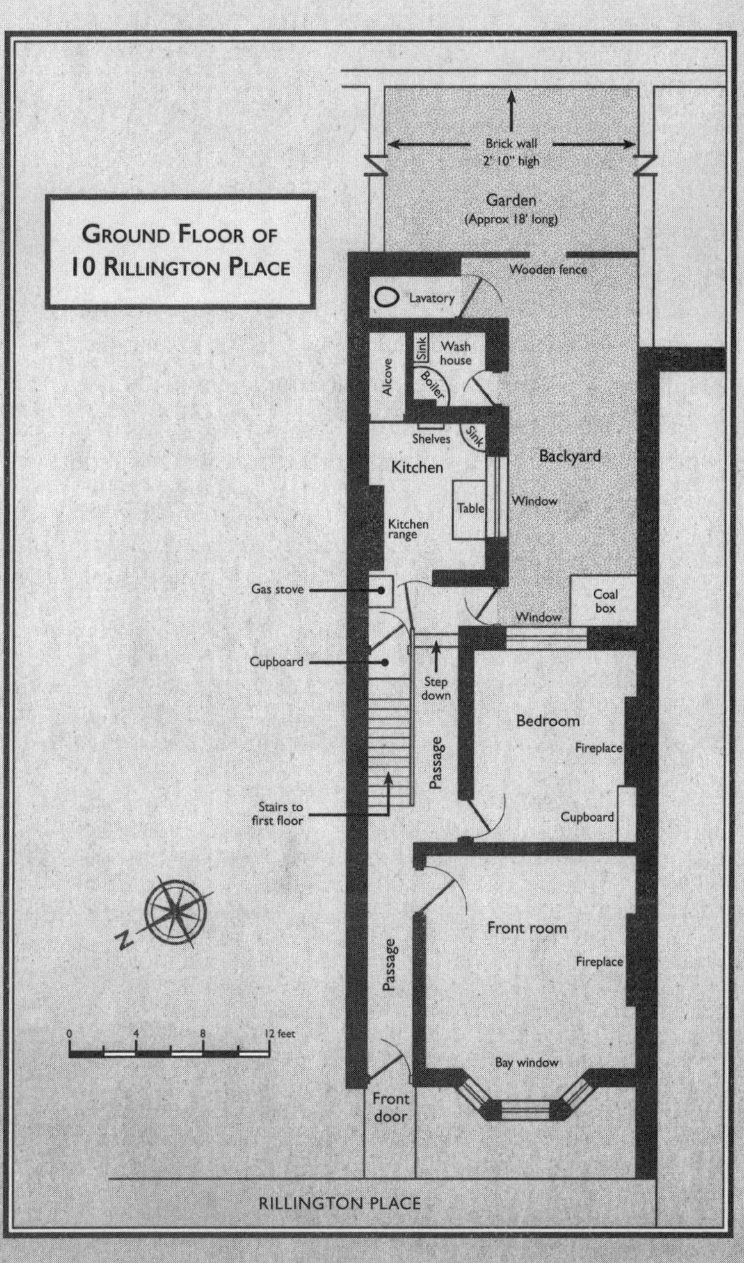

Ground Floor of 10 Rillington Place
Brick wall 2' 10" high
Garden (Approx 18' long)
Wooden fence
Lavatory
Sink
Wash house
Alcove
Boiler
Sink
Shelves
Kitchen
Backyard
Window
Table
Kitchen range
Gas stove
Window
Coal box
Cupboard
Step down
Bedroom
Fireplace
Passage
Cupboard
Stairs to first floor
Front room
Fireplace
Passage
0
4
8
12 feet
Bay window
Front door
RILLINGTON PLACE

A NOTE ON MONEY

£1 in 1953 is the equivalent of about £30 (or $40) today.

A shilling, a twentieth of £1, is the equivalent of about £1.50 ($2).

A penny, a twelfth of a shilling, is the equivalent of about 12 pence (15 cents).

PREFACE

At about 8 o'clock one foggy night in March, Christina Maloney was soliciting for custom outside the cheap hotels and boarding houses in Sussex Gardens, a dilapidated stucco terrace in Paddington, when she was approached by a thin man in spectacles. He was dressed in a suit, a brown overcoat and a brown trilby. Even with his hat on, she could see that he was going bald. They exchanged a few words on the pavement, shielded from the main road by a railed enclosure of plane trees and hedges.

Christina asked the man if he wanted to come home with her. He suggested that she come to his place instead. He was an estate agent, he said, who let out flats to girls like her, and he had a basement that he could show her. Christina declined his offer. She didn't go to strangers' houses, she told him.

The man said that he might come back the next morning, but he seemed first to want to know more about Christina's accommodation. 'Do you live in the basement?' he asked. No, she said, her room was on the second floor. 'Are there any other people on the same landing?' Yes, Christina said, but they were out during the day. 'Are you sure that there will be nobody else in tomorrow?' She said that she couldn't be certain.

Now the man changed tack.

'Have you got any photographs of girls in the nude?' he asked.

Christina said that she didn't.

'Well, there is always you,' he said.

'That's right,' she replied.

He asked her where she was from. She told him that she had just moved to London from Ireland.

The man proposed that he return to Sussex Gardens the next day at noon, and after he and Christina had done some 'business', she could come to his flat for a session with his photographers. He would pay her £2 an hour, he said. She agreed, and he left.

The stranger did not turn up the next day as promised. But just over a week later, on Sunday 29 March 1953, Christina recognised his photograph in the *News of the World*.

PART ONE

I

In the walls

In the evening of Tuesday 24 March 1953, Harry Procter, the star crime reporter of the *Sunday Pictorial*, drove over to a Victorian terrace in Notting Hill in which the bodies of three young women had been discovered. They were rumoured to have died accidentally, in botched back-street abortions, but Harry thought the story worth checking out anyway. He was used to working all hours, shuttling between his office in Fleet Street, crime scenes, pubs, courts and police stations. Over the past few years he had become known throughout Britain for his scoops and sensational exposés – 'Tell it to Harry Procter', people would say when they heard something outrageous. At thirty-six, after a decade and a half in Fleet Street, he looked like a weathered cherub. Harry drank, he smoked. He had tousled brown hair, pale skin, soft bags beneath his eyes.

Harry turned into Rillington Place, parked his car and switched off the headlights. The twenty small buildings in the cul-de-sac were lit by a single gas lamp, and the air was hazy with fog. Every few minutes, a Hammersmith & City Line train rumbled across a steel viaduct just out of sight above the roofs of the right-hand terrace. There were no railings outside the houses, no doorsteps, no plants, no trees. The chimney of a derelict factory rose over the high, blind wall that blocked the end of the street.

No 10 was the last building on the left, abutting the wall. Paint peeled from its sandstone portals, stains spread across its crumbling facade. A police constable stood guard at the front door, by a bay window hung with a dirty net curtain and a sagging sheet, while other officers moved in and out with tools and boxes. Neighbours peered from their windows, stepped from their houses to watch.

The police told Harry that the first body had been discovered that afternoon by a West Indian tenant who was cleaning the abandoned ground-floor kitchen. The lodger had torn a hole in the wallpaper as he tried to fix a shelf to the back wall, and in the shadows behind he saw what seemed to be the bare back of a white woman. He fetched a torch to make sure, then hurried with another tenant to a public telephone kiosk around the corner. The police came quickly. They ripped off the wallpaper, forced open a cracked piece of board that had been nailed to the wall and lifted out a body, only to find the corpse of another young woman beneath it, and behind that a third. The bodies at the back of the alcove were wrapped in cloth and smeared with earth and ashes.

The Criminal Investigation Department at New Scotland Yard despatched a squad of plainclothes detectives to North Kensington, and asked Dr Francis Camps, a well-known pathologist from the London Hospital in Whitechapel, to attend the crime scene. Camps was dining with the hospital's head of anatomy when he was summoned. In his dinner jacket and bow tie, he sped over to Rillington Place to inspect the bodies in the alcove, and then had them conveyed to Kensington mortuary, where he carried out post-mortems. Camps estimated that the women had been murdered within the past few weeks.

When the detectives searching the house pulled up the floorboards in the ground-floor front room, they discovered the corpse of a fourth woman. She was identified by a neighbour as Ethel Christie, a middle-aged housewife who had lived in the flat for fifteen years. Her husband, John Reginald Halliday Christie, had gone missing a few days earlier. Reg Christie was an accounts clerk and a former policeman, described by neighbours as the 'poshest' resident of the street. He immediately became the chief suspect in the murders.

Harry realised, with a shock, that he had not only been to 10 Rillington Place before, but had met the man the police were now seeking. Just over three years ago, as a reporter for the *Daily Mail*, he had been sent to interview Reg Christie when another tenant of the building was charged with the murders of his wife and child.

Back then, late one December evening in 1949, Harry had knocked at the front door of No 10. After a few minutes a balding, bespectacled figure opened the door a couple of inches and asked to see Harry's press card. The man peered at the card in the darkness, then gave a thin smile. 'I'm Mr Christie,' he said, holding out a clammy hand for Harry to shake. He led him down the communal hall and through a door into his kitchen. The walls of the house were thin, the floors uneven. There was no electricity in the property, so the rooms were lit with gas.

'Sit you down,' said Christie. He put a tin kettle on the stove. 'I know you reporters like something stronger,' he said, 'but I can only offer you tea.' He told Harry that his wife was asleep in the bedroom.

'You're a Yorkshireman, aren't you?' Christie asked, noticing Harry's accent. 'I was born in Yorkshire – many years ago, but you never forget the accent, do you?' There was no trace of the north in Christie's voice: he spoke with a genteel Cockney lilt.

Harry confirmed that he was from Leeds. Christie said that he had been born and brought up in Halifax, only twenty miles away.

Harry asked Christie about the murders of his neighbours. Christie said that he was happy to tell him what he had told the police. He and his wife had been friendly with the Evans family, who had rented the top-floor flat of No 10 for the past year. A few days ago, he had been horrified to learn that the bodies of Beryl Evans and her thirteen-month-old baby, Geraldine, had been found in a washhouse in the back yard, only a few feet away from where he and Harry were now sitting. Beryl's husband, Tim, had briefly accused Christie himself of killing her, but had since made a detailed confession to strangling both his wife and his daughter.

Christie told Harry that the upset had made him ill. He said that he hoped the killer would be punished.

He asked Harry: 'Who do you think murdered Mrs Evans and her baby?' He seemed nervy, Harry thought, almost ingratiating.

Harry saw Christie again a few weeks later, at Tim Evans's trial for murder at the Old Bailey. In court, Evans claimed that Reg had killed Beryl and Geraldine, but the jury did not believe him. There seemed no conceivable reason for Christie to have strangled another man's wife and child, nor for Evans to have made a false confession to their murders. Tim Evans, aged twenty-five, was convicted of murder and sentenced to death.

After the verdict, Harry found Christie in the lobby outside the courtroom, wiping tears from the lenses of his round, horn-rimmed spectacles. 'What a wicked man he is,' Christie had said to Harry, sadly.

The few crime reporters who attended the trial, recalled Harry, had considered it 'dull, sordid, unglamorous, dreary'. They dismissed Beryl and Geraldine Evans's killings as a 'fish and chippy' type of crime: a banal, vulgar, open-and-shut case of domestic violence that would quickly be forgotten.

But things looked different now. The latest discoveries at Rillington Place suggested that a serial killer of women was at large in London, and they also hinted at a terrible miscarriage of justice.

***

Harry had been inspired to become a reporter when, as a fifteen-year-old errand boy in a shoe shop in Leeds, he read Philip Gibbs's novel *The Street of Adventure*. He imagined newsmen racing for taxis as they investigated dastardly crimes, editors shouting into telephones, presses thundering in basements, vans speeding away with cargoes of crisply printed papers. He dreamed of working in Fleet Street.

One afternoon the shoe-shop manager caught him reading the book, for the umpteenth time, in the rat-ridden cellar that he was supposed to be sweeping. What did he think he was doing? his boss asked.

'I'm going to be an ace reporter,' declared Harry. 'One day you're going to see my name in big black letters across the front page of a national newspaper.'

Never before, the manager told him, had he had a lad in his shop whose head was filled with such rubbish. He fired him on the spot.

But Harry's mother encouraged his ambitions: she found the money to buy the youngest of her five children a typewriter and to sign him up for shorthand classes at night school. 'From now on you never go out without a pencil and some paper in your pocket,' she told Harry. 'Keep your eyes and ears open, write notes about everything you see. What interests you and me interests everybody, always remember that.'

Harry had only a basic education, but he was tenacious. He besieged local papers with stories, and then took to the road, sleeping in fields and hedgerows and hostels as he tried his luck as a reporter in different northern towns.

After a string of temporary jobs, Harry was hired back in Leeds by the *Yorkshire Evening News*. He learnt to work at speed, mentally composing a story as he investigated it so that he could dictate his copy straight down the line to the newspaper's typists: his mind, he said, was like a tape-recorder. And he was ruthless in getting a scoop. The novelist Keith Waterhouse, then working for the *Evening News*'s rival, the *Yorkshire Evening Post*, remembered that Harry beat him to the phone when they were both covering an inquest. As Harry emerged from the kiosk, he ripped the handset out of its socket, and passed it to Waterhouse, saying: 'All yours.'

In 1935, Harry fell in love with Doreen Vater, a tiny young woman from a village east of Leeds. She was already pregnant when they married that winter. She gave birth to a son, Barrie, in the spring of 1936, and twin daughters, Phyllis and Patricia, the next year. Harry couldn't spend much time with his family – he would leave home after breakfast and return long after the children had gone to bed – but thanks to his success at the *Evening News*, he was able to rent and furnish a nice house for them in Leeds.

In 1939, Harry was offered a week's trial at the bestselling London tabloid, the *Daily Mirror*. In great excitement, he caught the train to King's Cross, rented a room above an Italian café in Bloomsbury and presented himself at the *Mirror*'s offices off Fleet Street. His first story, about a watercress farmer who had taken his own life, did not impress the editor, but he was then sent to interview two very fat Australians on honeymoon in London. The photographer who accompanied him grumbled that they were on a fool's errand: there was no chance the editors would touch the story. But Harry was resolute. 'Not only will they touch it,' he said, 'they'll splash it.' His piece about the 'world's heaviest pair of newlyweds' filled that week's coveted centre spread. The *Mirror* offered Harry a permanent job, at nearly £10 a week, and he happily accepted.

By now the Procters had four children – the youngest, Valerie, was born in 1939 – and as soon as he could Harry moved the family down to a house in Beckenham, south-east of London. But Doreen suffered a stillbirth in 1940, when the neighbourhood was bombed by the Luftwaffe, and decided to move back to Leeds with the children. Harry rented a room for himself in Lincoln's Inn, a few minutes' walk from his office.

Harry soon learnt what was required of him. 'The *Mirror* wanted Sex,' he wrote. Sex 'sold papers – papers – papers by the million'. The *Daily Mirror* was pitched at a left-leaning, working-class audience, and it prided itself on a frank and unprudish approach to sexual matters. During the war it ran a campaign to raise awareness of venereal disease, as well as scores of photos of curvaceous women in swimsuits and underwear, and a risqué comic strip, 'Jane', whose heroine often ended up losing her clothes. Doreen was furious when a *Mirror* man turned up at the Procters' home in Leeds to photograph her legs – Harry had written a piece about the difficulty of buying his wife high-heeled size 2 shoes in Oxford Street.

Harry served at a Royal Air Force base in Yorkshire from 1940 to 1942, but spent the rest of the war as a reporter, becoming well known for his ingenuity and his nose for a story. In 1943 he took a new job at the *Daily Mail*, a more prestigious title than the *Mirror*. He proved a success there, too, and was sent to Europe as a correspondent with the American and British forces. During the Rhine Crossing of 1945, Harry was a passenger in an RAF aircraft bombing the German town of Wesel when he saw the plane carrying his *Daily Express* colleague explode in mid-air.

Later that year in a cinema in Leeds, said Harry, his mother, wife and son were startled to see him on the newsreel before the main feature. He was standing next to King George VI and President Truman, having sneaked on to an American warship moored at Plymouth. He grinned at the camera as the two dignitaries shook hands.

'Look, Mum, that's my Dad,' cried Barrie.

'A meeting of the Big Three,' said Doreen wryly.

After the war the newspaper trade became more frenetic than ever. Eighty per cent of the 50 million people in Britain read a daily paper, a greater number than anywhere else in the world. Professional photographers chased after film stars and criminals, snatching images to splash across the pages of the papers, and journalists were expected to do anything for a story. 'One minute a reporter may be trying to gatecrash an earl's wedding in a hired morning coat,' said one of Harry's colleagues; 'an hour later he is in Stepney, persuading a group of stevedores that he is one of them.'

As a Fleet Street journalist, a working-class man like Harry could go anywhere – and Harry did. When the *Express* bought a helicopter to give its reporters an advantage over the opposition, Harry's editor was sanguine: 'They've got a helicopter,' he said; 'we've got a Harry Procter.'

Shortly before Philip Mountbatten's marriage to Princess Elizabeth in 1947, Harry and a photographer blagged their way into Philip's stag party at the Dorchester Hotel, and some of their rivals stole in after them. As the photographers took pictures of the guests, Philip grabbed one of their cameras. 'You've had your fun,' he said, 'now let me have a go.' He took pictures of the newspaper men, then pelted them with the spent flashbulbs lying about the room. The papers ran one of his photos of the beaming hacks the next morning.

In 1951 Harry was hired by Hugh Cudlipp, the famously populist editorial director of the *Mirror* and the *Sunday Pictorial*, as the *Pictorial*'s chief reporter. His immediate boss was the news editor, Fred Redman, a rumpled, red-faced, genial figure who chain-smoked cheap cigars. 'Harry,' said Redman as he bought him a beer, 'you're going to have fun on the *Pic*. You're going to have a hell of a time.' Redman told new recruits that he would turn a blind eye if they got drunk at work, cheated a little on their expenses or slept with the secretaries, but they must never make mistakes in their copy.

At the *Pictorial*, Harry was expected to produce ever more sensational material. 'Though most English men and women cannot "let themselves go",' observed Geoffrey Gorer, who carried out a survey of the typical Briton for the *Sunday People* in 1951, 'they love to think and read about people who do throw off inhibitions, either with sex or violence.' From Tuesday morning to the early hours of Sunday, Harry plied his contacts with drinks, whisked his interviewees away from rival reporters, phoned his pieces in to the newsroom or rattled them off on his typewriter. One minute he was a sleuth, hardboiled as Sam Spade, and the next an impresario, staging a drama, engineering a confrontation. He was licensed to deceive.

There was plenty for Harry to investigate. The war had nearly bankrupted Britain and, though the Labour governments of 1945 to 1951 had introduced extensive health and welfare reforms, the living conditions of many Britons remained terrible. A severe housing shortage, caused partly by bomb damage and partly by the wartime moratorium on building, enabled landlords to charge huge rates for squalid premises. The crime rate doubled between 1938 and 1948, rising to more than half a million cases a year. The divorce rate rose more than tenfold, from fewer than 5,000 dissolutions in 1937 to 60,000 in 1947. The black market continued to flourish, as many goods were still rationed, and so did the sex trade: 10,000 prostitutes were thought to be working in London in 1951, making an estimated quarter of a million transactions a week.

'I exposed, and exposed, and exposed,' said Harry. 'I exposed the London Call Girl Syndicate, crooked financiers, white slavers, phoney doctors, peddlers in vice and drugs, unscrupulous landlords, swindlers, confidence tricksters; I exposed vile slums, black-marketeers, crooked politicians, dishonest officials in high places. I exposed husbands who deserted their wives, and wives who deserted their husbands.'

Harry's secret, wrote a fellow journalist, was that he did not just report a story; 'he infiltrated it, embedded himself, then owned it, then manipulated its protagonists as puppeteer-in-chief so that everything fell into place as, and when, and exactly how, he wished'. It was relentless, exhilarating work. For reporters, Gibbs wrote in *The Street of Adventure*, 'everything in life is but a peep-show'; they, as the observers, felt like 'the only real people in the world'.

Sales of the *Pictorial* rose by a million in the early 1950s, taking thousands of readers from the almighty *News of the World*. Harry's name regularly appeared in big black type on the front page, and he earned enough to secure a mortgage on a five-bedroom semi-detached house for his family in the pretty village of Pratt's Bottom, Kent.

But even Harry could miss a story, and he was afraid that the Evans case had been his worst miss yet. It suddenly seemed possible that the polite, soft-spoken clerk he had interviewed in 1949 had framed his upstairs neighbour for crimes that he had himself committed. By failing to suspect Reg Christie, Harry might have let an innocent man hang – and left Christie free to find more victims. He cursed himself for not having questioned him more closely at Rillington Place that night.

***

In the Scotland Yard press room on Thursday 26 March 1953, the police handed Fleet Street's crime reporters a photograph of

Reg Christie. He was a thin, pale-faced man with staring eyes, false teeth and spectacles, they said, who was wearing a mackintosh, a grey suit, a light brown trilby and a striped pink shirt with a blue tie. He was a little over 5ft 8in tall. 'Every hour he is at liberty,' the police warned, 'the life of a girl or a woman in any part of the country may suddenly come to a terrible end.' They hinted that Christie had sexually assaulted his victims: 'If the murderer is not caught, there is nothing to stop him carrying out his bestial practices. No woman is safe from outrage and death while he is at large.'

The press descended on Rillington Place. Outside No 10, a reporter from the *Manchester Guardian* saw a six-year-old boy pick a spent matchstick from the gutter and start gouging moss out of the gap between two paving slabs. 'Hey, Johnny,' the child called to a friend, 'let's play dig up the bodies.' A twelve-year-old lit a cigarette butt he had just salvaged from the gutter, and held forth to three journalists about the local prostitutes and 'abortioners' with whom he was acquainted. A stout woman in carpet slippers emerged from a doorway and snatched up a collection of metal biscuit-tin lids that had been left on the pavement. 'Get these out of here!' she shouted as she hurled the lids across the road. 'How can I keep this place respectable? Murders and dirt and filth all day long.'

Leila Dymond, who lived with her parents at No 13, told the *Kensington Post* that she had been too frightened to sleep since the women's bodies had been found. She hoped the police would be gone by the weekend, she said, as she was getting married on Saturday. The owner of the Rainbow Café, on the corner of Rillington Place and St Mark's Road, said the neighbourhood was rife with crime. 'I've been in plenty of tough areas in London,' Mr Wood told a reporter from the *Daily Mirror*, 'but this beats the lot. I've never seen such hooligans in my life.' Harry Procter, having shared a Notting Hill flat with a fellow journalist in the 1940s, was familiar with this local underworld: the prostitutes who worked the streets, the spivs and flash boys who frequented the drugs dens, gambling clubs, pubs and late-night cafés.

Nine police cars were parked outside No 10. Inside the house, policemen were dismantling the ground-floor flat, using crowbars and claw hammers to pull out fireplaces, tear down the flimsy walls and ceilings, lever up floorboards and linoleum. In the small back garden, a band of officers took off their jackets and sank their shovels and pickaxes into the earth, digging up the crazy-paving path, the rose bushes and the yellow-flowering forsythia. They sieved each spadeful of soil, using steel probes, palette knives and forceps to extract any objects they found.

Dr Camps, the pathologist, stood by in a belted raincoat, puffing on his pipe as he selected items to be sent to the laboratory at New Scotland Yard. He recognised some human bones among the finds; one of them had been propping up a broken fence at the back of the garden. The objects were packed in white paper bags, carried through the building in tea chests and cardboard boxes, and loaded into a van outside. Occasionally, a young woman came to the front door with cups of tea for the policemen, and plates of biscuits.

The Christies' dog, Judy, was missing, but the police found their black-and-white cat in the house, wild with distress. Tommy was taken to a shelter run by the Royal Society for the Prevention of Cruelty to Animals in Kensal Green, just north of Notting Hill.

***

The police interviewed the seven West Indian women and men who were still living in the upper storeys of 10 Rillington Place, the only black residents of the street, and their West Indian landlord, a 33-year-old pub and nightclub bouncer called Charles Brown.

Charles Brown had been the heavyweight champion of Jamaica when he moved to London in 1947. He had won thousands of pounds in boxing matches in Britain and Sweden, but eventually ran out of opponents. 'Charlie Brown came to England to make a name for himself,' reported the *Daily Mirror* in 1949. 'So far, the only name he has got is "the heavy-weight to be avoided". Charlie is a clever boxer. Joe Louis paid him that compliment when he had him as a sparring-partner on his exhibition visit to London. But Charlie wasn't quite clever enough. He failed to hide his ability. As a result he has been dodged by nearly every leading heavyweight in England.'

Brown decided to invest his winnings in property to let out to fellow West Indians, several thousand of whom came to Britain when the British Nationality Act of 1948 gave them the right to live and work in the country. Many gathered in Notting Hill, where Brown lived with his family.

When Brown bought 10 Rillington Place in 1950, Reg and Ethel Christie were the only tenants. The elderly man who occupied the first-floor rooms had moved out, and Tim Evans had just been hanged for murder. The Christies were legally entitled to stay at the rate they had paid since 1938: 12 shillings and ninepence a week for their three rooms and use of the garden. Brown, taking advantage of the different rules that had been brought in for furnished accommodation, charged the new tenants three times that – £2 a week – for a single room equipped with a bed, a wardrobe, a jug and basin, a couple of chairs, a frying pan, a saucepan, a baking tray, a teapot and some crockery and cutlery. The first-floor front room had a gas ring, but the other upstairs lodgers shared a kitchen on a landing between the first and second floors, and everyone, including the Christies, used the lavatory in the back garden.

Reg Christie had hated living alongside black people. He complained to the local sanitary inspector about the 'dirty habits' of the 'coloured people' upstairs, and he was disgusted to see white women visiting the tenants in his building. In 1951 the Notting Hill police marched two of the top-floor tenants down the stairs of No 10, having arrested them on a charge of stealing a loaf of bread and a tub of margarine from a nearby bakery. One of the men protested at his arrest: 'I study economics,' he told the police, 'and the persecution of the coloured people.' But Christie congratulated the officers as they led the suspects out of the house: 'It's time some of you blokes sorted out these bastards.'

When the police interviewed Charles Brown at the end of March 1953, he told them that Reg Christie had last paid his rent on 5 January. Brown said that he had supplied him that day with a bag of cement, a bucket of sand and a tin of whitewash, which Christie claimed to need to mend a hole in his kitchen wall. When Brown came over on Friday 20 March to collect the several weeks of arrears that Christie owed him, he found an Irish couple in his rooms. They told him that Christie had left earlier in the day, having rented his flat to them for the next three months. Brown informed them that Christie was not entitled to sublet the rooms, at which they agreed to leave the property. He then asked Beresford Brown, one of the top-floor tenants, to clear and clean the Christies' kitchen.

Beresford Wallace Brown, a moustachioed 43-year-old jazz musician, had made the six-week journey from Jamaica on a French 'banana boat' in 1950, and now worked at a dairy in Shepherd's Bush. The officers who took his statement recorded his middle name as 'Dubois' – maybe he gave his middle initial, and they were confused by his accent.

He told the police that he had come across the bodies while trying to put up a shelf for his transistor radio, on which he hoped to listen to music as he worked. He had tapped the wall to check for a place to fix the brackets, he said, and noticed that it sounded hollow. 'I thought then that there must be a hole there. I went out and looked at the construction of the house at the back. I came to the conclusion there must be a cellar of some sort on the corner of the kitchen.'

He went back in, pulled away the paper on the kitchen wall and saw a hole in the wooden panel behind it. 'I went to my room and got a torch,' he said. 'I shone it in the hole and saw it was a cellar and I also saw the bare back of a human being.' He asked Ivan Williams, a 22-year-old porter who lived on the first floor, to come downstairs to have a look. Williams shone the torch into the hole and said that he too could see a body. They called the police from the telephone box on the corner of Lancaster Road.

Beresford's common-law wife, Lena Louise Stewart, told the officers that in the weeks before Christie left she had often seen him pouring disinfectant in the hallway and under the bay window in the street. He had opened the front door for her on 3 January, she said, as she was taking her two-week-old daughter to the clinic. 'What a lovely little thing,' he had remarked, in a rare show of friendliness, 'and Mrs Christie is not here to see her.' Louise had last seen Ethel Christie in early December, shortly before the birth of the baby.

Louise's brother, Franklin, a railway worker who shared a top-floor room with his wife, Amy, told the police that he too had noticed Christie sprinkling disinfectant in the hall. He said that in February he and Christie had discussed the filthy condition of the lavatory, which Stewart had agreed was too dirty to use. Christie had told him that his wife was in Halifax, looking after her sick sister. 'He said she was happy where she was,' said Stewart, 'though she badly wanted to come back to him.'

Cyril Edwards, who lived with his wife and baby in the first-floor front room, said he and his wife had noticed a nasty smell in the house, which they had reported to the landlord. He had little to do with Christie. 'I was not particularly friendly with him,' he said, 'because I don't think he liked coloured people.' Sylvia Edwards, a dressmaker who had come to London from Jamaica in 1951, told the police: 'The Christies have never spoken to me at all.'

All the tenants were informed that they had to move out of No 10 at the weekend, so that the police could search the whole building. One family said they were already planning to leave – 'We couldn't stand it here another day' – but to others it was a blow. That week's *Kensington Post* carried just two accommodation notices that specifically excluded black and Irish applicants – a room in Willesden was available to 'British only', a room in Earl's Court to 'English only' – but the tenants knew that they were likely to be turned away from most of the properties in the *Post*'s pages. There was one welcoming ad: 'Coloured people, why be humiliated?' asked Afro-West Indian Services, offering rooms at £2 a week in a property in west London. Black migrants expected to pay a premium for lodgings. In the absence of any laws against racial discrimination, they were also routinely turned down for jobs, refused entry to clubs and pubs, and insulted on the street.

Two days after discovering the bodies, Beresford Brown received a letter addressed to 'Mr Beresford Brown (coloured), 10 Rillington Place'. 'Mr "Beresford" BLACK,' read the scrawled note: 'Quit England and our boarding houses, you dirty stinking Black niggers we dont want you here doing all your filthy breeding. Leave our white women alone or there will be trouble.'

***

In the national press, news of the murders at first competed for space with news of the death of Queen Mary, who had succumbed to 'gastric problems' (actually, lung cancer) in Marlborough House, Pall Mall, on the night that the bodies were discovered in Notting Hill. Winston Churchill, who had been returned to power as prime minister in 1951, paid tribute to the queen consort in the House of Commons. Mary had been the widow of George V, the mother of Edward VIII and George VI, and the last member of the family to have been close to Queen Victoria. Her dying wish, Churchill told Parliament, was that her granddaughter's coronation go ahead in June 1953 as planned – Elizabeth had become queen in 1952, on the death of her father, but had yet to be anointed.

Tens of thousands of people queued at Westminster Hall on Sunday to pay their last respects to Queen Mary, while a crowd of more than two hundred gathered at Rillington Place to watch the police at work, some settling in for the day with sandwiches and flasks of tea. William Lawrence of No 8 warned the police that a group of local lads was planning to cause a disturbance in the street. 'Let's get some milk bottles,' he had heard one of them say, 'and give the coppers a shaking up.' The police cleared the crowd and sealed off the street for the afternoon.

By now the Rillington Place story was dominating the papers. In the *Pictorial*, Harry reported on the detectives' intense search of Christie's garden and their efforts to identify the human remains that had been found there. 'Parents of young provincial girls who have gone to London and who have not written home,' he wrote, 'are asked to contact their local police stations.' The *News Chronicle* told its readers that officers were working feverishly to trace the killer before Monday, in case he was a 'sexual lunatic' whose madness was triggered by a full moon. The *Mirror* described him as 'the Bluebeard of Notting Hill', an allusion to the fairy tale in which a young bride enters a forbidden chamber in her husband's house and finds the dead bodies of his six former wives.

The police continued to scour London for Christie. They searched the crowds at the Oxford–Cambridge boat race on the Thames, and at the football match at Loftus Road between Torquay United and Queens Park Rangers, the team Christie supported. They sought information about the victims at hotels used by prostitutes in Bayswater, Portobello Road and Paddington.

Christie's house had become a scene of dark entertainment. 'Rillington Place', ran a *News Chronicle* headline: 'A London nocturne with the grim fascination of a thriller'. The paper published a panoramic photograph of the street, shadowy and stark as a film noir set. A chauffeur drove a large Daimler into the cul-de-sac that week, bearing six women, and asked a reporter to direct him to the 'murder house'. At the end of the road, he stopped so that his passengers could have a good look, then turned the car around and sailed away. Young men in drape suits dropped by to get the latest on the 'House of Horror' before repairing to the Juke Box Café in Lancaster Road to play pinball.

Harry Procter's great rival, Norman 'Jock' Rae, reported on 'the Ripper of Rillington Place' in the *News of the World*, the newspaper with the biggest circulation on the planet – it sold 8 million copies every Sunday, compared to the 4 or 5 million shifted by its closest competitors, the *Pictorial* and the *People*. Rae told his readers that he had staked out the 'dingy little Victorian house of doom' by watching from a neighbour's window as the detectives went about their work. His report was so thorough that Harry sent him a telegram. 'Congratulations on your magnificent story,' it read. 'You have beaten us all.'

Harry was not conceding defeat, but throwing down the gauntlet.

2

The man of a thousand doubles

Harry headed to the north of England to trace Reg Christie's friends and relatives. He hoped that he might even find Christie hiding out with one of them. He began by visiting Black Boy House, a solitary building on a bleak moor outside Halifax, in which the Christie family had lived at the time of Reg's birth in April 1899. Reg's father, Ernest, had been a town councillor and a designer at Crossley & Sons, the largest carpet manufacturer in the world. At the carpet factory, he was known as 'Doctor Christie' (for his proficiency in first aid and his work as an ambulance steward) and 'Mephistopheles' (for his goatee beard and his violent temper). Ernest's wife, Mary, used to comfort her children when their father harangued or hit them. In 1905 the family moved to a house in Boothtown, Halifax, where neighbours often heard quarrelling and once saw Mrs Christie run into the street in fear.

Harry sought out people who had known Reg as a boy. He had been an able student, he was told, though disliked by some fellow pupils for his 'sneaking' ways. Reg attended Sunday School, sang in the choir and gained the highest honour – King's Scout – in the local boy scout troop. At fourteen he left school to become an apprentice in a boot-making factory, then took a job as a cinema projectionist. He joined the army in 1916, when he was seventeen, and for three months in 1918 he served as a signaller on the Western Front, carrying messages from front-line troops to battalion headquarters. Near Ypres in June, his regiment was bombarded with mustard gas, and Christie was blinded and struck dumb. He was admitted to a hospital in Calais, his throat and eyelids severely inflamed by the sulphurous compound, and then to two military hospitals in Staffordshire. Though his eyes gradually opened and his larynx healed, the shock of the attack left him almost mute. He was diagnosed with functional aphonia, a psychosomatic condition, and discharged with a war pension of a few shillings a week. Unable to speak at more than a whisper, Christie communicated for the next three years with a notebook and pencil, or by mouthing words. He found work as a projectionist at another Halifax cinema, then as a clerk in a woollen mill.

In 1920, Christie married Ethel Simpson, a shorthand typist at the mill. He was twenty-one and she twenty-two. Reggie, as Ethel called him, promised her that he would soon be inheriting a house, and in the meantime they moved into a top-floor room in a poor part of town. Both took new jobs: Ethel as a typist at an engineering works, and Reg as a postman. He gained a reputation for efficiency, but his employers noticed that mail was going missing on his round. When investigators searched his lodgings they discovered that he had been taking home bags of post, raiding them for cheques and postal orders, then stuffing the empty sacks and envelopes into cupboards, under the carpets and the floorboards. In a foreshadowing of the crime scene at Rillington Place, he had lined his home with the evidence of his wrongdoing.

Reg served two-and-a-half months for the theft, at Strangeways prison in Manchester. By then his voice had become stronger, though he continued to speak very quietly. He was in trouble with the police again in 1923 when he absconded from a boarding house without settling the bill, and escaped a sentence only because his mother stepped in to pay what he owed. That year he accused Ethel of having an affair with her boss. He moved away from the city, and the couple spent the next decade apart.

By the time Harry visited Halifax, Reg's parents had died – Ernest in 1928 and Mary in 1944 – but his surviving siblings were still in the north. His sister Winifred was living near Manchester, and his sister Dorothy near Liverpool, while his brother Percy, a retired bank manager, was in Harry's own hometown, Leeds. None of them had stayed in touch with Reg. They had been glad to see the back of him when he left Halifax in 1923. Winifred had assumed that he was dead.

Harry called on Percy Christie in Leeds and urged him to strike a deal with the *Sunday Pictorial*. The law forbade direct payments to murder suspects, but Fleet Street reporters sometimes made surreptitious arrangements with prisoners' families. Harry told Percy that the *Pic* would fund Christie's defence in exchange for his exclusive story, to be published after the trial. If Reg was 'mentally sick', said Harry, it was his family's duty to get him the best possible medical and legal help. Percy, seeing that only he could help his younger brother, agreed to sign a contract with Harry's paper.

Back in London at the end of March, Harry hired Ambrose Appelbe, of Cliftons solicitors in Lincoln's Inn, to provide Christie with legal advice if he was caught. The small, dapper Appelbe had collaborated with Harry the previous year on a story about a man accused of passing government secrets to the Russians. Appelbe was a pacifist, and a founder (with George Bernard Shaw and H. G. Wells) of the Smell Society, which aimed to promote pleasant smells and to find new words to describe the aromas of roast turkey, mimosa and tar. Appelbe's chief clerk, Roy Arthur, agreed to carry out the work on the

Christie case. He and Harry were old friends. Arthur was 'charming, bearded, courteous, wise', said Harry, and he knew how to play a situation to a client's advantage while staying on the right side of the law.

With an inside track to Christie, Harry hoped that he might have the biggest story of his career, and a chance to make good on the shameful mistake he had made in December 1949. First, though, Christie had to be found.

***

The newspapers 'zithered with excitement' about the murders, said the reporter Molly Lefebure, 'and so did the public. In buses, shops, market-places and offices and over family breakfast tables the talk was all of Christie.' Women were more watchful on the streets, in cafés and cinemas; children lay awake worrying that the wicked man might burst into their bedrooms and carry them off. It was as if the country had been caught up in the closing frames of a horror film.

'The story was an all-time sensation,' wrote Lefebure: 'wonderful tales were passed around of the madman who, controlled by the moon, was now roaming at large, liable to leap upon and kill scores more women.' On their way home from work, people rushed to buy the evening papers, 'like sea-gulls swooping for food'.

Hundreds of real and phantom Christies were reported to the police – Harry described him in the *Pictorial* as the 'man of a thousand doubles'. On Thursday 26 March, two days after the bodies were found at Rillington Place, a coach driver said that he had seen Christie at 12.30 in the gents' lavatories at Golders Green station, north London – he had 'very piercing grey eyes'. At about 2 p.m. an estate agent saw a man like Christie waiting to alight the 607 trolley bus from Acton to Ealing, his hat in his hand: 'His nose was long and straight, and his eyes were staring.' At 6.30 p.m. an electrician on a Northern Line train to Edgware sat next to an agitated man who resembled Christie. 'His manner was strange and his conversation was about clothes and weather,' the electrician told the police. 'He got off at Hampstead.'

Many of those who reported sightings of Christie described a man who stared; others described a man who averted his eyes. He was the predatory watcher, but also, now, the watched-for. At 2.50 a.m. on Friday 27 March, a trolley-bus driver saw a man like Christie on the East India Dock Road: 'He had a hunted look about him.' A woman on the 6.25 a.m. from Brighton to London Bridge noticed a man who seemed startled when he heard the other passengers discussing the murders: he hid his face behind a newspaper, and when he got off the train almost ran to catch a taxi outside. A man from Bognor Regis thought that he saw Christie on the train to Victoria, walking up and down the corridor. 'Every time he passed our compartment he glanced at me as if he was frightened.'

At 12.20 that Friday, a secretary shared a table with a man who looked like Christie at a Lyons tea shop near King's Cross. 'I hope you don't mind me smoking at the table,' he said, as he tried to engage her in conversation: 'I believe they have found the fifth victim of the Notting Hill murder. I think men like that should be sterilised and let loose again.' He remarked approvingly that the Americans castrated 'black boys', 'like tom cats'. A man like Christie followed a young artist in Knightsbridge. 'Can I carry your case?' he asked her. Near Tower Hill at 1 p.m. a man resembling Christie offered to help a woman across the road. 'Where do you live?' he asked. 'Are you married?' Women were used to being pestered in the street, but the approaches of strangers now seemed more sinister.

At 3 p.m. on Friday, a housewife believed that she saw Christie in Hackney. 'I had to move out of the way otherwise he would have knocked into me. I thought for a moment he was blind and looked to see if he was carrying a white stick. Just then he looked round at me and I could see he was not blind.' At Euston railway station that afternoon, three detectives apprehended a man who looked like Christie; he told them that he had been stopped and asked if he was Christie four times in the previous twenty-four hours.

Later the same day, a young woman went into the King's Cross Road police station to say that she had met the man pictured in the *Evening News*. In the Star Light Café in Pentonville Road at 7 p.m. on Tuesday, the evening that the bodies were discovered, he had called her to his table and told her that he'd noticed her on Saturday night, very drunk. 'Do you know you are two months pregnant?' he asked. 'Do you want to keep it or get rid of it? If I can help you in any way let me know.' The man showed her a photograph of his wife, who he said had died, and told her that his father had been a doctor in Edinburgh. 'I'll see you in here tomorrow night at 10 o'clock,' he said as they parted, 'and if you want to get rid of the baby put your hand to your face.'

Three hundred calls came in to Scotland Yard on Saturday afternoon, and scores more people visited their local police stations to report sightings. In the morning a passenger on the Hammersmith & City Line had seen a man who looked like Christie, with 'glaring eyes' and a mild grin, getting off the train at Ladbroke Grove. In a house nearby, two young women were discussing the West Indians who had just moved into the ground-floor rooms, having been evicted from 10 Rillington Place, when a middle-aged white man walked in and asked to see 'the coloured man'. The women blocked his passage. 'That's the man the police are looking for,' one of them said to the other, at which the stranger quickly left the building. The same morning a pawnbroker in Battersea gave 10 shillings and sixpence to a man answering Christie's description, in return for a herringbone-tweed double-breasted overcoat.

On a train in south London at about 11.30 a.m., a woman asked her husband if he recognised the man sitting opposite them. 'Who do you mean – Christie?' he asked loudly. When the man hurriedly got off at the next station, other passengers agreed that he had looked just like the pictures in the papers: a middle-aged chap with drawn cheeks, horn-rimmed spectacles and glassy, staring eyes.

At 12.30 a carpenter thought he saw Christie with a dark-haired younger woman in an Italian café in Paddington. Another woman believed that she had encountered him in the same neighbourhood, at the ABC restaurant in Praed Street. He invited her to the pictures, and when she declined he seemed upset. 'I wish I'd met you years ago,' he said, taking her hand.

At about 1 p.m. in the Odeon Cinema in Harrow Road, just north of Paddington, a woman was irritated by a man sitting next to her who kept rustling his newspaper; when the lights went up at the end of the screening, she thought she recognised him as Christie. A 33-year-old widow was cleaning the area outside her basement flat in Paddington when a man startled her by silently coming down the steps and standing behind her before asking for a room. He looked very like the pictures of Christie, she said.

The police were told that a man with a shiny bald head had been seen in the Essoldo Picture House in Hackney that week, staring at a young woman a few seats away from him. They received an anonymous note: 'YOU WILL NEVER GET ME. I AM LEAVING ENGLAND. GOOD-BYE. STARING EYES.'

Christie was everywhere and nowhere. Starting to despair of finding him, the detectives at Scotland Yard discussed whether to make a television appeal for information – it might be worth a try, they thought, since hundreds of thousands of people had bought or rented TV sets in advance of the coronation.

On Monday, though, the police made a breakthrough. Alfred Arrowsmith, a pipe-fitter's assistant who was staying in the Rowton House hostel in King's Cross, reported that a few days earlier he had sold a coat to a fellow resident who looked like the man in the papers, in part exchange for a greasy mackintosh. Arrowsmith said that the two of them had tea together, and discussed the different stages of baldness. The man claimed to have come to the hostel to escape 'domestic trouble'. 'He seemed to be pretty well-educated,' said Arrowsmith. 'He spoke nicely and had a quiet voice.' He had seen him playing snooker in the hostel's games room and he knew that he frequented the Star Light Café in Pentonville Road. Arrowsmith had last spoken to him a week ago, he said. 'I got the impression that he was worried about something. He seemed on edge.'

When the police checked the Rowton House records, they discovered that Christie had registered at the hostel on Friday 20 March, the day he left Rillington Place, and stayed there until Wednesday 25 March, the morning after the murdered women were found in his house. There was a suitcase still in his locker, containing clothes and family photographs.

Officers at Scotland Yard gave the press a mocked-up photo of Christie wearing a coat like the one that Arrowsmith had described. They sent an update by telegram to every police station in Britain: 'Please have late or midnight enquiries made at common lodging houses, cafés, billiard halls, and other likely places to trace John Reginald Halliday Christie. May now be wearing double breasted overcoat, dark blue or purple with lighter diagonal stripe.'

By Tuesday 31 March, the day of Queen Mary's funeral at Windsor, the police had been hunting Christie for a week. 'Race Against Time to Trap Horror Killer', announced the front page of the *Mirror*. A man who knew Christie called at Notting Hill police station in the morning to say that he had seen him asleep in the back of a van in Powis Mews, less than a mile from Rillington Place. By the time the detectives checked, the van was empty. They sealed off the area and searched the front gardens, but could find no trace of the fugitive.

Later in the morning two brothers unloading timber from a barge on the Thames saw a gaunt, unshaven man in a battered brown trilby looking down at them from the towpath by Putney Bridge.

'That fellow up there looks just like Christie,' said Charlie Burgess.

'Hundreds of people look like him,' replied his brother George. 'Perhaps it's his double.'

A passing policeman also noticed the man leaning on the railings near the bridge, and asked him for his name and address. The man said that he was John Waddington of Westbourne Grove. PC Thomas Ledger asked him to take off his hat. When he did so, revealing the high white dome of his forehead, Ledger recognised him as Christie. He asked him to come with him to Putney police station.

In the van, Christie admitted his identity. At the station, an officer informed him that four bodies had been found at his house, including that of his wife. 'She woke me up,' he said softly, starting to cry. 'She was choking. I couldn't stand it any longer. I couldn't bear to see her suffer. You know what I did.'

Two Notting Hill detectives came to Putney to interview Christie. He answered their questions about the murdered women, and at the end of his statement he thanked his captors: 'I am grateful to the police in charge for the kindly way in which I have been treated in Putney station.'

The officers gave Christie a breakfast of tea, bread, butter and bacon before transferring him to Notting Hill. Word of his arrest had got out. The writer J. G. Ballard, who lived nearby, saw hundreds of people waiting near the police station on Ladbroke Grove. As the van from Putney drove up to the gates, the crowd drew back, leaving only a woman in a red coat standing in the middle of a side street. She stared after Christie as he was ushered into the station, shielding his face with his hat. Ballard was told that she was a sister of Timothy Evans. She believed that Christie had murdered her brother's wife and child.

The Notting Hill police took possession of the objects that had been found on Christie: his ration book, his rent book, his union card, his marriage certificate, a ticket for a week's stay at Rowton House, a QPR football badge, a silk scarf, a spectacle case, a few pawnshop tickets and a newspaper cutting about the death sentence passed on Timothy Evans three years earlier, in January 1950. Christie was no longer wearing the coat he had bought from Alfred Arrowsmith, having pawned it in Battersea on Saturday. The officers locked him in a cell overnight.

The crime reporters in the New Scotland Yard press bureau phoned the news of Christie's capture to their offices in Fleet Street. The police issued a telegram to local forces all over the country: 'Cancel Express message nos 9, 10, 11, 12, 13 concerning John Christie – Christie has been traced.'

***

At nine the next morning, Wednesday 1 April, Harry Procter met the *Pictorial*'s short, pot-bellied assistant editor, Reg Payne, at the West London Magistrates' Court near Hammersmith Road. Harry disliked Payne – he was an abrasive boss, especially nasty when drunk – but on a story this big even a hotshot reporter had to put up with his superiors sticking their oar in.

The streets around the courthouse thronged with people. Some had been waiting in the cold and drizzle for an hour or more, others had stopped on their way to the shops: women in headscarves, holding bags and baskets, boys and girls on their Easter holidays. The crowd lined the steep front steps to the houses that overlooked the back of the court, where Christie was expected to be brought from Ladbroke Grove.

Half a dozen newspaper photographers had climbed on to the low roof of the woodwork shop next to the courthouse, from which they hoped to get a shot of Christie. Others leant out of the windows of the facing terrace as the police van drew up, training their lenses on the court's back entrance. But Christie's escorts pressed around him as he emerged from the van, and even the best-placed observers could see only his hand stroking the top of his head.

When Harry and Payne entered the courtroom, they saw Christie in the dock, wearing a creased grey suit. Harry had already sent him a message, through the Notting Hill police, to say that his brother Percy had agreed for the *Sunday Pictorial* to pay his legal fees in exchange for his story. But Harry noticed, to his dismay, that Roy Arthur of Cliftons, the solicitors his paper had appointed, was arguing with a clerk from another firm, who claimed that the *Sunday Dispatch* had hired them to represent Christie. The magistrate asked the legal aides to retire to a side room to settle the matter.

Harry and Payne stepped out of the courtroom for an anxious smoke. James Reid of the *Dispatch* joined them in the hall. Though his paper had only half the circulation of the *Pictorial*, Reid seemed confident that Christie had agreed to appoint its legal team.

'Anyhow,' Reid said genially, 'this is a moment we shall all remember when we write a book.'

'I'm not writing a bloody book,' rasped Reg Payne. He was as bad-tempered as ever, Harry observed, and white with worry.

Harry was worried, too. To get his scoop and to find out the truth about the Evans murders, he needed Christie to endorse his brother's deal with the *Pictorial*.

When they went back into the court, Christie gave Harry a smile and a nod – 'as though he had missed me', said Harry – before he was taken down to the cells to choose between the two legal firms. When they returned, the magistrate announced that the defendant would be represented by Cliftons.

Harry was jubilant. Christie was his.

The hearing itself lasted just seven minutes. Christie sat in the dock, scribbling notes as the murder charges were read out. The magistrate ordered that he be detained in Brixton prison, a remand jail in south London, while the police gathered their evidence.

As Christie was led away, Harry turned to Payne. 'You can get the Christie poster ready,' he said. He knew that the paper would advertise this exclusive widely.

When Christie emerged from the court building, he was wearing a new blue pin-stripe suit, blue shirt and tie, which Harry had dropped off for him with the Notting Hill police. He put his face in his uncuffed hands as he was bundled into the back of the black prison van. Some of the children in the crowd booed. The high green gates swung shut behind the departing vehicle, clanged as an iron bar dropped into place.

Roy Arthur, the Cliftons clerk, gave Harry a note from Christie, expressing thanks for the clothes he had sent him, but observing that the shirt was half a size too big and that he did not care for the colour of the tie.

Harry and Reg Payne saw James Reid of the *Sunday Dispatch* in the street, raging about how Christie had been stolen from him. 'I shall protest!' he shouted.

'I wonder what's got into that chap?' Payne remarked drily.

'I haven't the vaguest idea, sir,' said Harry as the pair of them departed, suave as crooks who had just pulled off a heist.

***

In Pear Tree Cottage in St John's Wood, a well-to-do district a couple of miles north-east of Notting Hill, the acclaimed novelist Fryn Tennyson Jesse was gripped by the newspaper stories about the murders. One of her neighbours, Sally Speelman, had been among the many who had reported a sighting while Christie was at large: Mrs Speelman thought she had spotted him on Sunday in the queue at the Classic Cinema, Baker Street, reading a newspaper and wearing a fawn, rather grubby gaberdine coat.

On learning from the evening papers of 31 March that Christie had been caught, Fryn at once wrote to her old friend James Hodge in Edinburgh, asking to cover the case for the 'Notable British Trials' series. This was a lauded collection, published by the Hodge family since 1905, which printed transcripts of trials with introductions by eminent authors. Fryn had already written essays for five of the volumes.

'You can imagine the agitation we have all been in in London,' she told Jim Hodge. 'I must of course go to the trial at the Old Bailey.' The case, she said, might be the biggest crime story since Jack the Ripper. 'You must say you want me to do it for the Notable British,' she said, 'and get me a Press card.'

'James,' she wrote, both imperious and beseeching, 'do not fail me.'

Fryn was part of a golden generation of female crime writers. Among her successes were *Murder and Its Motives* (1924), a collection of essays about murderers, and *A Pin to See the Peepshow* (1934), a novel based on the life of Edith Thompson, hanged in 1924 for conspiring to kill her husband. Fryn's contributions to Notable British Trials included essays on Alma Rattenbury, charged with murdering her husband in 1935, and Madeleine Smith, charged with murdering her lover in 1857. Fryn was strikingly sympathetic to her female subjects. She depicted the women on trial as passionate, sexual beings who had been constrained by the societies into which they were born. Rather than write ingenious whodunits, like Agatha Christie and Dorothy L. Sayers, she produced books that tried to fathom a murderer's mind.

By 1953, though, several of Fryn's works had gone out of print, and she was in poor shape. She was sixty-five years old, frail, puffy and – she had just learnt – going blind. Nurses came to her white Regency villa to massage her swollen joints, a secretary came to help with her writing, and a doctor came to inject her with morphine. Fryn was a registered addict, having become hooked on opiates in her youth while being treated for an injury to her hand. Alarmed by her failing body, afraid that she was being forgotten, she hungered for a story that would restore her.

On 2 April, Jim Hodge replied to Fryn's letter to say that unfortunately he had already promised the Christie case to someone else. This trial was going to be so popular, he observed jovially, that the government ought to consider holding it in the new Festival Hall as part of the summer's coronation events.

Fryn was beside herself. 'Oh James, base James, Oh James, how could you let me down so?' she wrote. 'You have ruined my Easter. Oh James, James, how could you?'

On 3 April, just in time for Easter, Hodge called off the other writer and told Fryn that she could write about the Christie case for him. But he had no idea, he warned, whether he could get her a seat in the Old Bailey.

Fryn, delighted at least to have the commission, asked her friend Richard 'Joe' Jackson, head of the civilian staff at Scotland Yard, to help with her research. For as long as she could remember she had been fascinated by the psychology of violence. When she was twelve, she recalled, she and a friend caught a cabbage-white butterfly and 'pulled it to pieces very slowly, first taking off its wings and then its legs, feeling horribly sick as the oblong body wiggled a little before it lay still'. The sight aroused a 'strange excitement' in her, she said.

Some reviewers had expressed distaste for Fryn's morbid predilections. 'Miss Jesse has all a young author's passion for grim, ugly, speciously passionate subjects,' said the *Observer* when she published her first volume of short stories in 1915: 'Murder, lust, treachery are revelled in with that deliberate abandon which so rarely brings with it artistic conviction.' The *Nation* detected an 'abnormal strain of feminine eroticism' in her work. More sympathetically, the *New Statesman* noted in 1917 that 'there is something painful and terrible in her genius. She is preoccupied with pain.'

3

Dreams of dominance

The police gave Harry and the other crime reporters the names and ages of the three white women whose bodies Beresford Brown had found in Christie's alcove. One was Kathleen Maloney, twenty-six, whose fingerprints Scotland Yard had matched to their records. One was Rita Nelson, twenty-five, identified at Kensington mortuary by her older sister. The third was Hectorina Maclennan, twenty-seven, identified by her two older brothers.

Henry Waddington, a local government clerk, came down to North Kensington from Sheffield to confirm that the body found under the floorboards was that of his younger sister, Ethel, aged fifty-four.

All the women had died in the past three or four months, said the police. Ethel Christie was the first victim, and Hectorina Maclennan the last.

Roy Arthur, as clerk to the defence solicitors, was supplied with a copy of the confession that Christie had made to the police. Christie claimed in this statement to have woken at 8.15 a.m. on 14 December 1952 to find his wife choking and convulsing. He assumed that Ethel had taken an overdose, he said, as the bottle of sleeping pills on her bedside table was almost empty. 'My wife had been suffering a great deal from persecution and assaults from the black people in the house,' Christie told the officers, 'and had to undergo treatment at the doctor for her nerves. In December she was becoming very frightened from these blacks and was afraid to go about the house when they were about and she got very depressed.'

When he saw Ethel struggling for breath, he said, 'I did what I could to try and restore breathing, but it was hopeless. It appeared too late to call for assistance. That is when I could not bear to see her so. I got a stocking and tied it round her neck to put her to sleep.' After doing this, he said, 'I left her in bed for two or three days, and didn't know what to do. Then I remembered some loose floorboards in the front room. I had to move a table and some chairs to roll the lino back about halfway.' Then, he said, 'I believe I went back and put her in a blanket or a sheet or something and tried to carry her, but she was too heavy, so I had to sort of half carry her, half drag her and put her in that depression and cover her up with earth. I thought that was the best way to lay her to rest. I then put the boards and lino back.'

Even as he confessed, Christie tried to absolve himself – Ethel had wanted to die, he insisted, and he had strangled her as an act of mercy. His recall was sometimes precise (the carriage of Ethel's body across the room, the raising and lowering of the boards and lino) and sometimes clouded ('I believe I went back'), with jarring lurches into piety (he had been seeking 'the best way to lay her to rest').

Christie said that he had given up his job as an accounts clerk a week before killing Ethel, losing his £8 weekly wage and instead claiming £2 and 14 shillings in unemployment benefits. Three weeks after her death, having run out of money, he sold his furniture for £11, keeping just a mattress, sheets and blankets, a kitchen table and two chairs. He sold Ethel's wedding ring to a jeweller's in Shepherd's Bush for 37 shillings (just under £2). 'I was in a state,' he said, 'and didn't know what to do.'

In reply to the police's questions, he described the deaths of the three other women. One evening in January, he said, he went up to Ladbroke Grove to get some food for his dog and cat, and on his return was waylaid by a drunken woman who demanded that he 'take her round the corner' and pay her £1. Christie claimed that he replied: 'I am not interested and have not got money to throw away.' To the police, insisting on his propriety even as he described the prelude to another killing, he added: 'I am not like that.' The woman, he said, threatened to scream and publicly accuse him of 'interfering' with her if he didn't give her 30 shillings, 10 shillings more than the £1 she had originally demanded. 'I walked away,' he said, 'as I am so well known round there and she obviously would have created a scene.'

By his account, the woman followed him to Rillington Place and pushed her way into the house after him. 'I went to the kitchen,' said Christie, 'and she was still on about this 30 shillings. I tried to get her out and she picked up a frying pan to hit me. I closed with her, there was a struggle, and she fell back on a deckchair. There was a piece of rope hanging from the chair. I don't remember what happened, but I must have gone haywire. The next thing I remember she was lying still in the chair with the rope around her neck.' He left her there, had a cup of tea and went to bed.

Again, his narrative had absences, muddles, lapses, as if he lifted out of the scene at critical moments: 'There was a struggle', she 'fell back', he 'must have' gone 'haywire'.

In the morning, he said, he washed and shaved and made some tea, then pulled away a cupboard next to the kitchen wall and pushed the dead woman into the disused coal cellar behind it. 'I must have put her in there. I don't remember doing it, but

I remember pulling away the cupboard because it came away in two pieces.' This woman was Kathleen Maloney.

Soon afterwards, said Christie, he got talking to a young woman in a Notting Hill Gate café who asked him for a cigarette. When he learnt that she was looking for accommodation, he invited her to see his flat. She came over that evening and offered to 'visit him' for a few days if he would persuade the landlord to let the rooms to her when he moved out. 'I was rather annoyed,' claimed Christie, 'and told her that it didn't interest me. I think she started saying I was making accusations against her when she saw there was nothing doing. She was in a violent temper. I remember she started fighting.' She had 'Irish blood', he explained, and was threatening to set a local gang on him. 'I am very quiet,' he assured the police, 'and avoid fighting.'

Then his memory apparently went hazy. 'I know there was something. It is in the back of my mind. She was on the floor. I must have put her in the alcove straight away.' Again he portrayed his victim – Rita Nelson – as a woman who wanted to have sex with him and then attacked him. He blanked out the moment of her death, and erased his own aggression.

A few weeks later, he said, a woman he had met in Hammersmith came to stay in his flat with her husband. After three nights he asked them to leave, but the woman returned alone that evening, and insisted on waiting until her husband arrived.

'I got hold of her arm and tried to lead her out,' said Christie. 'I pushed her out of the kitchen. She started struggling like anything and some of her clothing got torn. She then sort of fell limp as I had hold of her. She sank to the ground and I think some of her clothing must have got caught round her neck in the struggle. She was just out of the kitchen in the passage way. I tried to lift her up, but couldn't. I then pulled her into the kitchen on to a chair. I felt her pulse but it wasn't beating. I pulled the cupboard away again and I must have put her in there.' This was Hectorina Maclennan, whose bare back Beresford Brown had seen when he tore a hole in the kitchen wallpaper.

Christie cast all three women as invaders of his home: they had forced themselves on him, he suggested, and had died as he resisted or tried to eject them.

When Harry read Christie's statement, he noticed that the police had asked him nothing about the killings of Beryl and Geraldine Evans in 1949. Scotland Yard, keen to rule out any suggestion that the police had made mistakes in that investigation, told the press that there was no connection between the two cases.

***

Few details about Christie's victims emerged in the newspapers, but the police gleaned some information about them from their friends and families. Scotland Yard also had a criminal record for Kathleen Maloney, the first woman whose body Christie had hidden in his alcove.

Kathleen, known to her friends as Maloney or Kay, was born in 1926 in Plymouth, a city in Devon. Her father, a stonemason's labourer of Irish descent, died when she was two and her mother when she was three. She was briefly taken in by an aunt before being sent to live at a local convent. Kathleen had been unruly, said the aunt; she was a wild girl, her uncle confirmed, full of pranks. In 1944, after a fling with a black American soldier, Kay started to roam the country, acquiring convictions for indecency, disorderly behaviour, an assault on a police officer, the use of obscene language, soliciting and drunkenness.

In a police mugshot distributed to the press after her murder, Kay looked heavy-lidded, dull-eyed and sullen – she was probably drunk, and annoyed to have been arrested. A picture taken a few years earlier showed her differently: a full-cheeked, pale girl with pursed lips and a narrow, wary gaze. She was 5ft 2in, and had dark brown hair – which she had dyed blonde – and a slight cast in her right eye.

When she first came to London in 1945, aged eighteen, Kay met a young woman called Sylvia Sowerby outside a dancehall in the Edgware Road, and they went drinking with some sailors. A couple of weeks later the two women found themselves in Holloway prison – Kay had been imprisoned for vagrancy, Sylvia for indecency. On their release they both decamped to Southampton, on the south coast, where they lodged together and earned a living as prostitutes.

Kay would go with any man at all, according to Sylvia, and she was careless about her safety. Most sex workers asked their customers to wear rubber sheaths, to guard against pregnancy and venereal disease, but Kay did not bother – maybe she couldn't afford to pay for condoms, nor to turn away customers. She was almost continuously pregnant between 1946 and 1950, and on one occasion was rushed to hospital while giving birth. Because she was unmarried and poor, each of her five babies was removed from her by the authorities – four were taken to a children's home in Southampton, and a fifth was adopted.

Kay wrote to her older sister, who lived with a Polish immigrant in Birmingham, asking if she could come to stay as she was in trouble with the law. Her sister did not reply. Kay told Sylvia that she was fed up with being harassed by the Southampton police and was going to hitchhike back to London. She didn't have much in the way of possessions when she left for the capital in 1952 – some cheap rings, a green and white wire bangle. She was a few weeks pregnant.

Kay fetched up in Paddington, a rough, busy district between Notting Hill and Hyde Park where it was easy to find lodging houses, alleys or bombed-out buildings in which to bed down or have sex. Kay dressed in plain, inexpensive clothes: a white T-shirt, a pleated skirt, a white cotton cardigan and flat black shoes. In Soho, streetwalkers wore bright lipstick, pendant earrings, nylon stockings and high-heeled shoes, but in Paddington they were less showy.

In the pubs around the railway station, Kay picked up men who were passing through the area. The going rate in central London was £1 or £2 for sex in a hired room, £1 or less for sex in a car or a back street or a clearing in the park; half that for a hand-job in an alley. The men faced no penalties if they were caught – it was not a crime to pay for sex – but a woman who offered herself to a man might be fined £2, or up to £5 if she was caught engaging in 'indecent behaviour'. Most women and girls treated the fines as a running cost: a streetwalker might be picked up by the police once every two or three months, so the penalties issued by the magistrates' courts amounted to a small fraction of her income.

Though Kay was sometimes imprisoned because she was unable to pay a fine, no other work could have funded her taste for alcohol so well. She was usually defiant about her drinking, telling anyone who criticised her that it was a free country, and she a happy-go-lucky kind of girl. But occasionally she referred to her desire for drink as an affliction: something that she could not help.

Kay made friends in the local pubs. At the Red Lion in Edgware Road she became close to the pub's cleaner, Kitty Struthers, who was also pregnant. Kay told Kitty that she had a two-year-old boy, Danny, who was being looked after in a children's home in Southampton – this was the only one of her children with whom she had managed to keep in touch. Danny's father was a Norwegian sailor, she said. When Kay was barred from the Red Lion, for 'exuberant singing', she and Kitty met up in other pubs in the area.

At the King's Arms in Edgware Road that summer, Kay met Maureen Riggs, known locally as 'Edgware Road Jackie'. Maureen and Kay realised that they were both 'on the game', so they set out on a pub crawl and picked up two American soldiers. The men gave them £2 apiece for a 'short time' in a Sussex Gardens hotel that hired out rooms for sex. After this the two women drank and solicited for custom together whenever they could. Kay confided in Maureen: she told her that her parents were dead, and spoke of her aunt in Plymouth and her baby in Southampton. 'We knocked around together all the time,' said Maureen. 'We never separated if we could help it.' They favoured the Mitre in Edgware Road but were barred when the publican realised that they were selling sex to customers.

When Kay was imprisoned in Holloway for drunkenness, she wrote to the aunt with whom she had briefly lived as a child, asking for the money to pay her fine and promising that she would go straight when she was released. The aunt did not reply. Perhaps Kay had disappointed her family too often. But the barman at the Mitre helped her out when she was next sent to Holloway for being drunk and disorderly. 'I felt sorry for her,' said George Noakes, who turned up at the prison in person to pay the £2 fine. Upon her release Kay went straight to the pub to thank him. She paid Noakes back his money in instalments.

At the Cider House in Harrow Road, a rustic, straw-strewn dive that dished out a powerful cider known as 'lunatic soup', Kay became friendly with Gladys Jordan, an older woman who earned a living as a cook. Gladys accompanied Kay to St Mary's Hospital in Paddington when she injured her finger, and she checked up on her most days afterwards. In November, Kay told Gladys that she was four months pregnant. Gladys worried about how much her friend drank. As well as strong cider, Kay liked fortified red wine (a favourite was 'Jelly Jump-Up') and a sharp, treacly Yorkshire ale known as Stingo. 'She used to get very drunk,' Gladys said, 'and I used to keep an eye on her in case she got arrested. I had told her that if she did get in trouble and was fined, I would help her.'

Kay met Reg Christie in November 1952, when her friend Maureen brought him into the Fountains Abbey pub in Praed Street. The two women later bumped into him in another Praed Street pub – the Great Western, where Maureen had first encountered him a few weeks earlier – and then on Praed Street itself, as they were emerging from the Standard. On this occasion he bought them some drinks, then invited them to accompany him to a photographic studio nearby.

Kay and Maureen followed Christie, walking a little behind him, until he told them to wait at a corner. They saw him knock on the door of a house off Marylebone Lane, which was opened by a woman in a dressing gown. He beckoned to them and they followed him in. At the top of the stairs was a room fitted out as a studio, with floodlights and a camera on a stand. Christie told Maureen to undress. Kay sat on a chair while Christie stood at the tripod, instructing Maureen to adopt different positions as he peered through the aperture and photographed her. In some shots Maureen was naked, in others dressed only in nylon knickers or a black suspender belt. Eventually Christie himself got undressed, told Maureen to bend over, naked, and asked Kay to photograph them as he pretended to push into her from behind.

At the end of the session, Christie said he didn't have enough cash to pay Kay and Maureen in full, as he owed money for the room. He gave them £1 each, promising that he would provide more soon, along with prints of the photos – prostitutes often carried pictures to sell to clients. Christie probably planned to sell some of the photos himself. He had thin lips, Maureen noticed, which he licked as he spoke.

About a week before Christmas, Maureen spotted Christie while she and Kay were walking to Sussex Gardens with two American servicemen who had agreed to pay them for sex. Maureen, who was drunk, shouted at him: 'There's the man that took the photos! Where's the photos and the money?' He walked away very quickly, she said, and she did not see him again. But she knew that Kay had met 'the photographer' once or twice since.

By December, Kay was spending most nights sleeping on the floor of the public lavatories in a subway at the junction of Harrow Road and Edgware Road. Homeless women and their children had started sheltering in the bathrooms during the Blitz, and the practice had continued ever since. Kay washed and slept there, and ate in cafés nearby. She was fond of the lavatory attendant, Lilian Shields, who she called 'Mum'.

For five days in late December, Kay didn't visit the bathrooms. When she returned, Mrs Shields asked her where she had been. Kay, while curling her hair with a pair of tongs in Mrs Shields's office, said that she had been staying with a man in Notting Hill. His wife had just died, she explained, and she felt sorry for him. But his landlord had told him to get rid of her, as he didn't want prostitutes on the premises.

At the end of the month Kay turned up at the lavatories with a suitcase full of women's and babies' clothes, a gift from the widower in Notting Hill. She shared out the contents among her friends. Mrs Shields accepted some frocks and babies' woollens. She assumed that Kay, being pregnant, was keeping some of these for herself.

One Thursday in early January, Kay came into the bathrooms to pay back a couple of shillings that she had borrowed. Mrs Shields offered her a free wash, but Kay declined, saying that her friend in Notting Hill had invited her over for the night; he had promised to give her his late wife's blouses and shoes. Kay set off in the fog, with her friend Kitty Struthers, to meet the man at the Westminster Arms. It was less than a month since a toxic smog had covered London, killing thousands of people, and the air was still acrid and damp.

In the pub, Kay and Kitty sat by a fire in the bar, and talked for a while to Augustine Murray, who was clearing glasses from the tables. Kay told Gus that a nice man had offered to put her up at his place that night. Soon enough – at about nine o'clock – this man came into the pub, joined the women at the fire and bought them a Stingo each. He had an upright posture, Kitty noticed, his shoulders pushed well back, and wore thick horn-rimmed spectacles, a suit and a trilby. Kay seemed very friendly with him, but then she was friendly to everyone after a few drinks.

The man bought a second round of beer for the women, and at 10 o'clock he and Kay got up to go. Before they left, Kay asked him for two shillings. He gave her the money, and she handed it to Kitty, telling her to buy herself another drink. Kay and the man crossed the road to the stop for the number 27 bus, which would take them to Notting Hill.

Kay's friends did not see her again. Later, when the police showed them pictures of Reg Christie, they identified him as the man they had met in the pub.

Christie's story of the drunken woman who accosted and followed him bore little relation to the facts. Kay was certainly drunk when she died (the pathologist found the equivalent of eight pints of beer in her body) but Christie had been meeting her for several weeks. He had bought her drinks that night, promised her clothes and a bed to sleep in. He had taken her to his place by bus, then killed her.

Kay had been pregnant since the summer, but by the time of her death in January she was no longer carrying a child. Dr Camps, in his post-mortem report, noted: 'uterus somewhat thickened suggesting pregnancy in past'. The lining of a uterus usually returns to its normal thickness within six to eight weeks of pregnancy. Perhaps Kay had procured an abortion shortly before she died.

Kitty Struthers went to Kensington mortuary to confirm the identity of her friend. Maureen Riggs, who was serving a fourteen-day sentence for drunkenness in Holloway prison, told the police that she had last seen Kay in early January, when she had left her drinking Jelly Jump-Up in the Westminster Arms, and she had assumed that she'd since gone back to Southampton, perhaps to see her son. A prison officer showed Maureen a picture of Christie, and she recognised him as 'the photographer'.

***

The police and pathologists who worked on the Christie case described the women found in his alcove as prostitutes, or 'of prostitute type', a designation that served both to explain and to diminish their deaths. Keith Simpson, a pathologist employed by Christie's defence team, observed that the 'wretched girls' who worked as prostitutes 'know very well the risks they run in their casual pick-up relationships with men of all sorts. Though paid well enough, they are roughly treated, often gripped fiercely by the neck, half strangled, punched, and suffer fierce "love" bites while giving satisfaction; and sometimes they die of the violence that they receive.'

The murder of such a woman was no loss to society, said Simpson: she had little chance of becoming 'a happy and useful citizen'. Sometimes, when he examined the corpse of a prostitute who had been strangled, he would reflect: 'Better out of this world.'

The capital's prostitutes congregated in Piccadilly and Soho, in Notting Hill, the East End and around the railway stations – Waterloo, London Bridge, Paddington, King's Cross, Euston, Victoria. They picked up customers in pubs and cafés or walked the pavements, murmuring to passersby: 'Hello, dear,' 'Are you looking for a naughty girl?', 'Would you like to come home with me?' Churchill's government feared that the coronation festivities in the summer of 1953 would be sullied by the spectacle of thousands of women offering their bodies to strangers. In the *Pictorial* in March, Harry Procter urged the police and the public to join together to 'stamp out the evil that is disgracing London'.

Women who sold sex may have become more visible because they were more desperate. The war had been a boom time for the sex trade, thanks to the hundreds of thousands of Allied troops passing through the capital. But now there was far less work to go round. Women began to cut their rates, work longer hours, solicit more openly and take more risks with clients.

In 1949 the British Social Biology Council commissioned Rosalind Wilkinson, a 24-year-old social researcher, to conduct a survey of prostitution from the perspective of the women themselves. Wilkinson studied the statistics for arrests and prosecutions in the city, and then, over several months in 1951 and 1952, she embedded herself in the world of London streetwalkers, befriending sixty-nine women who sold sex for a living.

Most of Wilkinson's interviewees were disparaging about the men who paid them for sex. Ena, who solicited for custom in Hyde Park, described her clients as 'babies and fussers'. She hated it, she said, when a punter tried to kiss her or touch her breasts. Margaret, who worked in Soho, said her customers were 'silly old fools'. Olive, from Euston, said: 'I think they are disgusting.' They laughed about some of their clients, felt sorry for others and were frightened by a few.

The women told Wilkinson that some men attacked prostitutes who wouldn't do the things that they wanted, and some seemed set on violence from the start. Ena said that she got a lot of sadists. Gwyneth, who also solicited in Hyde Park, kept a small knife clasped in her fist while having sex. She chose to work out of doors so that she could summon help if a punter turned nasty.

As Wilkinson carried out her research, she was herself sometimes approached for sex. If she was sitting on a bench in Hyde Park, men would sit down and proposition her, or slow their cars and honk their horns. This behaviour was far more intrusive, she thought, than the mild entreaties for which prostitutes were prosecuted and fined. In a pub one night a man mistook her for a prostitute and followed her home on the Tube to Earl's Court, keeping up a steady stream of insults about her loose morals: it seemed as though desiring her and reviling her went hand in hand. Wilkinson observed that there were men who sought out prostitutes because they wanted women they could despise and dominate.

The streetwalkers were vulnerable – to violent assault, venereal disease, unwanted pregnancies – and they were treated with contempt by the press and the public. Yet many told Wilkinson that their work was rewarding: they enjoyed the camaraderie with other women, the independence, the money. Most of them earned between £10 and £25 a week, which compared to the £3 or £4 a woman might take home from a job in a café or factory. It was no use trying to 'rescue' prostitutes, Wilkinson concluded: they chose to live this way. 'Even if she makes only £10 a week,' she wrote, 'the street prostitute is earning far more than she could in any job open to her.'

The women Wilkinson met were usually vague about their early lives, and she was reluctant to press them for details: it seemed rude to imply that they were emotionally disturbed by quizzing them about their childhoods. She began to understand them, she wrote, only when 'I ceased to ask myself "Why are these women prostitutes?" and began to ask "Why are other women not prostitutes?"' She came to see her subjects less as victims of personal damage than as rational beings making the best of an imperfect world.

Prostitution may have aroused so much public anger and unease because it exposed the underlying economic deal between men and women. If a man wanted a woman's company in a pub, he bought her a drink; in a café, he offered her a cup of tea or a cigarette; at the cinema, he bought her ticket; and in marriage, he gave her a portion of his wages in return for an undertaking to share his bed, run his household, care for him, and bear and raise his children.

To sustain this system, women were routinely paid less than men, to the extent that it was very difficult for a woman to feed, house and clothe herself without a man's support, and more or less impossible to bring up a child. In effect, most women sold themselves to men; the ones on the streets of London just did it more openly and more profitably. By undertaking this work, a woman made explicit the unspoken transaction between the sexes, and she chose the terms on which she took a man's money. For all the dangers of the profession, the logic of her choice was compelling.

***

Early in March 1953, three weeks before the discoveries in Rillington Place, Harry Procter had uncovered a network of upmarket call-girls in London. 'These women are not the unhappy prostitutes who appear day by day in the police courts,' he wrote. 'They are exceptionally attractive, often well-educated – many of them married to respectable, wealthy businessmen.' They worked in luxurious flats, Harry reported, owned by 'madames' who took telephone bookings, and they did business secretly while their husbands were at work, charging from £5 to £50 a session.

Having obtained the phone numbers and code names for thirty-seven high-class London brothels, Harry began to call them, with a colleague listening in on a second line.

'I am a friend of Patricia,' he told Madame Phyllis when she answered his call in her Knightsbridge apartment.

'Which Patricia?' asked Madame Phyl.

'Little Pat,' Harry replied, as he had been briefed.

Madame Phyl invited Harry and a friend to visit her flat, where she subjected them to questioning and then agreed to fix them up with two girls.

'You have asked for the best,' she said, 'and you will get them.'

On Madame Phyl's instructions, the undercover reporters met the young women at a fancy restaurant, where they treated them to a boozy four-course lunch. Harry's date was Little Pat herself, a petite eighteen-year-old with a sparkling smile and a blue-black pageboy crop, dressed for the occasion in an emerald-green tailored coat and high heels. Little Pat had married a naval officer a year earlier. 'I need a lot of money,' she explained to Harry. 'I like this job. I meet a lot of men. This way I get the clothes I have always wanted.'

Back in the Knightsbridge flat, having ordered bottles of gin and brandy for the guests, Little Pat led Harry to a private room. He observed 'how eagerly this young girl sought to play her part in this sordid deal'. Before things went any further, he said, he announced that he had to leave. Little Pat seemed disappointed. She gave Harry her home telephone number, encouraging him to call her any weekday before four, the time that her husband got home.

Little Pat chose to sell sex, according to Harry, even took pleasure in doing so. She and her kind were not impoverished; they were just dissatisfied with the pocket money their husbands gave them, and also, perhaps, with their boring lives as housewives. They brazenly defied their husbands' control over their bodies and their finances.

In the second instalment of the series, the *Pictorial* published a picture of Harry, rakish as a movie star, beneath the headline

'Women in Fear!' Word of his investigation had got out, Harry wrote, and the city's elite prostitutes were terrified that their identities would be exposed. 'Every call-girl in London, every Madame, every hanger-on of the racket – all are doing their utmost to stop my inquiries,' he claimed. 'A detailed description of me has been sent to them all.'

Harry's reports offered his readers the excitement of imagining a visit to a high-class prostitute, the righteousness of refusing her, the thrill of exposing her. His pieces were a kind of moral undressing, designed to arouse a heady mix of disapproval and desire. Hugh Cudlipp, the editorial director of the *Pictorial*, warned Harry not to make the women sound too exciting. 'I will not glorify sex,' Cudlipp told him. 'These girls are trollops, not glamorous creatures.'

In Philip Gibbs's *The Street of Adventure*, the novel that inspired Harry to become a journalist, a reporter saves a 'fallen' woman from the streets, giving her shelter and work so that she need not sell sexual favours. But Harry knew that the *Pictorial*'s call-girl campaign was less a rescue than a persecution, intended to instil fear and to shift copies of his paper.

Duncan Webb of the *Sunday People* had become famous in 1950 for uncovering a prostitution racket run by a Maltese gang in Soho. In a novel by one of Webb's colleagues, a crime reporter poses as a punter to infiltrate a prostitution ring, as Webb and then Harry had done.

'We're fighting vice,' the reporter declares as he reveals his identity to the cornered pimp, 'and rats like you who run it.'

'What do you mean, fighting vice?' retorts the pimp. 'You're selling it, same as me.'

The ruptures of war had transformed sexual behaviour in Britain. A Mass Observation survey commissioned by the *Pictorial* in 1949 disclosed that a quarter of British men admitted to having slept with a prostitute; a third of men and women approved of sex before marriage; half of men and a third of women had lost their virginity before marriage; and a quarter of husbands and a fifth of wives admitted adultery. Sir Harold Scott, the Commissioner of the Metropolitan Police, said he had observed 'a general slackening of sexual morals' in the city since 1945.

In *The Unfair Sex*, a book serialised in the *Pictorial* in the spring of 1953, 'Nina Farewell' advised single women on how to negotiate this new territory. She urged the reader to resist the pressure to have sex with a man: if she succumbed, he was likely to lose interest and move on, and if she fell pregnant, he might not marry but desert her. 'No genuine full-blooded male is trustworthy,' she warned: 'if he is a man, his motives and methods are base.'

Farewell listed sixteen pleasures that men took in women, among them 'the joy of ownership', 'the joy of conquest' and 'the joy of destruction' ('A proud or inaccessible girl fills the male with an inexplicable desire to "knock her off her high horse", to see her with her hair disarranged, her make-up blurred, and her poise shattered'). Her book depicted relations between men and women as a battle, in which women had to defend themselves – against men's blandishments and their own desires – with dissimulation, deflection and lies. This was a handbook for resistance.

Nina Farewell assumed that her readers aimed to marry, but wives were themselves increasingly discontented. Eighty per cent of married women had entered the workplace during the war, and some had been unhappy to return to domestic duties when the men came home. Dr Doris Odlum told the *Mirror* in April 1953 that the 'put-upon wives of Britain' were turning up in hospitals every day, exhausted and depressed. Many felt taken for granted by their husbands, said Dr Odlum – they were humiliated, frustrated and resentful at their lack of autonomy.

'They only get housekeeping money, and out of this they have to pinch and screw whatever they can for their own needs.' But now, she said, women were 'beginning to think for themselves – the result is the dawn of revolt in the home'.

The married call-girls described by Harry were dramatic examples of these restless new women. On the one hand, a woman who hired out her body played to male fantasies of control: she was subject to a man's whims and desires, in thrall to his money. But on the other, she was a threatening figure: independent, experienced with other men, unsentimental and pragmatic about sex.

Alongside Dr Odlum's article, the *Mirror* ran a short piece about a forthcoming 3-D film, *House of Wax*, in which Vincent Price played a disfigured sculptor who murders women, coats their bodies with wax and puts them on show in his museum. Next to this item the paper published a large photograph of Reg Christie arriving at the magistrates' court: a man who had acted on just such dreams of dominance.

In *Woman's Own* in 1950, the film star Dirk Bogarde outlined what he required from his ideal woman. 'Do not smoke in public,' he wrote. 'Do not wear high heels with slacks. Wear a little skilful make-up. Never draw attention to yourself in public places by loud laughter, conversation, or clothing. NEVER try to order a meal from a menu when I am with you. Never laugh at me in front of my friends... Never welcome me back in the evening with a smutty face, the smell of cooking in your hair, broken nails, and a whine about the day's trials and difficulties.'

A woman from Essex responded on the letters page: 'After reading Dirk Bogarde's article, I find that I am his ideal woman. The only snag is, I breathe. Do you think it matters?'

4

The washhouse

While Harry waited to see Christie again, he continued to turn out stories for his paper. He wrote them up in the *Pictorial* and *Mirror* office at Geraldine House, a 1920s block off Fleet Street, at a long table furnished with typewriters, Anglepoise lamps, paper trays, ashtrays and banks of black Bakelite phones. Light washed in through the slanted windows and glowed from the globes on the ceiling.

On Saturday 4 April, Harry filed a story about Ruby Crocket, a housemaid whose wedding he had attended that afternoon. Ruby had concealed from her groom that she had just been convicted of theft at Croydon Magistrates' Court. On Sunday, as she awoke in her honeymoon suite, Ruby and the *Pic*'s readers would share a secret of which her new husband was seemingly oblivious. Harry also filed a short item for the edition to announce that Cliftons solicitors had been appointed to defend Christie, not mentioning that his paper was paying their fees.

Harry reacquainted himself with the details of the Evans case. There were a few articles on the murders in the newspapers' cuttings library, and Roy Arthur, the Cliftons clerk, had been given a transcript of Evans's trial by the barrister who had represented him in 1950. Christie may have chosen Harry over his rival at the *Sunday Dispatch* because he was impressed by his fame as a reporter – 'I want Harry Procter to have my story,' he had told Roy Arthur in the magistrates' court. Or he may have considered him an ally, even a pawn, after their encounter in 1949. But Harry was determined not to be fooled by Christie this time.

***

Beryl Susanna Evans, the twenty-year-old Jewish woman found murdered with her baby at 10 Rillington Place in December 1949, was brought up a few streets away, in Cambridge Gardens. She and her younger brothers and sister were evacuated to Surrey during the war, and on her return to Notting Hill in 1943 she helped to nurse her mother, who suffered from pleurisy and bronchial pneumonia.

Beryl was a lively, affectionate girl, according to her youngest brother. She used to whistle and sing Bing Crosby's 'White Christmas' around the house, loud and out of tune. Their mother died in March 1947, and Beryl soon afterwards met Timothy Evans on a blind date. Tim, like Beryl, was slight and dark-haired. They were married that September, when he was twenty-three and she had just turned eighteen.

The couple lived at first with Tim's family at 11 St Mark's Road. Beryl worked as a telephonist at the Grosvenor Hotel in Victoria, and Tim as a van driver for Lancaster Foods in Notting Hill. After the birth of their baby, Geraldine, in 1948, they moved round the corner to the two top-floor rooms at 10 Rillington Place.

Tim drank at the Kensington Park Hotel and Elgin pubs on Ladbroke Grove, where he was known as a cocky lad, given to exaggeration and tall tales. He could put away as many as ten pints in a Saturday session. By the summer of 1949, he and Beryl were constantly arguing. She complained that he spent too much time at the pub, wasted money on drink and gambling, and chased after other women; he accused her of being spendthrift and untidy. In August, Beryl was distressed to find that she was pregnant with a second child, whose birth would tie her even more tightly to their home and stretch their income still further.

The whole family went missing in November, and at the end of the month Tim Evans surrendered himself to the police in Merthyr Tydfil, near his birthplace in South Wales. 'I want to give myself up,' he announced to the constable on duty on 30 November. 'I have disposed of my wife.'

'What do you mean?' asked the officer.

'I put her down the drain,' said Tim. 'I can't sleep and want to get it off my chest.'

Tim Evans said that Beryl had threatened to kill both herself and Geraldine if she couldn't end her pregnancy, so he had given her a bottle of abortifacient medicine that he had been handed by a man in a roadside café. On his return from work on 8 November, he said, he found Beryl lying dead on their bed. He assumed that the potion had killed her.

He fed Geraldine, who was in her cot, sat down and smoked a cigarette, and in the early hours of the morning, he said, he carried Beryl's body down the stairs and pushed it headfirst into a drain in front of the house. He then left for his aunt and uncle's house in Merthyr Vale, having found someone to look after his daughter.

The Notting Hill police, when this information was relayed to them, went to Rillington Place to inspect the drains in front of No 10 – the manhole cover was so heavy that it took three officers to raise it, using tyre levers and screwdrivers that they borrowed from the garage at the end of the street. There was nothing inside.

Evans, on being told that the drains were empty, conceded that he had misled the Welsh officers. 'No,' he told them. 'I said that to protect a man called Christie. It's not true about the man in the café either. I'll tell you the truth now.'

In his second statement, he claimed that Reg Christie had offered Beryl an abortion, assuring her and Tim that he was qualified to carry out the procedure – he showed Tim the medical books in his flat – but warning them that one in ten such operations was fatal. Tim hadn't wanted Beryl to go through with it, he said, but she was determined. As he left for work on 8 November, Tim told Christie 'everything is all right': he could proceed with the abortion.

Tim said that Christie was waiting for him in the hall when he came in at 6.30 that night. 'Go on up,' said Christie. 'I'll come behind you.'

Upstairs, Christie warned: 'It's bad news. It didn't work,' and showed him his wife's body on the bed. Beryl, said Tim, was bleeding from the mouth and 'the bottom part'.

According to Tim, Christie carried Beryl's corpse to an empty room on the first floor – its elderly tenant, Mr Kitchener, was in hospital – and said that he would later put it down the drain. 'You'd better go to bed,' said Christie, 'and leave the rest to me.' (Tim later amended this story, to say that he had helped Christie carry the body to the first-floor room when he heard him puffing and blowing on the stairs.)

Christie fed the baby while Tim was out at work on Wednesday, Tim claimed, and told him in the evening that he had found a childless couple in East Acton, west of Notting Hill, who would take her in. When Tim got home from work on Thursday, Christie said that the couple had collected the baby, and he would soon send on her highchair, pram and clothes. Tim sold the rest of his furniture, and on Monday 14 November he headed for Wales. He returned to London briefly a week later, with the intention of seeing Geraldine, he said, but Christie told him to let her settle in for a bit longer at her new home.

The police in Notting Hill, on being informed of Tim's second confession, returned to Rillington Place. They searched the Evanses' top-floor flat, where they found a stolen briefcase, and asked Reg Christie to come to the station in Ladbroke Grove to be interviewed. Some of the Notting Hill officers knew Christie, as he had served as a reserve constable in a neighbouring police station during the war.

In his interview on 1 December 1949, Christie denied any involvement in the disappearance of Beryl and Geraldine. He had always considered Tim 'a bit mental', he told the police: he knew that Tim hit Beryl and he had heard him threaten to 'do her in'. Christie said he had been aware that Beryl was taking drugs to bring on a miscarriage: 'I said to her, in my wife's presence, that she was looking a physical wreck and advised her to stop it. We warned her of the consequences and she promised both of us that she would stop taking the stuff.' He dismissed Tim's claim that he had offered her an abortion. Ethel Christie, who was interviewed at 10 Rillington Place that evening, gave the police a similar story.

On 2 December, Detective Inspector James Black was despatched to Wales to arrest Tim, on the pretext that the police had found a stolen briefcase in his flat. Meanwhile, his fellow officers in London returned to No 10 to search the premises more thoroughly. In the washhouse in the back yard, they found the bodies of Tim's wife and daughter, partly concealed by some pieces of wood. Both had been strangled to death. Beryl's face was bruised and swollen. A sixteen-week-old male foetus was in her womb.

The Notting Hill police telephoned Inspector Black in Wales to tell him that they had discovered two bodies at Rillington Place. He was told not to mention this to Tim Evans, but to bring him back at once. Black took Tim to London by train. At Notting Hill station, Chief Inspector George Jennings informed

Tim that they had found the bodies of his wife and child in the washhouse. He showed him two piles of clothes – on top of one was the necktie that had been wrapped around Geraldine's neck.

Tim now said that it was he who had killed them. In a long statement to Jennings and Black, he explained that he and Beryl had a fight about money in the evening of 8 November, and he had used a rope from his van to strangle her. He bundled up her body, took it to the first-floor room and then to the washhouse. For the next two days he had left the baby alone while he went to work, and in the evening of 10 November, he killed her: 'I picked up my baby from her cot in the bedroom, picked up my tie and strangled her with it.' At midnight, he said, he placed her body next to that of her mother in the washhouse. 'I then slipped upstairs, and laid on the bed all night, fully clothed.'

'It's a great relief to get it off my chest,' said Tim as he finished his confession. 'I feel better already.'

Tim Evans was charged with the murder of his wife. 'Yes,' said Tim. 'That's right.' At Brixton prison, he confirmed to the medical officer that he had killed her.

Tim was appointed a solicitor, under the new legal aid system, and a barrister to represent him in court. Now he changed his story again, reverting to his claim that Beryl had died at the hands of his neighbour, who he now said had killed Geraldine, too. 'Christie done it,' he insisted. But the lawyers feared that Tim's case was hopeless. He had signed a detailed confession to two murders.

The Crown decided to prosecute Tim Evans for the killing of his daughter. Under English law, a person could be tried for only one murder at a time, and they guessed that Evans might mount a defence of manslaughter, on the grounds of provocation, if charged with killing his wife. There could be no such defence for the murder of a child.

At Tim Evans's trial at the Old Bailey in January 1950, Harry had watched Christie give evidence for the prosecution. The

Crown's barrister portrayed Christie as a model citizen, who had been wounded in action in the First World War and commended as a police officer in the Second. He appeared so frail that the judge invited him to sit down in the witness box. The defence barrister tried to discredit him by asking him about his criminal record, but was unable to make much of this; he had learnt of Christie's previous offences only just before the trial, and the most recent of them dated from 1933.

Christie rejected all of Tim Evans's accusations. He insisted that his many physical ailments would have made it impossible for him to move a body. He said that Tim had told him that Beryl and Geraldine had gone to Bristol. Tim had seemed 'extremely angry', said Christie; 'upset, really wild, as though he had had a terrific row, I should say'. Christie claimed that he had heard a 'thud' upstairs on the night of 8 November, 'as though something heavy was being moved'.

Ethel Christie, in her evidence, confirmed her husband's account, saying that she too had heard a 'bump' upstairs that night.

When Tim Evans went into the witness box, he said that he had left London on Christie's advice, believing that Beryl had died during an attempted abortion. Why then, asked the prosecution counsel, had he told the Notting Hill police that he had himself killed his wife and daughter? 'Well,' he said. 'I thought that if I didn't make a statement the police would take me downstairs and start knocking me about.' He claimed to have been in a state of despair when he made his confession: 'I did not know my daughter was dead till Detective Inspector Jennings told me about it. I had nothing more to live for.'

But he could not explain why he had tried to protect Christie in his first statement to the Welsh police – nor why Christie might have committed the murders.

'Can you suggest why he should have strangled your wife?' the prosecutor asked him.

'Well, he was home all day,' Tim offered.

'Can you suggest why he should have strangled your wife?' repeated the prosecutor.

'No, I cannot.'

'Can you suggest why he should have strangled your daughter two days later?'

'No.'

The jury took just forty minutes to agree that Tim Evans was guilty. He was executed in March 1950.

But now that Christie had confessed to killing four women at 10 Rillington Place, Harry thought that Evans might have been innocent after all. Perhaps Tim had been telling the truth in his second confession in Wales, when he said that Beryl had submitted to an abortion, and he had later – for some reason – lied when he revoked it. Harry knew that his Christie exclusive would be all the more electrifying if he was able to show that Tim Evans had been hanged in error.

***

George Stonier of the *New Statesman* visited North Kensington as dusk was falling one Monday in the spring of 1953. He walked past a nun, in a black-and-white coif and tunic, and a couple of West Indian men 'with strange gaieties of shirt peeping out from raincoats', before he turned into Rillington Place. There he joined more than twenty bystanders, most of them women, who were watching No 10 in silence from the facing pavement. Every detail of the house seemed sinister to him: the cracks in the front door, the shiny patches where its green paint had worn away, the five windows shrouded with curtains.

All of a sudden a man emerged from No 9, propped a ladder against its front and set to work cleaning the windows. 'How his rag whirled!' wrote Stonier. 'What polishings and squeakings!' The small crowd of onlookers relaxed a little and began to chat – about their gardens, the races at Newmarket, the price of cauliflowers. The man continued to rub vigorously at the glass, observed Stonier, as if to signal 'that *he* had nothing to hide, *his* windows weren't afraid to let the light in'.

The residents of Rillington Place were annoyed by the attention that their road was attracting. 'There is a stigma on the street now,' complained one. 'We are all honest, working-class folk, and we don't see why we should suffer for other people's crimes.' Alice McFadden of No 3 said that they needed to protect the children, who were being teased at school. Her husband, Dave, told reporters that his workmates were ribbing him about whether any more bodies had been found at No 10. 'It's terrible,' he said. 'As soon as I arrive they ask what the "score" is.' Dave's brother, Alex, was furious to find a photographer in the street when he came home from the pub one Saturday night. He grabbed the man's camera and threw it to the ground.

Mrs McFadden sent Kensington Council a petition to change the road's name, signed by eighty-three of its adult residents. Only John Clark of No 13 abstained, because he had just printed his address on 1,000 flyers for his window-cleaning business.

When interviewed by the police, the neighbours said that Reg and Ethel Christie had seemed respectable people, almost too good for the area. Mr Christie dressed nicely, observed Leila Dymond of No 13, and Mrs Christie was a quiet lady. William Swan of 9 Rillington Place said that Reg always set off for work in a suit, often carrying a rolled-up umbrella. Another neighbour described him as a polite man who raised his hat to every woman he knew. Margaret Ploughman of No 14, a widow in her late seventies, said that the last time she saw Mr Christie he had stopped to inquire after her infected eye.

For the most part, his neighbours recalled, Christie had kept himself to himself. He went on long walks at night, and ignored knocks at the door unless he expected callers (the house had no doorbell, but it was so cheaply constructed that sound carried easily: visitors rapped the large black knocker once for the ground-floor tenants, twice for the first floor, three times for the second).

Some of the local children knew Christie as 'Spoil-sport' or 'Grumpy', because he told them off when they kicked balls against the wickets and goalposts they had chalked up on the wall at the end of the street. 'I'll have the police on you!' he would shout. But Ruby Newman, a thirteen-year-old who lived directly opposite No 10, said that Mr Christie was kind to her: he once gave her a flower pot, and he advised her on how to look after her plants. Ruby's father, Albert, was a lorry driver who had founded the Kensington Poultry and Rabbit Club in the late 1940s, having taken to breeding animals during the war; he had won several trophies for the chickens he kept in the back garden of No 11.

When Christie was working for the Metropolitan Police war reserve force, from 1939 to 1943, he had taken pleasure in his role as a law-enforcer. Mrs McFadden remembered how bossy he had been, in his high-collared blue uniform and peaked cap. He would chastise neighbours for the slightest chink in their blackout curtains, she said: 'He threatened to report practically everybody in the street.' A colleague at the Harrow Road police station agreed that Christie's uniform 'gave him a certain status and a sense of power over ordinary people'. He flashed his warrant card about, said his fellow officer, and boasted about the number of people he had arrested.

Christie appointed himself the official photographer at street parties, among them the celebration of Victory in Europe Day in May 1945, and he developed photographs for his neighbours – the

McFaddens' niece, Patricia, had pushed a roll of film through the letterbox of No 10 shortly before he went missing. The police had also found a cache of negatives hidden in the chimney stack in Christie's kitchen. He was a man who liked to watch others.

Christie's colleagues told the police that he liked taking charge in the workplace, too. He had volunteered as a first-aid officer when he worked at the Post Office Savings Bank in Kew in the late 1940s. 'He always made a terrific fuss over just a scratch,' said a fellow worker. 'I've gone to him with only a little cut on my thumb and came away with a huge bandage over it.' At British Road Services, the government-run haulage firm for which he had worked as an invoice clerk since 1950, he became chairman of the union and acted as referee at football matches. He 'would trot about the pitch', said one of the players, 'very much in command of the game'.

After a spell of ill health, Christie had been transferred in September 1952 from British Road Services in Shepherd's Bush to the depot in Cressy Road, Hampstead. A female worker there said that Christie had told her to come to him if she ever 'got in trouble'. By this, she said, 'I understood he performed abortions.' Abortion was illegal, but some women resorted to back-street procedures if their own attempts to induce miscarriage failed. Christie also told a man at the depot that he could help out if he got a girl pregnant, and informed both a waitress and a customer at the Panda Café, in Westbourne Park Road, that he was a former doctor who had been struck off the medical register for 'helping a girl out of trouble'. One woman told the police that Christie had stopped her in Portobello Road in early March 1953, when she was out with her baby and child, and asked her if she was pregnant. 'If you were,' he said, 'I know how to get rid of it for you.'

But to most of his neighbours and his colleagues, Christie had seemed restrained, punctilious, above reproach. He had duped them, as he had duped Harry Procter and the jury at the Evans trial, into thinking him an upright, proper and faintly prudish member of the community.

***

When Ethel Christie disappeared in the middle of December 1952, Reg variously told his neighbours that she had gone to Birmingham, or Bristol, or Halifax, or Sheffield. By now he had packed in his job and was living on unemployment benefits. On Christmas Day he called at 9 Rillington Place with Christmas cards and a box of handkerchiefs for Ethel's friend Rosina Swan and her family. Rosie and her husband, William, shared the house with her niece, Louisa Gregg, and Louisa's husband and children. Mrs Gregg, realising that Reg was at home alone, invited him to come over in the evening to watch television. The BBC showed a couple of children's programmes that night (*The Flowerpot Men*, *Andy Pandy*) and then a festive variety show with Norman Wisdom, Frankie Howerd, Tommy Cooper and Petula Clark. Reg was 'all nerves', Rosie Swan recalled.

In early March, Christie told Louisa Gregg that he was lonely and didn't know what to do with himself. She reassured him that he would feel better when Ethel came home. A week or so later, her husband was emptying their waste bucket in the garden when he saw Christie over the fence. Christie told him that he was feeling a bit restless and wanted a smoke. John Gregg passed him a packet of ten cigarettes.

Bessie Styles, who lived above the Newmans at 11 Rillington Place, spotted Reg Christie shining a torch in his front room in March. 'I could see him through a gap in his curtains,' she said. 'I saw him moving the light up and down.' Other neighbours noticed him with unfamiliar women. Emily Lawrence of No 8 saw him taking a woman with red-tinted brown hair to his house. Jennie Grimes, a waitress who lived at No 19, saw him walking along Lancaster Road at 11.30 p.m. one night with a woman in black. The next morning, he sought out Mrs Grimes and said that he hoped she didn't think the woman was anything to do with him: he was only showing her the way to Ladbroke Grove station.

Other residents of North Kensington came forward to report meeting Christie when he was trying to rent out his flat in the first weeks of 1953. A woman had been to see the property with her husband and mother-in-law one evening in January. The hall was dark – Christie, explaining that there were no mantles on the gas lamps, used a torch to show the visitors through to his rooms. He poured them glasses of Irish whiskey in the kitchen, where they saw two pink corsets hanging from a clothesline. Another prospective tenant noticed a peculiar smell in the building. 'I asked Mr Christie if there were coloured men in the house,' she said, 'and he said there were and I put the smell down to this.'

***

Fryn Tennyson Jesse wondered how Reg Christie had started to kill. 'How do people like Christie find out that they *are* like that?' she wrote to her fellow novelist Rebecca West. 'The opportunities for finding out seem so limited. Or do they just feel peculiar one day when passing Kensal Green?'

Fryn had been told by her friend Joe Jackson, at Scotland Yard, that the police were still confident of Tim Evans's guilt. But she thought that Christie might have helped Evans to hide the bodies of Beryl and Geraldine, and she wondered whether those murders had inspired his own: this would account for the coincidence of two men in the same house committing such similar crimes.

'Perhaps stranglers attract other stranglers,' Fryn reflected in her letter to West. 'I don't know. Perhaps seeing Evans strangle his wife and child first attracted Christie's attention and gave him the experience and the practice he needed to discover he was like that?' She believed it possible that both men in the house had murdered their wives.

Fryn was married to the well-known playwright Harold Marsh Harwood, a bear-like man whom she adored, but their relationship had been fraught from the start. They had met in 1913, when he adapted her short story 'The Mask' for the stage. She was a pretty and vivacious young woman. 'When she came into a room,' said a friend, 'she brought with her a golden ambience. She glowed. It was not only the whorl of gleaming hair, or the warmth of her resonant voice, or the flashing humour that lit her words.' Rebecca West thought her the loveliest girl she had ever seen.

But Fryn was insecure about her looks. She felt that her features were too coarse, her forehead too wide. She was ashamed of her artificial right hand, which had been fitted when she lost several fingers to an aeroplane propeller in the year that she met Harwood. The accident left her feeling 'most horribly mutilated', she said. 'I thought no one would be in love with me again.' When the *Daily Mail* sent her to report on the women serving at the Western Front in 1918, she marvelled at the volunteers' indifference to their appearance. The drivers would return to the barracks windblown and reddened, throw their caps down and push their hair back off their brows. 'What blessed freedom!' Fryn wrote. 'This at last is what it is to be free as a man.'

That year Fryn married 'Tottie', as everyone knew Harwood, but he at first insisted that their union be kept secret. He told Fryn that he had a child by a married woman, who he feared might stop him from seeing his son if she knew that he had taken a wife.

Slowly, Fryn came to realise that Tottie was still sleeping with this woman. She became desperately jealous of his mistress and their child, and one night in 1921, while Tottie was visiting them, she took an overdose of barbiturates. He afterwards agreed to make their marriage public.

Fryn suffered three miscarriages in the 1920s and 1930s, each more painful and distressing than the last. She felt humiliated by her failure to bear Tottie a child, and sometimes wondered if her miscarriages were a punishment for her literary ambition. But she kept writing. In stories about murder, she could escape into emotions – a killer's fury, a victim's terror – that outstripped her own.

She often took barbiturates, on top of the morphine to which she had become addicted after her accident, and occasionally doped so much that she became paranoid and vicious. She more than once had to be taken to hospital to have her stomach pumped.

'Come back and love me,' Fryn pleaded with Tottie after one of her breakdowns. 'That is all I mind, except your work and my work. I have no child to share you with – you are everything – that has to be my distinction now.'

Fryn and Tottie travelled round the United States in the early 1930s, while he was writing the screenplay for the Greta Garbo film *Queen Christina*, and in 1937 they moved into Pear Tree Cottage. The house lay in a cul-de-sac in St John's Wood, north of Marylebone, its wrought-iron front gate giving on to a fountain and a pear tree in a garden enclosed by rose-pink walls. Tottie continued to produce plays and scripts, and to draw a handsome income from his family's cotton-spinning business in Bolton, Lancashire.

In 1952, when she discovered that she was losing her sight to cataracts, Fryn became terrified that Tottie would stop wanting her. She begged him to tell his secret son that she and no one else had been the love of his life. 'I know all this sounds very egoistic,' she wrote to him, 'but my love is all I have had in my life except my writing, and I love you so terribly it hurts me to look at you.'

In his reply, Tottie urged Fryn to put the past behind her. He had long since broken up with his mistress, he said. 'I told you a short time ago how much more I loved you than ever before,' he wrote, 'and it is true.'

Fryn wondered whether Ethel Christie, like her, had felt needed only by her husband. Perhaps this was why she had returned to Reg after their decade-long separation, and stayed with him until he killed her. 'The heart of a woman is a strange thing,' wrote Fryn. 'Human beings, especially women, are bound not only by money, by loneliness, but by the hope that they are needed.'

In March 1953, while Christie was on the run, a married man had contacted the Sheffield police to disclose what had become of Ethel in the years that she and Reg were apart. At the letter-writer's request, the information was not made public. But his account showed how Ethel's life, like Fryn's, had been blighted by childlessness. Just as an unwanted pregnancy could destroy a woman's happiness, so could her failure to bear a child.

In 1928, five years after splitting up with Reg, Ethel went to Sheffield to live with her brother, Henry, who worked as a clerk for the city council, and she found a job as a shorthand typist in a steel works. Her sister, Lily, lived next door, having moved to the city after separating from her husband, and now ran a grocer's shop from her home. Ethel was very fond of Lily's baby, Edwin.

At a dance at the Abbeydale ballroom one night, Ethel met Vaughan Brindley, a radio engineer and the son of a prosperous tool manufacturer. They were instantly drawn to one another. Ethel let Vaughan believe that she was twenty-six, like him, and single, rather than a married woman of thirty. He took her to dances, to the theatre and the cinema. After they had been dating for three months, Ethel realised that she was falling for Vaughan and decided to reveal at least some of her history.

Ethel wore her wedding ring one day, and when Vaughan noticed it she burst into tears, telling him that she had married when she was very young, and her husband had died after being gassed on the Western Front. Ethel claimed that she had concealed her former marriage in case, as a young widow, she attracted unwelcome attention from men. She had only been looking for a good time when she met Vaughan, she told him, but now she was falling in love.

Once Ethel had declared her feelings, she and Vaughan became closer. They continued to live separately – she with her sister, he in a rented room – but they started to have sex, registering as 'Mr and Mrs Christie' in bed and breakfast hotels in Bournemouth, Blackpool and Derbyshire. Ethel kept a shorthand diary, in a notebook with golden edges, in which she recorded each sexual encounter. They discussed getting married when they had saved enough money, but it was a slow process – Vaughan was earning £3 a week at his radio shop, where business was poor, and Ethel received about £3 and ten shillings as a typist.

Vaughan was everything Ethel had hoped for: a kind, hard-working man who was much more amorous and sexually confident than Reg had been – she and Reg had not had full intercourse in the three years that they lived together. Vaughan introduced his shy, pretty girlfriend to his family and friends, and Ethel introduced Vaughan to her sister; perhaps Lily agreed to go along with her claim to be a widow.

By 1932 Vaughan's father had given him a well-paid post as head operator at a cinema that he owned, and Vaughan had saved almost enough money to marry. But he had started to have doubts about Ethel: he wanted a family, and she had not become pregnant in the four years that they had been sleeping together. When he told Ethel his concerns, she insisted that she could conceive: she had been pregnant during her first marriage, she claimed, but had a miscarriage at six months. Vaughan warned her that he would only marry a woman with whom he could have children.

Ethel made a direct approach to Vaughan's father, begging him to intervene. She told him that she and his eldest son had been living as man and wife for four years, and he was now refusing to marry her. William Brindley told Vaughan that it was his duty to marry Ethel, and offered him money towards their first home. But Vaughan was furious that Ethel had gone to his father behind his back. They quarrelled bitterly and he told her that the relationship was over. Ethel was devastated. She wrote to Vaughan, enclosing a photograph of herself. He destroyed the letter and the picture.

In his letter to the Sheffield police in 1953, Vaughan Brindley expressed regret about how his relationship with Ethel had ended. 'I regarded her as a refined, well-bred and educated young woman,' he wrote. 'She was extremely attractive, but I know that she never associated with any other men and she would not go into public houses or even smoke. She had a timid, sensitive nature, and was an extremely competent shorthand typist.' They had fallen out, he said, only because of his 'obsession about having a childless marriage and the great quarrel after she had told my father what had happened'.

He asked the police to keep his identity to themselves, as his wife and two children did not know about this episode in his past. But by writing his letter, he put on record that Ethel had once been happy, and loved.

After being ditched by Vaughan in 1933, Ethel was desperate. She learnt that Reg was in Wandsworth prison, serving a sentence for car theft, and she went to London to see him. In the visitors' room, Reg asked Ethel to come back to him – he needed her, he said – and she consented. On his release in 1934, she was waiting for him at the prison gate. They agreed not to discuss anything that had happened in the decade they had spent apart.

The Christies took a room in Oxford Gardens, Notting Hill, and in 1936 Reg became foreman of the Commodore cinema in Hammersmith. Early in 1937 they moved into the top-floor rooms at 10 Rillington Place, which the Evans family would later occupy, and after a year and a half moved down to the ground-floor flat. During the war, when married women were encouraged to work, Ethel took a job at the Osram light bulb factory in Hammersmith. The couple seemed contented. Ethel's sister, Lily, said that Ethel never said a word against Reggie. Her brother, Henry, observed that she would have kept it to herself if there had been any difficulty between them.

Ethel remained close to Lily and her son, whom she used to visit in Sheffield. She was fond of the local children, too. After the war, she enjoyed watching television with Louisa Gregg's children at No 9 on Thursday afternoons, and when the Evans family moved into No 10, she would offer tea and sticky buns to Beryl's fourteen-year-old brother, Peter, if he called by on his way home from school. Peter would sit in a rope deckchair to play snap and rummy with Reg at the kitchen table. He sometimes went out to the garden to throw a ball for the Christies' leggy mongrel, Judy.

Ethel was especially attached to Tim and Beryl's daughter, Geraldine, who she often looked after when Beryl went out. The baby would giggle at the antics of Judy the dog. When Ethel realised that the Evanses' marriage was in trouble, she told Beryl that she and Reg would be happy to adopt Geraldine if they split up. Beryl told her that there was no need: her mother-in-law had already offered to take her in.

On 2 December 1949, Ethel watched the police search the washhouse in the back yard of No 10. As they lifted up the first bundle, she saw Beryl's feet slip out of the blanket. Then she saw the body of the baby.

5

My Sweetest Darling

On the advice of Cliftons solicitors, Harry appointed Derek Curtis-Bennett QC, a balding man with round black spectacles, to represent Reg Christie in court. Curtis-Bennett was a well-known barrister. In 1946 he had helped to defend William Joyce, or 'Lord Haw-Haw', a Nazi propagandist who had been charged with high treason. Curtis-Bennett's life had taken a downward turn since then. He frequented Soho clubs and bars, as well as gentlemen's clubs in Piccadilly, and his colleagues noticed that he sometimes slurred his words in court. A hearing into government corruption in 1948 had to be adjourned when Curtis-Bennett, who was appearing for the defendant, was found dead drunk in his rooms. In 1949 his marriage ended in divorce. But he still had a reputation as a powerful advocate, well equipped for a case as big as the defence of Christie.

Harry returned to Leeds to tell Percy Christie that the *Pictorial* had hired lawyers for his brother. He asked Percy if he would give him an interview, but Percy said that he and his sisters did not want to speak to the press. Nor did they wish to attend their brother's trial.

At 1.40 p.m. on Thursday 9 April 1953, Harry turned up at Brixton prison in the hope of interviewing Reg Christie. Rather than identify himself as a journalist, he said he was a friend of the prisoner. He was admitted through a high wooden door in the arch of the perimeter wall, and was asked to wait while the guards consulted their superiors. The prison governor called an official at the Home Office, who told him to turn Harry away.

Before he left, Harry wrote a letter for Christie. 'I am terribly sorry they would not allow me to see you when I called at Brixton prison today,' he said. 'I waited for 2 hours, but it was of no avail.' He was polite about the staff, who he knew would vet his letter: 'the prison authorities were kind enough to let me leave some cigarettes, sweets and apples for you, and I do hope you get them'.

'I hope it will be possible to see you in the future,' he continued, 'but meanwhile let me assure you that, if there is any little personal thing you want, or little private service you would like doing, you can count on me. For instance, if you have any particular brand of cigarettes, if there are any special sweets you like, or if there is anything you want bringing or buying I will get it for you and drop it in at once... How about clothes? Anything you want in the clothing line?... How about reading?' He advised him not to see or write to any strangers: 'But you can drop me a line any time you feel like it.' Harry finished his letter by passing on best wishes to Christie from his brother – a coded reminder of the deal that he had struck with Percy.

The governor consulted the Home Office about Harry's letter and about a contract that the *Pictorial* had submitted for Christie, in which the paper promised, in exchange for his exclusive story, to pay his £500 defence costs and to make a payment of £1,150 to his family. The Home Office forbade Christie from signing the contract, and ruled that all correspondence between him and Harry Procter be prohibited.

But Roy Arthur, who as Christie's solicitor had free access to the jail, encouraged Christie to start writing an account of his life for Harry, on the understanding that the *Pictorial* would pay his costs as promised. Christie readily agreed. 'I wish the *Sunday Pictorial* exclusively to have my story,' he wrote in a note for Arthur. 'Please see they get it.' He started to compose a statement for Arthur to smuggle out of the jail. The prison authorities could not inspect documents that an inmate entrusted to his solicitor.

In the first instalment of his statement, Christie ranted about the 'niggers' in 10 Rillington Place. They were an 'insistent torment', he wrote. They had 'persistantly persicuted' him and his wife for the past two and a half years. 'These coloured people used to kick and dance and make noise continually until we just could not sit in the front room in evenings or weekends. Complaints to the landlord were useless. He encouraged it in an effort to make us leave.' When Charles Brown called round for his rent, said Christie, Ethel would refuse to open the door to him – 'She was too scared' – and the landlord would go through the hall to the back garden to grin at her through the kitchen window.

Christie insisted that if only London County Council's housing committee had arranged alternative accommodation for him and Ethel, they would still be very happy together. He seemed to be trying to blame her death, and the deaths that followed, on the black men in 10 Rillington Place.

In his statement, Christie boasted of his expertise in first aid – his colleagues at British Road Services had great faith in his medical abilities, he said. He described himself as a good husband – 'not what is described as "sexy" never was', but helpful around the house, 'washing scrubbing polishing floors and cooking meals when my wife was not well or tired'. He enjoyed repairing clocks and radios, he said, and used to make spinning tops for the local children.

He alluded only indirectly to his aggressive impulses. 'For many years I have had many dreams at night and are nearly always mixed up with some form of violence,' he wrote. 'Sometimes I have helped to check it, but mainly I have just been looking on.'

Harry locked Christie's statement in a safe at Geraldine House. If the *Pictorial* were to publish any of it now, the paper might be prosecuted for contempt of court. The editor of the *Daily Mirror* had been jailed for three months in 1949 for disclosing details of John Haigh's 'Acid Bath Murders' before the case came to trial.

So far, Christie had made no reference in his notes to the women he had killed, nor to the Evans case. Harry urged Roy Arthur to impress on him that, since a plea of insanity was his only possible defence, it would be in his interests to confess to the murders of Beryl and Geraldine: the more people he had killed, the more likely he was to be found mad.

Harry hoped to get hold of some of Christie's family photographs for the paper, but Roy Arthur was allowed to take only documents out of the prison. The two of them arranged for Francis Ross, a self-styled journalist with several criminal convictions, to act as an intermediary. Ross had met Christie during the war, when the mobile canteen on which he worked was sent to Harrow Road after a bombing raid. He had also worked briefly for Cliftons.

When Francis Ross visited Brixton the next week, Christie gave him some photos from his family album, which Ross then sold to Harry. On the front page of the *Pictorial* that Sunday, Reg and Ethel were shown smiling in a park, her hand through his arm; he wore a suit and held a hat, while she wore a frilled floral dress and a pair of white gloves. On the back page, they were pictured separately: Reg leaning against the iron railings of the Palace Pier at Brighton, his left hand in his pocket, his right holding a cigarette; Ethel standing next to two swans on a lake.

At the prison on Monday 20 April, Roy Arthur introduced Christie to Dr Jack Hobson, a forensic psychiatrist and founder member of the Society for the Abolition of Capital Punishment, who had been hired by the defence to assess whether Christie was insane. Dr Hobson had recently helped to secure the acquittal of a man charged with sexual assault and attempted murder – he had testified in court that the defendant's 'brain worked abnormally'. Hobson and Christie spoke for four hours. Christie seemed to enjoy talking about himself, observed the psychiatrist. But when asked if he had anything to do with the Evans murders, he dismissed the suggestion as 'monstrous'.

***

Harry had been barred from seeing Christie in Brixton because of a murder he had investigated five months earlier – a case that had caused a furore about the workings of the British justice system, as he hoped that the Christie case might do.

In November 1952, Christopher Craig, aged sixteen, and Derek Bentley, nineteen, had been chased by police while they were trying to burgle a warehouse in Croydon, south London. Craig pulled out a gun. 'Let him have it, Chris!' shouted Bentley, and Craig shot one of their pursuers dead. Both youths were arrested.

This was an explosive story, not only because a police officer had been killed, but also because of the widespread anxiety about a new generation of violent young men, armed with the thousands of firearms that had been circulating in Britain since the war. Harry described it as 'the terror-problem of the times'.

Harry befriended the Craig family and persuaded them to introduce him to Chris, who was awaiting trial in Brixton prison. The boy was lying on his bed when Harry arrived. 'Brought me any comics?' he asked. 'I'm mad about comics. Have you brought some apples? How is my girlfriend?' He boasted about his liking for guns and gangster movies.

During Craig and Bentley's trial in December, Harry drove Craig's family to the Old Bailey in the paper's Rolls-Royce, and at lunchtime shepherded them to a local pub, making sure that no other reporters got near them.

In court, Derek Bentley's defence team argued that their client was an impressionable young man who had been led astray by Christopher Craig and had played no part in the killing of PC Sydney Miles. He had not been urging Craig to shoot when he cried: 'Let him have it!', they said, but to surrender his weapon.

None the less, on Friday 12 December Craig and Bentley were both found guilty of murder. Craig, though he had fired the fatal shot, was spared the death penalty on account of his age, and instead sentenced to imprisonment 'at Her Majesty's Pleasure', for a minimum of ten years. Bentley was sentenced to death.

Harry was shocked by the verdict – it seemed obvious to him that Bentley was innocent of the murder.

As soon as the court dispersed, Harry bundled the Craigs into the Rolls-Royce and drove them to a hotel in Shepperton, Surrey. That night the *Pictorial*'s news editor, Fred Redman, phoned Harry at the hotel to ask for a piece by Christopher's father. Harry composed a story based on what Niven Craig had confided in him over the previous few weeks – his heartbreak over his son's actions and his regret about how he had indulged the boy – and Niven, reluctantly, signed off the ghost-written article. He had already taken the *Pictorial*'s money, after all, accepted its hospitality, entrusted it with his family's story. He begged Harry to make sure that the piece would not be sensationalised.

On Sunday 14 December, the *Pictorial* published Harry's interview with Chris in his prison cell. 'He tossed back his coal-black hair,' wrote Harry, 'turned his strikingly handsome head. "What a handsome youth!" I thought. And then he grinned. The grin broke the spell. As I saw the left lip curl and the impudent flicker creep into his eyes I knew I was watching just another of those brass-faced little hooligans of which this post-war world is so bitterly ashamed – a lazy, cowardly, selfish young lout.' The piece by Niven Craig that Harry had ghost-written was splashed across the front page, under the dramatic headline: 'My Failure: By Craig's Father'. When the Craigs saw how the paper had represented them, they refused to speak to Harry again.

In the House of Commons, an MP demanded to know how Harry Procter had been allowed to interview Christopher Craig while he was on remand in Brixton. The Home Secretary agreed that no journalist – and especially not Procter – should be given access to a prisoner again.

Harry believed that it had been his duty to expose Chris Craig as a callous thug, partly to show that he, and not Bentley, was responsible for the policeman's murder. But he felt ashamed of himself for betraying the Craig family's trust, and angry with his editors for forcing him to do so – it was all right for the newspaper bosses, he thought, smoking their cigars in Geraldine House, uncorking a celebratory bottle of champagne at morning conference while he had to contend with the family's pain.

He hoped at least that his next assignment – to get the scoop on Derek Bentley – would help rather than hurt the young man's relatives. As soon as his pieces on Chris Craig had appeared in the *Pictorial*, Harry introduced himself to Bentley's parents and his eighteen-year-old sister, Iris. On 27 January 1953, the night before Derek was due to be hanged, he drove the family to the House of Commons, where 200 Members of Parliament had petitioned the Home Secretary, Sir David Maxwell Fyfe, to ask the Queen to spare Bentley's life. Late that night, the Bentleys learnt that Maxwell Fyfe had refused the petition. Harry took Mrs Bentley and her daughter home, and sat up with them while they waited for the moment at which Derek would die. They were silent and dry-eyed.

On 29 January, a day after Derek Bentley's execution, Harry asked Mrs Bentley to show him the letter that her son had dictated in the death cell. She refused, but Harry asked again the next day, assuring her that the *Pictorial* would pay for the letter and that its publication would help to show Derek's innocence. To his relief, Mr Bentley persuaded his wife to agree. She retrieved the envelope, which she had hidden under a cushion on an armchair. 'There is the letter, Mr Procter,' she said, handing it to him, 'the letter from my boy.' She burst into tears.

Derek's last words to his mother were published in the *Pictorial* on Sunday. 'I am still keeping my chin up,' he told her, 'as I want you and all the family to do. Don't let anything happen to the dogs and cat and look after [them] well as you always have.'

'I tell you what Mum,' he wrote, 'the truth of this story has got to come out one day.'

Many MPs were agitating for capital punishment to be abolished in Britain, but the Conservative government insisted that it was an essential deterrent in an increasingly violent society. Maxwell Fyfe assured the public that the justice system was exceptionally robust. He had told the House of Commons in 1948 that anyone who thought that an innocent man could be hanged in Britain was living in 'a realm of fantasy'.

But Harry thought that Derek Bentley had been innocent, and that Timothy Evans might have been too. Both were illiterate, working-class young men of low intelligence, whose families believed that they had been manipulated by their associates and failed by the courts. The public disquiet about the hanging of Derek Bentley had strengthened the case for abolishing the death penalty; Harry hoped that doubts about Tim Evans's guilt would strengthen it further.

***

Dr Lewis Nickolls, director of the forensic laboratory at New Scotland Yard, examined the samples that Dr Camps, the pathologist, had taken from the bodies found in 10 Rillington Place. He studied the clothes and other items found on Reg Christie, and the objects from the garden: an array of bones, many of them charred and broken; a rusted dustbin; a square glass jar attached to rubber tubing; buttons, hair clips, large clumps of hair; a dark coat and skirt; several teeth; strips of newspaper dating from July 1943; a small tin containing four clusters of pubic hair. The forensic analysis in this case was to be more extensive than any in Scotland Yard's history.

Dr Nickolls started by picking out the human bones from those of chickens, rats and other animals, and passed them to Richard Harrison, the director of the anatomy department at the London Hospital in Whitechapel. Dr Harrison separated the bones according to age, and assembled them into the skeletons of two people: a small woman in her early thirties, whose skull was missing, and a tall woman in her twenties. From these, he and his team constructed three-dimensional plastic 'ghosts' of the women. By carrying out a spectrographic analysis of the teeth, Harrison discovered that one had been crowned with a palladium silver alloy used in central Europe. To assess when the bones had been buried, he asked a botanist at Kew Gardens to study the roots of a bush that had grown through one of them.

At Scotland Yard, Dr Nickolls analysed the clothes that Christie had been wearing when he was arrested, and those inside the suitcase he had left at Rowton House. He detected semen on almost all of them. 'I have examined Package No 4 and found on the Trousers an area of seminal staining containing spermatozoa on the inside of the right fly opening near the bottom,' wrote Nickolls in his report. 'I found a spot of seminal staining on the lining of the left pocket. On the front flap of the shirt there are extensive areas of staining: semen containing spermatozoa was identified in this staining.' He found semen even on Christie's vests and plimsolls.

Nickolls compared the pubic hair in the tin to that of the murder victims. One bundle might have been taken from Ethel, he thought, but he could not find a match for the others. It was possible that Christie had obtained these sinister trophies from the bodies in the garden, or from victims as yet unknown. Nickolls could find no trace of barbiturates in Ethel Christie's organs – she had not overdosed on sleeping pills, as her husband claimed.

Dr Camps had thought that the women in the alcove had been gassed to death, because their skin was so pink, but Nickolls told him that the quantity of carbon monoxide in their blood was not lethal. The saturation levels were 30 to 40 per cent – enough to make the women lapse into unconsciousness, perhaps, but not to kill them. Camps returned to Rillington Place to test the temperature of the alcove, and realised that it was as cold as a refrigerator. It was this, not the gas, that accounted for their flushed skin. The cold conditions had also disguised the severity of the marks on their necks. Though the women might have been knocked out with gas, Camps decided, the cause of each death was strangulation.

Dr Nickolls found sperm inside the women's bodies. It, too, had been preserved by the low temperature in the alcove. Its quantity suggested to Nickolls that the victims had remained horizontal after intercourse: they must have been raped as they died. He and Camps concluded that Christie was not only a killer but a necrophile. He liked to have sex with dead or unconscious women.

***

In a letter to Rebecca West on 13 April, Fryn Tennyson Jesse referred to Rita Nelson and Hectorina Maclennan, Christie's last victims, as 'poor little tarts', members of 'a sad floating population in London, where girls can disappear and never be missed'. She thought of them as interchangeable types – 'murderees', in her phrase – whose lives had been bound to end in violence.

But the statements taken by the police gave a more complex picture of Rita and Hectorina's histories. Both had tried, however chaotically, to find freedom and independence in London. They may have traded sex for money or favours, like many women of limited means, but neither earned a living by prostitution.

Rita Elizabeth Nelson was born in Belfast in 1927, the second of three daughters. She saw little of her father after her parents separated in 1930, but she and her mother remained close. Rita was charged with theft when she was thirteen, and acquired other convictions in her late teens – one for soliciting, one for drunkenness, one for an assault on a policeman. A local officer described her as 'childish in her habits', while her mother observed that Rita 'was funny in her way of going' and had a 'kink' for men. In 1949 Rita gave birth to a baby, George, who was taken into care at a children's home in County Antrim. She was very fond of the child, her mother said, and soon after his birth she was detained for two years in a psychiatric hospital in Belfast. Her mother reported that the treatment had done her good: it left her 'less keen on men'. Rita spent the next couple of years under the watch of the mental health authority, working as a maid in hospitals and hotels.

Early in 1952, Rita escaped her supervision order by moving to London. She worked as a live-in attendant at Great Ormond Street Hospital, then as a waitress in a café on the Goldhawk Road, Shepherd's Bush. During quiet periods in the café, she would stand with a drawing pad, a cigarette between her teeth, and make sketches of the clientele, many of them lorry drivers from the local British Road Services depot. 'I want to capture life as it really is,' she would say. She told customers that she was studying art in Kensington.

Reg Christie, who was then working as an accounts clerk in the British Road Services office, was a regular at the café. He introduced himself to Rita as a keen photographer who shared her interest in art. He had already befriended several young women in the cafés along the Goldhawk Road, among them Lilith 'Lolly' Campbell, a 20-year-old art student from Skye, and her tall friend Kay, who lived with her grandmother in Shepherd's Bush; another Rita, a small, well-spoken young woman of about eighteen who wore green corduroy trousers; Elsie Morris, a 29-year-old factory hand from Notting Hill; and a young woman who accompanied him to Rillington Place to see the fireworks in November 1951. A café proprietress said that Christie once came in with his glasses broken and his face scratched, as if someone had fought him off.

Rita Nelson had a playful, lively manner. She dyed her hair blonde and liked to wear red lipstick, red nail varnish and delicate jewellery (floral earrings, a thin yellow metal chain round her ankle, a white metal watch on her wrist). Her colleagues teased her about her clashing clothes – a purple skirt, for instance, teamed with a red scarf. 'I like brightness and colour,' she said. 'I think it is one of the nicest things about life.' Each week without fail, she wrote to her mother back in Belfast, often enclosing money.

By the end of the year, Rita was working as a live-in kitchen maid at the Devonshire Arms in Notting Hill Gate, but when she was dismissed (as 'unsuitable'), she moved to a furnished room in Shepherd's Bush. One of the young women in the boarding house heard that Rita worked as a photographer's model – perhaps she had posed for Christie, who used to advertise for subjects on noticeboards outside newsagents in Paddington: 'Christie, photographer, 10, Rillington-place'.

In November 1952, Christie apparently showed photographs of Ethel Christie, Rita Nelson and Kay Maloney to a woman in a Lyons Corner House in Marble Arch, describing them as his wife and daughters. The woman reported this to the police four months later, saying that the pictures were similar to those she had seen in the newspapers. If she was right, Christie had photographed Rita and Kay several weeks before he killed them.

Rita went back to Northern Ireland to see her mother for Christmas, taking 30 shillings as a gift. On her return to London she became a server on the counter of the J. Lyons tea shop in Shepherd's Bush, at £3 and eleven shillings a week. After a few days the manageress noticed something 'peculiar' about her figure and transferred her to the kitchen – it was not considered proper for pregnant girls to serve customers. At the end of the week Rita's boss saw her sweating while she was drying some cutlery, took her aside and suggested that she leave. When Rita collected her final week's wages from the Lyons head office on 10 January 1953, she was sent to the company's medical officer, Dr Dorothy Symers, for an examination. Dr Symers, having confirmed that Rita was six months pregnant, gave her a letter to take to the Samaritan Hospital in Marylebone Road, which accommodated unmarried pregnant women and took their babies into care at birth.

Rita disappeared in the next few days. Her landlady in Shepherd's Bush reported her missing on 17 January, and three days after that broke into her room by unscrewing the lock. All of Rita's belongings seemed to be there. She had left the drawers and cupboard full of clothes, cosmetics and other items, among them a tartan bolero, a bottle of scent, twelve pairs of stockings, six pairs of shoes, eight scarves, two yellow metal trays depicting the Queen and Prince Philip, a red cardigan, a pair of brown slacks, five skirts, five coats, two lipsticks, a powder compact, various necklaces, brooches, rings and earrings, and a white cigarette case. The letter to the Samaritan Hospital was still in the room, along with Rita's sketches of café customers.

In late February Rita's mother wrote to the landlady from Belfast, worried that she hadn't received a letter from her daughter for several weeks.

'I deeply regret not being able to give you any news (good or bad) about your daughter Rita!' the landlady replied. 'It is a most mysterious thing which has ever happened in my house. It is now six weeks since she was last seen. Had she taken her necessary belongings with her, such as her wrist watch, ration book & all her clothes and shoes (6 pairs of them) I could quite understand her disappearance! All I know about her is (am so sorry to have to write this) that she was pregnant.'

The landlady had learnt of Rita's pregnancy only after she had gone missing, she said. She had found several letters from boyfriends in her room, 'including Americans, naturally'. She seemed to assume that Rita had vanished of her own accord, and that by falling pregnant she had forfeited her right to sympathy.

'I shouldn't distress myself too much if I were you!' she wrote. 'A daughter behaving like that towards her mother does not deserve any tears to be shed. I have a daughter of my own, and thank God one of the best He ever created. She's my only child – very happily married – no children, but a beautiful home and all the good things life has to offer. I only wish mothers like yourself could share my joy & happiness in having an ideal child.' This was a cruel kind of compassion to extend to an anguished mother, but perhaps the landlady was seeking to reassure herself that her own child, being a good girl, would be safe.

When Rita was found in Christie's alcove, she was dressed in a fawn dress, a pink slip, a blue knitted cardigan; the nails on her toes and fingers were painted red. She was still carrying a baby. Christie had claimed to the police that she had come to his house because she wanted to rent a room, not mentioning that he already knew her. Rita may well have been looking for accommodation in January, fearing that her landlady would throw her out when she realised that she was pregnant and had lost her job. Or perhaps Christie had told her that he could end her pregnancy, despite it being so far advanced. She might have been desperate enough to take the risk. Her circumstances made it impossible for her to keep the baby, so she faced not only the ordeal of childbirth but the pain of again being parted from her newborn child.

Hectorina Mackay Maclennan, Christie's final victim, was born in Glasgow in 1926. At twenty-one she gave birth to an illegitimate baby, Marion, and at twenty-two she moved with her family to England. She and her daughter, her parents, her two sisters and her two brothers took up residence in Earl's Court, west London. Ina, as she was known, was tall and dark-haired and wore striking, if dishevelled, clothes: a brown tweed suit, a white blouse, a red tie, leather gloves, high-heeled black shoes, a red coat. She smoked heavily.

Ina and her younger sister Benjamina started dating a couple of Burmese airmen, who they used to visit in Portsmouth at weekends, and Ina became pregnant in 1950 by her beau, Khin-Maung Soe Hla. They got married in Portsmouth that year, according to Ina, and Hla used to visit her in Earl's Court after the birth of their daughter, Juline, in January 1951. When he returned to Burma, Ina applied for a passport so that she and the children could join him. She began to save money for the trip.

Over the next two years, Ina found employment as a maid and a cinema usherette, but she struggled to make ends meet. Towards the end of 1952 she took a job looking after the baby of Alex and Dorothy Baker in Notting Hill, at £1 a week. Alex, a 44-year-old lorry driver, became besotted with Ina, and in January he left his family to move into a room in Hammersmith with her. They had a fight two weeks later, because he was angry that she had not come home one night. Ina walked out on Alex, and he returned to his home.

Within a few days, Ina was approached in Holland Park by a small-time crook called Frank Colyer, known as Ron. Noticing that Ina looked 'shabby', Ron offered to buy her breakfast. The two knocked about together for several weeks, staying in lodging houses and occasionally with her family in Earl's Court.

At the end of the year, Ina's parents moved back to Scotland with her daughter Marion, now five. Her youngest sister Annie followed them in January 1953 with Ina's daughter Juline, who was nearly two. Ina was by now pregnant with a third child. She told Ron that the father was a bookmaker called Bill Weird, who drank at the George and Dragon in Hammersmith. 'He's not a bad-looking bloke,' she said, 'but he ripped my clothes off.' She was dismissed from her job as a waitress, as Rita Nelson had been, because she was 'showing' too much.

In mid-February, at a milk bar in Notting Hill, Ron noticed Ina blush with discomfort when she recognised a man in 'horn-rimmers' at the counter. Ron asked her who he was. 'He's a chap I had some trouble with,' said Ina. 'He gave me an unpleasant time.' Ron later identified him as Reg Christie.

In Hyde Park a couple of days later Ron was stopped by a policeman and charged with burgling a house in Acton. He immediately confessed and produced some of the stolen goods from his pockets. The officer, as he arrested Ron, noticed the tall girl in a red coat who was with him. She had 'crossed eyes', the detective constable recalled, and 'a dirty look about her'.

That day Ina went to the flat of her old boyfriend, Alex, waited outside until his wife went out, then told him that she wanted to get back together. Though he knew that she was pregnant with another man's child, he agreed to again leave his family for her.

Alex and Ina had nowhere to stay, so they spent the next few nights in all-night cafés or with friends. On Friday 20

February, Alex accompanied Ina to Brixton prison, where Ron was awaiting trial. She gave Ron some tobacco and cigarette papers, and told him that she was broke and desperate. She was 'on the floor', as she put it. He advised her to seek help from his estranged wife, Florence, in Ealing, and from a Methodist minister in Marylebone who had been good to him in the past. Ina called on both of them, claiming that she was pregnant with Ron's baby. The clergyman did not offer her any assistance, but Ron's wife, a social worker, was helpful: Florence Colyer bought Ina a cup of tea in a café, gave her 35 shillings to rent a room, and a week later provided her with clothes and a further £1, urging her to use the money to join her family to Scotland.

Alex Baker told the police what he knew of Ina's movements in the week that she was killed. On Tuesday 3 March, a day of heavy fog in London, Ina was standing alone outside the Gaumont Cinema in Hammersmith when Reg Christie approached and asked her whether she needed somewhere to stay: he had seen her earlier with a man in a café, he said, and noticed that she looked miserable. Ina agreed to visit his flat later. They met opposite Ladbroke Grove station at 7.30 p.m., but when Christie saw Alex with her, he started to walk away. Ina followed him, and persuaded him to let her 'husband' accompany them to the house. According to Alex, Christie said to her: 'I told you not to tell anyone, even your husband, about this, because I don't want a lot of people making inquiries about the flat.' He agreed to let them stay for a few days, but said that they could not share a bed because his wife would disapprove if she happened to come home.

The temperature fell below freezing that night, and they all stayed in the kitchen, the only warm room in the flat. Ina sat in the deckchair strung with rope, Christie perched on a wooden board laid over a coal bucket, and Alex sat in a small wooden armchair. Ina and Christie remained in the kitchen for the next two nights, while Alex slept on the mattress in the bedroom.

In the morning of Friday 6 March, another foggy day, Alex and Ina collected their welfare payments from the Labour Exchange in Shepherd's Bush. Ina told Alex that she was going back to Rillington Place to meet Christie at noon – 'She didn't know what for,' Alex claimed – and would join Alex in a snack bar at 3 p.m. She didn't turn up at three, so Alex went to find her at No 10. Christie told him that he hadn't seen Ina. After giving Alex a cup of tea, he helped him search for her in the streets round Shepherd's Bush.

Later, in his police confession, Christie claimed that Ina had come to his house in the evening and refused to leave until Alex arrived. But according to Alex she visited Rillington Place in the daytime, by arrangement, and knew that her boyfriend was waiting for her elsewhere. Christie must have killed her that afternoon. He abandoned his house a fortnight later.

Alex was the sole source of information about Ina's last days, and he may have disguised the real nature of her dealings with Christie, not wanting to tell the police that Christie had in fact offered to terminate Ina's pregnancy rather than to rent her a room. This would explain why she had promised not to tell anyone that she was visiting his flat and why Christie was annoyed that she turned up with her 'husband'. If Alex and Ina stayed in Rillington Place while she underwent the procedure, she may have returned on Friday for a follow-up examination, or to do something for Christie in payment. Alex may have lied about all this because he did not want to admit to having colluded in a criminal enterprise.

'Although not now pregnant,' noted Dr Camps, who carried out Ina's post-mortem, 'thickening of the uterus suggested a past pregnancy.' He added that 'secretion could be expressed from both nipples'. The police made nothing of this, but it suggested that Ina had very recently lost or 'got rid of' a baby.

Ina was scruffy and wayward, but she was adored by her lovers. When she broke up with Alex in February, he sent her longing letters. 'Hello Ina Darling,' began one. 'I don't like writing these letters because you might get in trouble, but honestly Ina, I love to do this because I can't see you, or speak to you... I hope you are OK and I am dying to see you.' He begged for a word of encouragement from her. 'I am completly lost around here. Ina Darling.'

Ron sent notes to Ina from Brixton prison. 'My Sweetest Darling,' he wrote. 'If you ever know how much I love you – you will probably burst into flames.'

6

The rooms upstairs

Outside the Clerkenwell Magistrates' Court in King's Cross Road on Wednesday 22 April, Harry was among more than two hundred people, many of them women, waiting to see Reg Christie. It seemed strange that women, the targets of Christie's violence, were so keen to set eyes on him. Perhaps they took satisfaction in seeing him captured. Perhaps they wanted to know their enemy. Three policemen patrolled the courthouse roof to stop anyone from climbing up to peek in through the skylight.

At 9.40 a.m. a police car pulled up sharply at the side entrance and Christie got out. He hid his face with a newspaper as he was led into the building.

In the courtroom, Harry saw Christie make a half-bow to the magistrate, then sit down in the cramped dock and start to scribble notes for Derek Curtis-Bennett, the barrister the *Pictorial* had hired to represent him.

Ethel's brother Henry and her sister Lily were among the nineteen witnesses to appear before the magistrate that day. Both had made the journey to London from Sheffield. Henry was so upset that he could hardly read his oath. As he gave his evidence, he glanced at Christie, who twitched and looked down, his fingers fidgeting on the dock's iron bar.

When Lily took her brother's place in the witness box, she stared at Christie and he turned away. She explained how Reg had tricked her into thinking that Ethel was still alive after 14 December 1952, by postdating a letter that she had written before her death, then sending a Christmas card with a note from himself: 'Dear Lil. – Ethel has got me to write as her rheumatism in her fingers is bad just now. The doctor says she will be OK in 2 or 3 days. I am rubbing them for her and it makes them easier… Don't worry. She is OK. I shall cook the Christmas dinner. Reg.' Lily broke off her testimony to stare across the courtroom at Christie, who again averted his eyes.

Rosina Swan of 9 Rillington Place told the court that Christie had deceived her, too. In mid-December she had asked after Ethel, who usually came over on Thursdays to watch television with her niece's children. Reg told Rosie that Ethel had gone to Sheffield, where he would soon be joining her. On 19 December she saw Reg over the garden fence, and he held up a slip of paper that he claimed was a telegram from his wife: Ethel sent her love to Rosie, he said.

Rosie Swan's evidence, like Lily's, suggested that Christie had deliberately and cunningly concealed his wife's death.

In the lunch break Christie was taken to a cell in the courthouse. That afternoon's *Evening Standard* reported that he was served a plate of roast beef, Yorkshire pudding, roast potatoes and peas, supplied by 'a friend'. His prison visitor, Francis Ross, had provided the meal, having first taken a photograph to sell to the paper.

After lunch, Kay Maloney's friend Maureen Riggs, a thin, raven-haired young woman dressed in black, gave evidence. Her back turned to Christie, she testified that she and Kay had been friends since July 1952. They used to pick up men together in bars, she said.

'Is that how she earned her living?' asked the prosecutor.

'That's how we both earned our living,' Maureen replied, defiantly.

'Have you ever seen this man?' asked the lawyer, gesturing to the dock.

At this, Maureen slowly turned to look at Christie, her shoulders trembling, and she began to sob.

'Yes,' she said. 'I introduced Miss Maloney to him. She was in the pub with a sailor, and I introduced her.'

The prosecutor tried to calm her – 'You need not upset yourself' – but Maureen continued to cry. Once her deposition had been read to the court, a policewoman escorted her from the room.

After the hearing, Christie was returned to Brixton prison. There would be two further sessions at the magistrates' court, on consecutive Wednesdays, before the case was committed to the Old Bailey.

In her police statement, Maureen Riggs had expressed contempt for Christie. She remembered him as a mean and pathetic man, a phoney. He only feigned intercourse with her, she said. When she saw him in the street, she had called him out as a cheat, demanding the money that he owed her and the pictures that were hers. None of this had been aired in public. On the advice of the Director of Public Prosecutions, who briefed the Crown lawyers on which parts of the police evidence to use, no mention was made in court of the women's nude photography session with Christie. The DPP may not have wanted to expose the public to even more unsavoury material.

After Maureen's testimony at Clerkenwell, the DPP advised the prosecution lawyers that she might not be a desirable witness at Christie's trial, as she had become 'somewhat hysterical' while giving evidence to the magistrate, with guilt and grief.

***

In the notes that he was writing for Roy Arthur to give to Harry, Christie claimed that an 'unknown force' had compelled him to kill. He still insisted that he had strangled Ethel as an act of mercy, though he now acknowledged that her death had left him free to kill others. 'The incident of my wife,' as he described her murder, 'just removed the one obstacle. After she was gone, the whole business seemed to come to the fore again.' His phrasing seemed to confirm that Ethel was not his first victim.

Christie pointed out how kindly he treated animals. While serving as a police officer in 1941, he wrote, he had seen a man in a side street hit a dog with a stick: 'Although *in uniform*,' he said, 'I caught hold of the man and hit him with my fist.' He had once looked after a sick cat belonging to the Newmans of 11 Rillington Place, he added, and, though the vet had declared it beyond help, he had nursed it back to health.

He continued to deny that he had murdered Beryl Evans. Killing her would have been a 'physical impossibility', he said. In November 1949, he had been suffering from such severe back pain that he was 'crawling about'.

He reflected, a little, on his past. When he was about eight, he recalled, he had been taken to see his grandfather's body laid out in a parlour. 'I remember I was not in any way worried or perturbed,' he wrote. 'All my life I never experienced fear or horror at the sight of a corpse. On the contrary I have seen many and they held an interest and fascination over me.'

He claimed to feel a similar detachment, now, when he read reports of his murders in the newspapers delivered to Brixton prison. 'It just didn't seem to be me. I have no recollection of it. I just don't seem to believe it.' But some memories of the killings had come back, he said: he thought that he had wrapped Kathleen Maloney's body in a blanket to make it easier to shift, and because he remembered that this was how Tim Evans had wrapped up his wife after killing her – 'but I did not tie them as he did', he added.

Had Christie really been inspired by Tim Evans's example? Or was this a ploy to account for the similarities in how the murders in the two cases had been carried out and concealed? Harry was becoming convinced that Christie had strangled Beryl Evans to satisfy his sexual perversion, and that he had then silenced the baby by killing her, too.

***

Harry arranged to meet Tim Evans's mother, Agnes Probert, who still believed in her son's innocence.

Agnes's first husband, a coal haulier in Merthyr Vale, had abandoned her and their daughter Eileen shortly before Tim's birth in 1924. Agnes went on to marry Penry Probert, by whom she had a second daughter, Maureen, and in the mid-1930s the family moved from Wales to Notting Hill. The children were raised as Catholics. Tim suffered from tubercular infections and inflammations, having cut his foot on a piece of dirty glass when he was eight, and missed so much school that he could barely read or write.

Tim was not conscripted during the war, because of his poor health, but he served in the Home Guard and as an Air Ministry lorry driver. When he and Beryl were married in 1947, Agnes said, they lived with her and her husband and daughters at St Mark's Road, paying £2 a week for board and lodgings. Tim earned about £7 a week as a van driver, including overtime.

Though the couple moved with their baby to the top floor of Rillington Place in 1948, Agnes still saw Beryl almost every day. She felt as close to her as to her own daughters, she said. She sometimes secretly gave Beryl cash, and she helped her out in the flat. Agnes described her daughter-in-law as a poor housekeeper – she prepared only one hot meal for Tim a week, on a Sunday; he had to wash his own shirts and socks; and she let dirty dishes pile up by the sink and empty milk bottles beneath it.

Tim and Beryl had bought some furniture, on a hire-purchase scheme, but their rooms were shabby. Beryl complained that the foundations of the building were sinking so much that objects rolled off the kitchen table. She also sometimes complained about her downstairs neighbour, Reg Christie: he crept around the house, she said. But she was friendly enough with the Christies. She sometimes gave them her sugar ration, as she didn't sweeten her tea, and they let her park Geraldine's pram in their front room.

Beryl used to leave Geraldine with Ethel Christie or with Tim's family while she worked shifts at the counter of an outfitter's in Ladbroke Grove, and Agnes sometimes looked after the baby in the evenings. She adored Geraldine, her only grandchild.

At first Tim and Beryl were on good terms, Agnes said, though they sometimes quarrelled about money. But the marriage came under strain in July 1949, when Beryl told Tim that she had been kissed by a painter who was decorating the shop at which she worked. Agnes reprimanded her: 'You little fool,' she said. 'What you tell him for?' Tim struck his wife in the face, then went to the outfitter's to complain. Beryl was sacked.

In her next job, as a telephonist at an Oxford Street department store, Beryl became friendly with a sixteen-year-old colleague called Lucy Endicott. Lucy came to stay with her for a couple of nights in August, while Tim was out of town on a long-distance delivery job, and stayed on after his return. When Beryl told her mother-in-law that she thought Tim and Lucy were sleeping together, Agnes came to the flat to confront them. During the row that followed, both Beryl and Agnes slapped Lucy in the face and Lucy slapped Agnes. Tim and Lucy left the house together.

A few days later, having been dumped by Lucy, Tim returned to Rillington Place. He and Beryl muddled on unhappily. They were almost £40 behind with the payments on their furniture, and £12 behind with their rent.

Beryl realised that month that she was pregnant again. She tried to bring on a miscarriage by taking pills, then by using a syringe. Neither method was successful. Beryl told her sister-in-law Maureen that she had heard of someone nearby who could get rid of her baby for £1. Maureen warned her that a local woman had died recently after an abortion.

Agnes, Tim and Beryl went shopping in Hammersmith with Geraldine on Saturday 5 November, and parted on the corner of St Mark's Road and Rillington Place. This was the last time that Agnes saw her daughter-in-law or her granddaughter, who was just starting to talk.

Tim called on his mother in St Mark's Road at 5.30 p.m. on Wednesday, the time that he and Beryl usually dropped off Geraldine with her while they went to the pictures.

'Mam,' he told her, 'you won't see Beryl or the baby for a week or two. She has gone to Brighton to her dad's.'

'She might have brought the baby round for me to have a look at before she went,' said Agnes.

'She didn't have the time, Mam,' replied Tim, 'but she will write to you.'

Three days later he called in the afternoon, saying that he was going to join his wife and child in Brighton. Agnes, noticing that he seemed moody, asked him what was the matter. 'Nothing,' said Tim. 'I am just going to get my shopping.'

He visited his mother and sisters again in the evening, saying that he was on his way to the pictures. He followed Agnes into the scullery, and looked strangely at her.

'What is the matter, son?' she asked. 'Are you in any trouble?'

'No, Mam.'

He mentioned that he had received a letter from Beryl, in which she said that Geraldine was asking for her grandmother.

On Monday 14 November, Tim left London for Wales.

A week or so later Agnes learnt that she was liable for the overdue payments on Tim and Beryl's furniture, for which she was the guarantor. A week after that, she received a letter from her sister-in-law in Merthyr Vale saying that Tim was staying with them.

Agnes immediately wrote back: Tim, she said, 'is like his father no good to himself or anyone else so if you are mug enough to keep him for nothing that will be your fault I don't intend to keep him any more I have done my best for him & Beryl what thanks did I get his name stinks up here everywhere I go people asking for money he owes them I am ashamed to say he is my son'.

In Merthyr Vale, Tim's aunt read his mother's letter to him over breakfast. Later that day – 30 November – he handed himself in to the Welsh police, telling them that he had 'disposed of' his wife, then changing his story to say that she had died while Christie was performing an abortion.

The Notting Hill police turned up at St Mark's Road to interview Agnes and her daughters the next evening. One of the officers passed on a message from Tim: 'Tell mother to ask Christie to get the baby from East Acton.' Agnes sought out Christie, but he would not see her.

On 3 December, Agnes learnt that Beryl and Geraldine were dead, and that Tim had confessed to killing them. She had lost her daughter-in-law, her grandchild and the unborn child that Beryl had been carrying. But when she saw Tim in Brixton prison the next day, he assured her that he hadn't touched them. 'Christie done it. I didn't even know the baby was dead until the police brought me to Notting Hill. Christie told me the baby was at East Acton.' He said that he had falsely confessed to everything because he had been so upset when he learnt that Geraldine was dead. 'Tell Christie I want to see him,' Tim said. 'He is the only one who can help me now.'

After Tim had been condemned to death, Agnes shouted at Reg Christie outside Court No 1 of the Old Bailey: 'Murderer! Murderer!' Ethel came to his defence. 'Don't you dare call my husband a murderer!' she said. 'He is a good man.'

Agnes said that Tim had protested his innocence to the last. On the eve of his execution she asked him: 'Son, for my own peace of mind, did you do it? Make your peace with God now.' He looked straight at her and said: 'Mam, I did not do it. Christie done it.'

Agnes was sure that it was Reg Christie who had murdered Beryl and Geraldine. She knew that her son was a liar, but she did not believe him capable of killing the child he loved.

***

Roy Arthur and the defence psychiatrist, Jack Hobson, interviewed Christie again at the prison on 23 April 1953. To their surprise, he offered to help identify the human remains found in the garden at Rillington Place, which he had read about in the papers. He could not remember the names of the women, he said, but one was an Austrian refugee who had lived in Oxford Gardens, not far from his house; he had killed her in 1942, a decade before the latest murders. The other was a woman from Putney who had worked with him at Ultra Electronics, a factory in Acton that made radio transmitters and aircraft parts; he killed her in 1943. In his notes for Harry, he corrected these dates to 1943 and 1944.

Christie seemed tantalisingly close to changing his story about Beryl Evans. 'Perhaps I was mistaken about Mrs Evans,' he told Arthur and Hobson. 'I cannot really remember. There is something about Mrs Evans which I cannot quite remember.'

He said that while he was sitting in the magistrates' court, the thought kept running through his mind that he had something to do with her death.

'Well, don't try too hard,' advised Dr Hobson. After almost three hours of discussion, he and Roy Arthur were exhausted. 'This memory will come back. Perhaps you will remember when I come again next week.'

In his notes for Harry, Christie was making similar hints about Beryl's murder: 'Normally I could not have done it but if I was ill mentally I could possibly have killed her using force that came to me without feeling the pain in my back. I believe actions like that one are known to occur.

'But I did not attack the baby,' he wrote. 'My wife and I were far too fond of it to harm it and we both wanted to adopt it, and Evans admitted it in court and to police when and how *he* did it and there is no mistake about that. The charge against the wife was not proceeded with. I *did not* – most emphatically I say this – harm the baby. Doubts have come into my mind about the wife of Evans. Weighing all things up I could be.'

Harry told Roy Arthur to put more pressure on Christie: he was frustratingly speculative, as if proceeding from deduction rather than memory, but he seemed to be edging towards a confession to Beryl's murder.

Arthur returned to Brixton on Friday 24 April and urged Christie to tell the whole truth. His accounts so far, he said, were not credible.

'We are the defence,' said Arthur. 'We must know everything that you can tell us. I want you to spend the weekend in thinking the whole thing over. That means that I want you to tell me exactly how you killed these six women. I want to know exactly the circumstances. There are scientific difficulties.' These difficulties included the fact that no barbiturates had been found in Ethel's body, which undermined Christie's claim that he had assisted her suicide, and the discovery that three of his other victims had been gassed, then raped at the point of death. Christie had so far made no mention of gassing or sexual assault.

'I also want to remind you that three years ago there was the Evans case,' said Arthur. 'There is a good deal of opinion that you may have had some sort of connection with it. You have so far said "no", but I want you to think over the weekend exactly what you had to do with this case.' He asked Christie if he understood the defence team's strategy.

'You are going to suggest that I was sick,' said Christie.

Arthur confirmed that they would be pleading insanity, and intended to bring up as many murders as possible.

Roy Arthur told the police what Christie had disclosed about the bodies in the garden. Scotland Yard was already trying to identify the two women by searching the missing persons files, and had appealed to dentists on the Continent for lists of patients whose teeth had been capped with a crown like the one that they had found. Now they also began to search the Register of Aliens and the staff records at Ultra Electronics. Dr Camps, in an attempt to locate the skull that was missing from one of the skeletons, returned to Rillington Place with a group of police officers. They dug down five feet in the yard, sifting nearly a ton of earth.

***

When Roy Arthur visited Brixton on Monday afternoon, Christie all at once confessed to killing Beryl Evans. He had put her to death, he said, only because she had asked him to do so. Beryl had been pregnant, he said, and was desperately unhappy because Tim was having an affair with a young friend of hers. Christie claimed that he found Beryl trying to gas herself from a pipe in her front room – the inhalation of household coal-gas, which was high in carbon monoxide, was a common means of suicide. He returned the next day to help administer the gas, then strangled Beryl with a stocking, which he afterwards threw in the fire. He might have cut off some of her pubic hair, he said, and put it in the tin the police had found.

Arthur, checking whether Christie was inventing this story to prop up his insanity defence, asked: 'Are you saying this on the basis of the more the madder?'

'No, no,' said Christie, 'not at all.'

Arthur told him to write down everything that he could remember and not to disclose any of it to the prison authorities. When Dr Hobson joined them at the jail, Christie repeated his story to him. He said that he believed he had sexually assaulted Beryl while she was unconscious. 'I must have been intimate with her then and strangled her afterwards,' he told him. 'I must have been intimate with all of them.'

Harry was relieved to hear from Roy Arthur that Christie had confessed to killing Beryl Evans. If he had murdered her, he had surely murdered the baby too. It must be only a matter of time before he admitted it.

***

Harry's wife, Doreen, was afraid of how far he might go in pursuit of a story. In a Leeds pub in 1938, Harry's colleagues at the *Yorkshire Evening News* had dared him to apply for a job at a newspaper run by Joseph Goebbels, Hitler's chief of propaganda. After drinking three light ales, Harry returned to his office to write a letter to the Nazi minister. A few weeks later he received an acknowledgement from the German paper, which he laughingly showed to the other reporters.

Several months after that, in July 1939, a package from Germany was delivered to the Procters' house in Leeds. Harry was by now working in London, so Doreen opened the parcel. She found inside an English translation of Hitler's *Mein Kampf*, tickets from Leeds to Berlin and an invitation to take up a highly paid post in Goebbels's Ministry of Propaganda. Doreen knew how impetuous Harry could be. Rather than forward the parcel to him, she burnt the lot.

Seven years later Doreen was reminded of the episode when the Nazi propagandist William Joyce was hanged for treason. She told Harry how she had opened and destroyed the parcel from Germany. 'Are you cross with me?' she asked. 'You know,' she added, squeezing his hand, 'you're a lad who needs some looking after.'

Doreen sometimes pleaded with Harry to take a break from Fleet Street, but he said that he could not risk it. The paper required complete dedication from its reporters. The news editor, Fred Redman, 'puts the *Pic* first, foremost, last, then first again', said Harry. 'He expects every other member of the staff to feel the same way.' Despite his success at the paper, Harry could never shake the feeling that he was about to be sacked. 'Get yourself a desk behind the door on the hinge side,' he advised a rookie reporter, 'where they will never see you when they come in to fire somebody.'

Doreen also worried about the stories that Harry was covering. In a bar near Fleet Street on Wednesday 19 June 1946, a colleague had introduced him to Neville Heath, a handsome airman with whom he shared a few lunchtime beers. Harry and Heath hit it off, and in the evening they met up in the smoky saloon of the Nag's Head, a snug little pub in a side street in Knightsbridge. Heath, having bought Harry a pint of mild-and-bitter, took a call on the pub phone, then announced that he had to leave to see a woman. 'Have one before you go?' asked Harry. Heath said that he hadn't time, but they arranged to meet again.

That Friday, Harry noticed a cluster of reporters outside the Pembridge Court Hotel, near his flat in Notting Hill, and he learnt that a woman had been found dead in one of the rooms.

He was told that it wasn't a murder – just an abortion that had gone wrong. But that night, over a drink at the Sun in Splendour in Portobello Road, a local policeman told Harry that the dead woman had seventeen whip marks on her back, and her ankles had been tied with a handkerchief. When Harry phoned the *Mail* with the story of the woman's murder, the night editor refused to run it, saying that he had been assured that she had died during an abortion. Harry was furious. He raced over to the office and pressed his case with every executive he could find, but they were unmoved. 'You're wrong,' they told him. 'Go and have a drink.'

It soon emerged that Margery Gardner, the woman in the hotel, had indeed been murdered, and that Harry's new friend, Neville Heath, was the chief suspect. Harry received a phone call from Heath while the police were trying to trace him, asking him to bring £50 to a remote spot in Surrey. Harry alerted Scotland Yard before he set out, and on reaching the meeting place was promptly arrested by two plainclothes officers who mistook him for the killer. Neville Heath went on to murder and mutilate Doreen Marshall, a young woman in Bournemouth, before he was arrested, tried and put to death.

Three years later, one Sunday in February 1949, Harry confronted the suspected murderer John Haigh in a hotel room in South Kensington. Haigh went white, Harry said, when he accused him of lying about his whereabouts at the time of a rich widow's murder in Sussex. Soon afterwards Haigh was charged with killing six acquaintances, whose bodies he had dissolved in sulphuric acid, and in August he was hanged.

In his essay 'Decline of the English Murder', published in 1946, George Orwell lamented the demise of the 'good murder' beloved of newspaper readers: a juicy story in the *News of the World* for a chap to settle down with on the sofa on a Sunday afternoon. The classic English murder, said Orwell, was inspired by passion and carried out with cunning: the killer might be a married dentist or solicitor, consumed by desire for another woman, who slowly poisoned his wife in a quiet suburban home. But Orwell observed that a different kind of murderer had now emerged in Britain: a ruthless spree-killer who chose his victims at random and despatched them without compunction. Such crimes, Orwell suggested, were products of a country deadened by war and corrupted by the 'false values' of American films.

Neville Heath, John Haigh and Reg Christie were exemplars of Orwell's modern murderer. They seemed vacant, vicious; creatures of a brutish new era. And yet Christie also resembled the domestic murderers of old. He may have been an unhinged serial killer, picking out strangers as he stalked the streets of London, but he was also the wily wife-killer, the apparently respectable neighbour who hid dark secrets in his home. The British public was transfixed by his story. Alfred Hitchcock, who was preparing to shoot his thriller *Rear Window* in Hollywood, was relishing the revelations too. 'Oh,' he told an interviewer, 'England's fantastic for this kind of thing.'

7

An unearthing

Since Fryn Tennyson Jesse's editor, Jim Hodge, couldn't assure her of access to Christie's trial at the Old Bailey, she approached everyone else she could think of who might help. The courtroom in which big trials were usually held – Court No 1 – was closed for renovations, having been bombed in the war, and she knew that in Court No 2 there would be even less space. She wrote to Sir Norman Birkett, a judge of the Court of Appeal, to ask if he could secure her a seat. Birkett was a famous criminal defence barrister, who had served as a judge at the Nuremberg trials of Nazi war criminals. Fryn had never met him, but he had recently described *Murder and Its Motives*, her book of essays on crime, as 'a classic' that shed light on 'one of the dark places of national life'.

To Fryn's relief, Birkett wrote back promptly, promising her a place in the court. 'I have long admired your writing,' he said. 'I will most certainly see that you get a reserved seat at the Old Bailey when the trial of Christie takes place.' He could confirm it, he added, only when the date was set. As backup, Fryn also wrote to Derek Curtis-Bennett, Christie's counsel, to see if he could get her a seat; and she asked her osteopath to make the same request of a well-connected lawyer in Surrey.

Fryn decided at least to get a glimpse of Christie at the magistrates' court. She had heard that the pathologist Francis Camps, who was known to enjoy murder trials, was due to take the stand when the hearings resumed on Wednesday. 'I am told that Camps is beaming all over his face,' she wrote to Jim Hodge, 'and saying "Delightful, delightful" as he rubs his hands.' Even the medical witnesses in this case seemed to be treating it as an entertainment.

On 29 April, Fryn's secretary, Joanna, drove her from Pear Tree Cottage to Clerkenwell in her open-topped Daimler. Joanna was a practised chauffeuse, having driven ambulances and desert vehicles for the First Aid Nursing Yeomanry in Africa during the war. She had started working for Fryn in 1950, as a 41-year-old divorcée, and had since married the London correspondent for a Dutch newspaper, with whom she lived in Hampstead.

A large crowd was again waiting for Christie. He wrapped a newspaper around his head as he got out of the police van, flanked by six burly officers, and he crouched between his guards as he was led inside.

With Joanna's help, Fryn made her way into the court. She was wearing a large crêpe bandage round her ankle – which she referred to as 'Alibi Alf' – to distract strangers from the fact that she could barely see: if she walked slowly, or tottered in a doorway, she hoped that bystanders would attribute her unsteadiness to her apparently injured leg. She was determined to keep her poor sight a secret from everyone outside Pear Tree Cottage.

In the courtroom, Fryn watched as Christie climbed into the tiny dock, in his neat blue pin-stripe suit. She imagined that he had never looked so smart in his life. None the less, she said, 'I saw and felt the monster.'

Bernard Tussaud, the great-great-grandson of Madame Tussaud, was also in court, to make notes and sketches for the wax model of Christie that he was preparing for his museum in Baker Street. He was accompanied by the Tussauds' hair specialist, Vera Bland. Harry Procter was watching from the press seats. For the time being, this was as close to Christie as he could get.

The magistrate listened to evidence that morning from a few people who had been acquainted with Christie's last victims, Rita Nelson and Hectorina Maclennan.

Dr Dorothy Symers, the medical officer for the J. Lyons restaurant chain, testified that she had examined Rita Nelson in January, and found that she was twenty-four weeks pregnant.

'Is this the girl?' asked the prosecution lawyer, holding up a picture of Nelson.

'It could be,' said Dr Symers, 'but I was not very interested in her and don't remember her clearly.'

In the cells at lunchtime, Christie was presented with another meal from his anonymous friend. This time Francis Ross sold a photograph of the spread to the *Daily Mirror*: the tray was set with roast lamb, mint sauce, baked and boiled potatoes, peas, cabbage, two mince pies and two cream cakes.

As Dr Camps gave evidence that afternoon about the bodies that he had examined in Kensington mortuary, Christie fiddled with his spectacles, leant forward and started to make notes.

The pathologist said that before being strangled, each of the three women in the alcove had been gassed with carbon monoxide, and the presence of semen in their bodies suggested that they had been raped at the time of their deaths. Neither carbon monoxide nor semen had been found in Ethel Christie's body, he said. He added, gratuitously: 'She was rather a fat woman. She had large breasts.'

Camps testified that most of the victims had been bundled up: Ethel in a flannelette sheet, Kathleen Maloney in a blanket, tied round the ankles with a sock, Rita Nelson in another blanket, tied at her ankles with plastic wire. They had diapers of cloth over their genitals, and their faces had been covered: Ethel's with a pillowslip, Kathleen's with a piece of cloth, secured at the neck with a stocking, and Rita's with a bloodstained towel. Christie may have wrapped the bodies to make them easier to pull across the floor, but the purpose of the maskings was unclear: perhaps he hadn't wanted to see the women looking back at him.

Christie had not wrapped Hectorina Maclennan's body, but her wrists had been tied with a handkerchief. Vertical scratch marks on her back and buttocks suggested that she had been dragged across a rough surface.

As Camps spoke, Christie stared at him, a puzzled look sometimes passing across his face; occasionally he yawned.

***

Christie's murders seemed to be inspiring copycat crimes. The *Pictorial* of Sunday 26 April reported that John Haskayne, a 39-year-old hotel porter who wore horn-rimmed spectacles, was wanted for the murder of Grace 'Babs' Darrington, a Bayswater prostitute found strangled with a nylon stocking. The two had been seen together in a pub in Praed Street the previous Tuesday, and Haskayne's fingerprints were detected on a beer bottle in the murdered woman's flat. On Monday he gave himself up to a police officer at Piccadilly Circus: 'I want you to take me in,' he said. 'It must have been me done that job in Bayswater. I saw my name in the newspaper.' He was sent to Brixton to await trial.

The *Pictorial* continued to publish the photographs that Harry had obtained from Francis Ross. In its edition of 26 April, the paper showed Christie in his garden, dwarfed by hollyhocks, his cat Tommy on his shoulder and his dog Judy at his feet. It also reproduced a letter that Christie had written in Brixton on 8 April, his fifty-fourth birthday. He was 'really glad to be alone to settle a bit', he told Francis Ross, 'as I am still somewhat "fuddled" and dazed'. He would feel better, he said, if he could only have an apple, and a few sweets and cigarettes.

The *Pic*'s photo of 3 May showed Christie at the age of about ten, posing with his boy scout troop in Halifax. He looked like a serious, obedient child, as he had seemed a devoted husband. The most shocking crimes of the century had been committed not by an insolent young lout like Christopher Craig, but by a former choirboy and boy scout who had served his country as a soldier and a policeman. Far from being part of the new wave of unruly hooligans, Christie had seemed typical of the generation that censured such youths.

A Home Office official, on seeing the photos in the *Pictorial*, noted irritably that every acquaintance of Christie seemed to be selling material to the papers. He advised the prison to stop any further communication between Christie and Francis Ross.

The governor of Brixton jail cracked down. He barred Ross from visiting the prison, and sacked a guard who had passed information about Christie to the *Pictorial*'s sister paper, the *Daily Mirror*. He summoned inmates who were friendly with Christie, and asked them what he had told them and whether he had asked them to contact the press when they were out on bail. He interviewed Christie himself to ask who was funding his defence and whether he was in contact with a newspaper. Christie replied, disingenuously, that his brother had appointed his solicitors and he knew of no other arrangement.

***

In the last session at the Clerkenwell court – on Wednesday 6 May – Harry watched Derek Curtis-Bennett cross-examine Detective Inspector Griffin, who was leading the investigation of the Rillington Place murders. Curtis-Bennett, knowing that Christie had confessed to killing Beryl Evans, asked the detective to confirm that the bodies of Beryl and Geraldine had been found within a few feet of the alcove in which three of the bodies in this case had been found.

'Yes,' said Griffin. 'Just the other side of the wall.'

'They were tied up?'

'Tied up.'

'From all this,' said Christie's counsel, 'it follows, if the Crown is right in both cases, there were two stranglers in the same house?'

'Yes.'

'And two people who tied up and killed people, tied them up similarly?'

'Yes.'

As the hearing closed, the magistrate told Christie that he was committing him for trial at the Central Criminal Court at the Old Bailey, on a charge of murdering Ethel Christie. The Crown lawyers, who could proceed with only one murder charge at a time, had chosen the crime for which they had the most evidence that Christie had acted with calculation. The magistrate asked Christie if he had anything to say. Curtis-Bennett jumped to his feet.

'He pleads *not* guilty,' he said. 'Reserves his defence and calls no evidence here.'

Immediately after the hearing, Curtis-Bennett took Harry down to the courthouse cells to meet Christie. They had only a moment together. Harry shook Christie's hand, and felt the same damp clasp that he remembered from their encounter in 1949, at once limp and insistent, with 'a tug like a reptile might give'. He knew that it might not be he who was using Christie, but Christie who was ensnaring him.

'Tell me one thing,' Harry said, 'one very important thing. Did you kill Mrs Evans and her baby? It is best for all concerned if you tell the truth.'

'Mrs Evans, yes,' said Christie, 'I had an affair with her.' He turned away as he added: 'But not the baby.'

This was the first time that Christie had claimed to have had a sexual relationship with Beryl Evans, though a couple of other people had suggested the same. Robert Hookway, a local furniture dealer, told the police that he thought the two were sleeping together, and that Ethel knew about it. An anonymous woman wrote to Scotland Yard on 26 April to say that Beryl had warned her in September 1949 not to have anything to do with Christie: he was sly, Beryl had told her, 'a very bad man' who paid only five shillings for sex.

Christie remarked to Curtis-Bennett that he had felt quite calm throughout the hearings, unaffected by all the 'sordid details' that had been rehearsed. Curtis-Bennett told him that this might be for the best – a lack of emotion would only help an insanity defence.

The prison guards took Christie back to Brixton, where he would be held until the summer sessions at the Old Bailey.

***

The next day, Harry was despatched to the Mediterranean to interview a high-society Englishwoman who had married a handsome Corsican. The *Sunday Pictorial* often splashed out on foreign stories, and this one played to its readers' fascination with relationships that crossed lines of class, nationality or race. Before he left for Corsica, Harry encouraged the defence solicitors to apply for an exhumation of Beryl and Geraldine's bodies. He hoped that a new post-mortem might confirm Christie's claim to have killed Beryl. Perhaps the pathologists could match some of the pubic hair in the tin to hers – or establish whether she had been killed in a similar way to the women found in March: it might have gone unnoticed in 1949 that she had been gassed, as Christie's recent victims had been, or that she had been sexually assaulted at the time of her death.

Roy Arthur asked the Home Office for permission to exhume the bodies of Beryl and Geraldine Evans, and he asked the Director of Public Prosecutions to supply Cliftons with the photographs and post-mortem reports from 1949.

Harry's story from Corsica – 'Mayfair Girl Weds Fisherman' – ran on the *Pictorial*'s front page on 10 May 1953. He hadn't enjoyed his trip, despite the beauty of the island, because he was desperate to resolve the question of the Evans murders before the trial in June. He urged Roy Arthur to renew the pressure on Christie. 'Do get this man to confess to the murder of the baby,' he told Arthur. 'Honest, I don't ask for it as a newspaper story. You and I must get the truth.' It was crucial to prove that Christie had killed Geraldine, since this was the murder for which Tim Evans had been hanged. Harry wanted to see justice done. He also wanted to assuage his guilt about the Evans case, and to justify the tactics he was using to get the scoop on Christie.

The Home Office, to avoid being accused of a cover-up, agreed on Wednesday 13 May to exhume the bodies of Beryl and her baby.

That weekend the police supplied the press with photographs of the two women whose bodies had been found in the garden of No 10. They had identified the victims as Ruth Fuerst, a Jewish refugee from Austria, and Muriel Eady, a factory worker from Putney. The *Pictorial* published their pictures on 17 May. 'Do you know these women?' the paper asked its readers.

***

Just before dawn on Monday 18 May, four men at Gunnersbury cemetery in Acton began to dig up the grave of Beryl and Geraldine Evans. They worked behind a canvas screen, by the light of arc lamps and torches, so that they could not be seen from the windows of the houses overlooking the burial ground. The weather that morning was warm, and the grass dotted with daisies. The undertakers and gravediggers who had performed the burial in December 1949 were on hand to confirm the position of the coffin. It was the second down in the plot, three and a half feet beneath the surface.

Watching over the disinterment were Christie's representatives – the solicitor's clerk Roy Arthur, the defence psychiatrist Dr Hobson and the defence pathologist Dr Keith Simpson – and the government-appointed pathologists Dr Camps and Dr Donald Teare. Camps, Simpson and Teare were the most prominent pathologists of their day, sometimes referred to in the press as 'The Three Musketeers'.

Dr Teare, when he carried out the original post-mortems on Beryl and Geraldine Evans in 1949, had identified bruises on Beryl's face, her left calf and her left thigh. He had also noticed an injury to her vagina that might have been inflicted at the time of her death, but Tim Evans's solicitor had advised the barrister against mentioning this in court: 'The case is sufficiently horrible,' wrote Geoffrey Freeborough in his brief, 'without disgusting surmises of this nature being put in the minds of the jury.'

Once the gravediggers had raised Beryl and Geraldine's coffin to the surface, they opened it slightly, to allow the escape of noxious gases. The coffin was then conveyed to Kensington mortuary, where the pathologists inspected the bodies – Geraldine was lying across her mother, covered with a shroud – and took samples of skin, nails and hair. They removed Beryl's reproductive organs to re-examine them for injuries and traces of sperm. The police photographer took pictures.

The bodies and their parts were restored to the coffin, which was fitted with a new lid of waxed and polished elm, secured with brass bolts and returned to the cemetery to be buried again after dark.

***

On Wednesday 20 May, Dr Desmond Curran of St Thomas' Hospital, a psychiatrist who had examined Tim Evans in 1950, visited Christie on behalf of the Home Office. He had been asked to determine whether he was sane.

Christie spoke in a low voice, Curran noted, and became almost inaudible when he replied to a difficult question. He told the doctor that he had gassed and strangled Beryl Evans because she wanted to die. He mused about what lay in store for him after his trial: death by hanging, incarceration in Dartmoor prison or – his preference – admission to Broadmoor, a hospital for criminal lunatics. 'I have heard people are happy there,' he said. 'Good treatment and that is what I want.'

Christie wept easily, Curran said, especially at any mention of his wife. He described pubs as 'dreadful places', and masturbation as 'a terrible thing'. When recounting how he met one of his victims, he said: 'We had a little cup of tea' – holding up a thumb and forefinger to indicate how very small it was. Dr Curran was appalled at Christie's self-importance and snivelling propriety. He disliked him, he said, as much as any man he'd met.

Dr John Matheson, the chief medical officer at Brixton, was also repelled by Christie: he got 'goose-skin' in his presence, he said. Christie was sometimes irritable, he noticed, sometimes wheedling and obsequious. In speaking of his childhood, he was particularly unreliable. At their first interview, Christie had described his father as an alcoholic; six weeks later he said that Ernest Christie barely drank at all. He claimed to the doctor that he had been his mother's favourite child. Matheson learnt that Christie had spent three weeks in a Notting Hill hospital in 1952, suffering from severe diarrhoea and back pain, and that his doctors, concluding that his conditions were psychosomatic, had referred him to a psychiatric hospital in south London.

When Matheson asked Christie about his sexual history, he reported that he had always found it difficult to have erections. As a young man in Halifax, he said, 'I was considered by the girls to be too slow, as all I would do would be to put my arm round them. I did manage sexual intercourse eventually. I could never do it standing up as some girls wanted it, but I was all right if we lay in the grass.' He and Ethel had not had intercourse in the first three years of their marriage, Christie reported, nor in the last three. He said that he had no homosexual impulses, had never had a wet dream and had never masturbated. 'When talking about his sex life he was hesitant and did not appear frank,' noted Matheson. He gave Christie an IQ test on which he scored 128 points, well above the average of 100 (Tim Evans, who Matheson had examined in 1949, had scored a very low 65).

Christie implied to Matheson that he had more to disclose about the murders. 'I think there is something in my mind but I can't get it,' he said. 'It seems to be forming a picture and then before it gets clear it gets all jumbled up again. My head starts hurting as the picture is getting clear and that's what stops me getting it clear. I know there's something.'

Matheson observed in his notes that Christie was a compliant prisoner: 'Arranges his bedside table with meticulous care. Has retained all his cigarette ash for one week.' Christie bragged to the doctor about his prowess at chess and dominoes, and claimed to be very popular with the other men.

On the prison ward, he was full of himself. 'I don't suppose any man who's ever been in this ward has had a bigger charge sheet against him, or more crimes,' Christie boasted to one inmate, who subsequently sold his story to *Empire News*. 'Look, I must be the first man in the country to be charged with four murders.'

He seemed pleased by the extent of the press coverage – the detailed reports of the magistrates' hearings, the photos adorning the pages of the *Pictorial*. 'Look at the space I'm getting,' he said as he leafed through the newspapers. 'No film star ever had such a show. This puts Haigh and Neville Heath in the shade.' His fellow prisoner advised him to be less flippant: 'You're going to get yourself topped for sure if you go on like this. You can't be light-hearted about murder. Whether you remember doing them or not, you can't laugh about it.' Christie turned on him angrily, asking him who he thought he was to tell him how to behave. 'I know my manners,' he said haughtily, 'which is more than I can say of some of the people in this place.'

Christie occasionally indulged in self-pity. 'The mob's against me,' he lamented. 'They take it all too serious. They don't understand me, that's what the trouble is.' But he was confident that he would be spared the death penalty. 'So long, George,' he told a prisoner who was being sent to Broadmoor on the grounds of insanity. 'Let's not say goodbye because I'll be seeing you again.' He chatted easily to the guards, telling one that, as a war reserve policeman, he had turned a blind eye to the activities of West End prostitutes, who in return would give him a 'good time'.

Christie adopted a suave, worldly manner with new arrivals, according to *Empire News*'s informant, offering them smokes and predicting what sentences they would receive. 'You'll get six months, my lad,' he told one young man. When John Haskayne, who had been charged with strangling Grace Darrington in Bayswater, was admitted to the prison, he told Christie that he was lucky to have killed so many women, as it improved his chances of being found insane. In a business like this, Haskayne observed enviously, it was a question of 'the more the merrier'.

One day Christie noticed a stack of pictures of women in the locker of a younger prisoner. Since no knives or scissors were allowed on the ward, the man had cut them out of newspapers and magazines with a pin, carefully piercing the outline of each body. Photographs of half-dressed young women had become a staple of the popular press since the war, especially in the *Pictorial*, the *Mirror* and their sister weekly, *Reveille*. 'Look here, my boy,' admonished Christie, 'there's no satisfaction in this sort of thing – it's the real thing that matters.' He picked up one of the photos, pushing his glasses up his forehead to examine it more closely. 'I must say,' he conceded, 'she's a smasher all right.'

***

Christie was 'an excessively inquisitive creature', observed Fryn, 'well used to minding other people's business'. He watched his neighbours from the front window of No 10, spied through the kitchen door on tenants passing through the hall, photographed women in his studio, his garden and his bedroom.

In the film that Harry Procter said was Christie's favourite, *The Seventh Veil* (1945), a series of men seek to control a spirited young pianist. The woman's guardian, played by James Mason, demands that she keep to the house and obey his rules. A portraitist insists that she sit still as a statue as he paints her. A doctor injects her with narcotics to elicit her secrets. Christie adopted all these roles: the benefactor, who lured young women with money, clothes and drinks; the photographer, who posed them for stills; the doctor, who stupefied them.

He, meanwhile, made himself almost invisible. Christie 'was perfectly camouflaged for the people amongst whom he lived', wrote Fryn. 'In his neat but shabby clothes he had complete protective colouring. People hardly saw him come and go. He might have been one of the many thousands who pour out of tube trains or out of buses every day.' After his capture, he hid his face from the photographers who waited for him at courts and police stations. It was fitting that spectacles became his defining feature: horn-rimmed, National Health-issue glasses that shielded his eyes while sharpening his vision.

Fryn was an inquisitive creature herself. She had been rebuked for her curiosity when she was a child. Once, when she asked her mother how hens laid eggs, her mother turned on her, saying she had always had a nasty mind, and now she had proved it by wanting to know about nasty things. For Fryn, to study crime was a way of indulging her curiosity, of breaking the bounds of fit subjects for a woman's inquiry. The Christie case gave her the perfect excuse – the perfect cover – for delving into nasty things.

In her novel *A Pin to See the Peepshow*, Fryn described a girl's rapture when a boy in the playground let her look into a toy peepshow that he had built, a cardboard box with two eyeholes and an interior furnished with miniature figures. The scene was 'at once amazingly real and utterly unearthly', Fryn wrote. 'Everything was just the wrong size – a child was larger than a man, a duck was larger than a horse; a bird, hanging from the sky on a thread, loomed like a cloud. It was a mad world, compact of insane proportions, but lit by a strange glamour. The walls and lid of the box gave to it the sense of distance that a frame gives to a picture, sending it backwards into another space.' She was gazing privately, almost illicitly, on the secret scene.

The heroine of Fryn's novel delighted in peering into strangers' homes, 'especially when the curtains were drawn back and you could see into the room; see the angle of a table, perhaps, with people sitting at it'. From this distance, she 'could imagine anything about what went on in these strange hollow shells called houses that looked so solid by day; she could feel herself part of every drama played there'.

Though Fryn came from a middle-class household, a world away from the rank squalor of Rillington Place, she had been brought up in an atmosphere of hostility and deceit. Her father, Eustace, a nephew of the poet Alfred Lord Tennyson, was a wistful, gloomily romantic man. He married Edith James when he was thirty-three and she nineteen. They had three daughters: Stella, born in 1887; Fryn, christened Wynifried, born in 1888; and Ermyntrude, born in 1891, who died as a baby. Eustace was rector of a Suffolk church, with a living paid for by his wife's parents, but many of his parishioners disapproved of his penchant for incense, flowers, music and poetry. In 1891, sick and exhausted, he gave up the seat. 'No name was put to his illness,' wrote Fryn.

Perhaps there was a scandal attending Eustace, because after his resignation Edith refused to share his bed again – 'the outrage to her lofty religious stance', wrote Fryn cryptically, was 'matched by the outrage to her sexual nature' – and the four-year-old Stella was sent to live with Edith's parents, who refused to let Eustace cross their threshold. He travelled the world in search of new clerical posts, finding work in Cape Town, Guernsey, Ceylon. Fryn and her mother took lodgings in a series of suburban villas.

Fryn became fanatically attached to her mother, fearing that she might otherwise share the fate of her sisters: one dead, and one farmed out to grandparents. But Edith was capricious and sometimes cruel. 'Your breath is vile today,' she would tell Fryn. 'Don't lean over me, for pity's sake!' She recoiled from her daughter's touch: 'Why don't you take proper care of your hands?' she said. 'The skin is like a crocodile's.'

'I loved my mother passionately of course,' Fryn recalled – 'a child can't live in an emotional vacuum – until she made it impossible with her temper.' Edith underwent an ovariotomy in

1904, when Fryn was sixteen, and afterwards began to behave like 'a fiend'. Fryn dared not tell anyone the things that her mother did; she thought that she would not be believed anyway. But she became 'horribly afraid' of her.

If Fryn saw something of her mother in Reg Christie – the coldness, the temper, the cruelty – she may have seen something of her father, too.

While Eustace was staying with Fryn in London after the First World War, he liked to walk in Kensington Gardens if the weather was fine, and on returning from his jaunts he would tell his daughter how he loved to see the little girls running about in their black stockings. One day, according to Fryn's autobiographical novel *The Alabaster Cup*, she came home from a weekend away to find that her father had invited one of these girls to the house and shown her French picture books of female nudes. He had explained to the girl, 'that the nude was the most beautiful thing in the world, that God never made anything more beautiful than a naked woman'. His daughter warned him that such behaviour could lay him open to blackmail.

'Papa sat as one stunned,' wrote Fryn. 'His faded but beautiful blue eyes filled with horror, his handsome Arab profile bent down upon his chest, his silvery froth of hair standing out like a halo around his head.'

'My dear child,' he said. 'You must have had a very unfortunate experience to make you think about anything like that? I have never heard of such a thing in my life.' But he agreed not to have any more little girls to tea.

Fryn recalled the passionate sentimentality with which her father used to address her. 'Your love made my short visit one of great happiness,' he wrote to her soon after her marriage to Tottie. 'To be so close to you, and to cuddle, and to talk so seriously yet so lovingly! No wonder that I think this intimacy between father and daughter is the greatest pleasure in the world.' He thanked Fryn for doing her best to 'give me the happiness which should have come from elsewhere'. Eustace was a man, Fryn recalled, 'in great need of demonstrative affection'.

She admitted to a cousin in the 1950s that her father's sex life 'was probably less well-adjusted than anybody's I have ever heard of'. His surface rectitude, like Reg Christie's, had masked wayward impulses.

Fryn had only dimly understood what was going on in her family home, sensing her mother's pain and fury, her father's disgrace. For her, as for others who were fascinated by Christie, to study the murders at Rillington Place may have been a way of returning to a house in which something bad and odd had happened, but this time as a beady detective rather than a bewildered child.

8

A symbol rather than a girl

In his latest notes for Harry, Christie was more forthcoming about his murder methods. He said that he had gassed his victims while they were sitting in the rope deckchair in his kitchen, behind which he had placed a rubber tube attached to a gas pipe on the wall. He would remove the bulldog clip on the tube, releasing the gas, and seat himself near the slightly opened kitchen window as he let the fumes rise. Only when a woman began to lose consciousness would he assault and kill her. He was keen to point out how mercifully he had despatched his victims. 'You will no doubt see that in all the cases my intention was to avoid *hurting* them all. They were rendered semi-conscious first and that in each case would eliminate the possibility of hurting them, or causing pain at all.'

Afterwards, he said, he forgot about them. 'Once in the alcove I appear to have dismissed them from my mind and commenced to plan another. I perhaps looked on each case as another job done.'

Christie said that he remembered giving Kay Maloney whisky and brandy in January, in an attempt to subdue her, and that she 'may have got to her feet and got hold of a pan *to protect herself against me*'. This was a revision of his first account, in which he said that she had initiated the violence. He now said that Rita Nelson might not have attacked him either. He had sex with her, he claimed, then gave her a drink in the deckchair, turned on the gas, and when he saw her eyes go 'a bit strange', quickly pulled a rope around her neck. He suggested that he might not have tried to push Ina Maclennan out of his flat in March, as he had previously stated, but rather had stopped her from leaving. After strangling her, he thought that he had shoved her body roughly into the cupboard, without wrapping it up as he had the others, because he was afraid that Alex Baker might turn up at any minute.

Christie described his murder weapon. 'The length of rope I spoke of was about 18" long with a double knot at each end. These knots would enable me to get a good grip and a far better pull. I kept this hidden away in a tool box. Do you think I may have come across the rope after years and the sight of may have started me off again. When any of these girls came to the flat one of the first things I did was to conceal the cord in my pocket. It was then perfectly handy at the right time.'

He went into more detail about Beryl Evans's death. He said that he had found Beryl trying to gas herself in her front room on Monday 7 November 1949. He had revived her, given her a glass of water and a cup of tea, and promised to return the next day to help her do the job properly.

On 'the fatal day', said Christie, Beryl confirmed that 'she wanted to go through with it and said she would do everything I asked if only I would help her. I think she knew I felt like making love to her and she got down on the eiderdown in front of the fire and said if I wanted to I must get down too but I must promise to help her after.'

Having had sex with her, he said, 'I got the tube and put it near her and was talking to her and she told me to keep on with the gas. She then started to become unconscious and convulsive and I strangled her at that moment. I believe I had intercourse again just then.' Christie said that he told Tim Evans that his wife had killed herself, and warned him that he would be suspected of having murdered her, so Tim agreed to use his van to dispose of her body. Christie claimed to have no idea of what had happened to Geraldine.

Christie seemed to have adapted his recollections about his latest victims to conform with the forensic scientists' deductions about how they had been killed. He was weirdly compliant, at once indifferent and obliging, as if the truth was conjecture, as if none of it meant much at all.

Yet on some points he was stubborn. He indignantly rejected the testimony that Kay Maloney's friend Maureen Riggs had given to the magistrates' court. He had never seen Riggs in his life, he said, and had certainly not met her in pubs. He insisted on how little he drank.

'I very seldom touch the stuff,' he wrote. He acknowledged that he had accepted some 'port etc.' on Christmas Day 1951, when he and Ethel visited Rosie Swan and her family at 9 Rillington Place, and on three occasions in 1952 he had a glass of beer with members of his union branch, of which he was chairman. But he said that he never went for a drink with the other union chairmen after their regular meetings near London Bridge: '3 or 4 of the Delegates and I used to always make for a late night cafe (app 9.30 to 9.44 p.m.) and have cups of tea. Mr Gould who was my Vice-Chairman will bear this out and will furnish names of other delegates. I invariably was taken home by Gould and more often than not after we had talked still sat in his car it would in any case be too late. All pubs were closed.'

He kept whisky and port in his flat, he said, only to give to women he intended to assault. 'I just kept those bottles to help me *not* because I like drink.' To Christie, it seemed, it was more shameful to be thought a habitual drinker than a man who kept alcohol at hand to facilitate rape and murder.

By now Harry had read thousands of words of the prison statement. Christie wrote in a neat fastidious hand, his phrasing measured and even, spooling out an enervating, self-serving monologue as if he were repeating the stifling he performed on his victims. His killings seemed to express a riot of emotion, yet his account disowned all rage, fear or desire. He identified aggression and lust only in the black men and young white women in his orbit; terror and despair only in Beryl and Ethel. In the gap between Christie's passionless telling and his victims' assaulted bodies, Harry had to imagine what he – and they – had felt.

***

On 2 June, 3 million people watched from pavements, windows, stands and scaffolds – under grey skies and bursts of rain – as a golden carriage drove the 27-year-old Queen Elizabeth from Buckingham Palace to Westminster Abbey to be crowned. Millions more watched the ceremony on television sets and cinema screens across the country.

After years of war, austerity and imperial decline, many hoped that the coronation would usher in a new Elizabethan Age of peace and progress. Princess Margaret described her sister's accession as a 'Phoenix-time' in which 'everything was being raised from the ashes'. Winston Churchill gave thanks for the 'gleaming figure' with whom England had been blessed. That morning's newspapers announced that a British expedition had just completed the first successful ascent of Mount Everest.

In an ice-cold gallery high up in Westminster Abbey, the society photographer Cecil Beaton was sucking on barley sugar to combat a horrible hangover. He had been commissioned to take the official photographs of the Queen after the service, and was so nervous about the job that he had drunk too much the night before. Beaton leant over the balcony to watch the peers and peeresses process up the aisle. They formed a magnificent tide of dark velvet and foam-white fur, he wrote in his diary, the vaulted stone rising around them like a silver forest. He saw Churchill lurch up to his pew, 'a fluttering mass of white ribbons and white feathers in the hat in his hand'. Most striking of all, Beaton said, was the Queen herself, her cheeks pink, her hair curled tightly around the diadem on her brow, her hands folded meekly on a dress embroidered with amethysts, pearls and opals. 'She is still a young girl,' he observed, 'with a demeanour of simplicity and humility.'

The Queen had only reluctantly assented to the proceedings being televised, insisting that there be no close-ups of her. But even with the TV cameramen at a decorous distance, the BBC footage of the monarch was more intimate, more intrusive than any seen before. At the Commodore picture house in Notting Hill, the audience were amazed at how close the cameras took them. 'We knew, of course, that it was all done by means of special lenses,' said the *West London Observer*. 'But, for the moment, the wild thought came that the cameras had sprouted wings, flown over the heads of the crowd and were actually peering with their implacable electronic eyes into those of Elizabeth II.' The Queen was caught in a close, unblinking stare.

Fryn was watching at the home in Primrose Hill of her friend Rosie, the Dowager Marchioness of Headfort. They had drawn the curtains before the broadcast started. 'We sat in the dark entranced,' wrote Fryn in a letter to an American friend, '(but very very cold because Rosie does her central heating by electricity and she was so afraid of anything affecting the television she had turned it off).'

The Queen looked 'defenceless and very lonely' as she approached the altar, said Fryn. 'A gold canopy was held over her and she knelt and was anointed on the palms of her hands, on her breast, and on the top of her head. It was so simple, so humble, so quiet.' Her attendants dressed her in a girdle and a tunic of cloth-of-gold, building her up 'piece by gold piece, till she became a symbol rather than a girl'. Elizabeth 'will make a marvellous Queen we all know', wrote Fryn, 'but, poor darling, freedom is over for her for ever'.

Cecil Beaton popped home to his London flat after the service, to sleep off his hangover, and an hour later headed to Buckingham Palace. He set up his lights and camera in the Green Drawing Room, in front of some screens depicting the interior of Westminster Abbey, and asked the Queen to sit next to several bunches of roses and clematis that he had picked in his garden in Wiltshire. Prince Charles and Princess Anne, aged four and two, were 'buzzing about in the wildest excitement', Beaton said, 'and would not keep still for a moment'. The Queen looked very small in her robes, he thought, her nose and hands a little reddened, her eyes tired. 'Yes,' she agreed, 'the crown does get rather heavy.' He placed a 1,000-watt bulb behind her, to make her face shine, and then snapped away at speed.

When Beaton developed his portraits of the new queen, he was surprised at how well they turned out. The photos that appeared in the papers that week showed a young woman in jewels and furs, her skin lustrous and dewy. Here was a pure, glowing figure to counter the desecrated female bodies that had been pulled out of 10 Rillington Place in March.

***

At the request of Scotland Yard, Dr Camps visited Rillington Place with a gas engineer to test the truth of Christie's account of Beryl Evans's murder. Having examined the gas pipes, windows and dimensions of the top-floor rooms, he concluded that it was 'highly improbable if not impossible' that Christie had gassed Beryl into unconsciousness as he described: if the front room had made an effective gas chamber, which seemed very unlikely, Christie would have himself succumbed. Camps also doubted Christie's explanation of how the other women were gassed from a pipe in the kitchen. Surely they would have smelt the gas? Surely Christie would have been affected by the fumes? And yet significant levels of carbon monoxide had been detected in three of the bodies.

Thanks to information provided by the public and the victims' families, the police were able to piece together the biographies of the two women whose remains had been found in Christie's garden.

Ruth Margarete Christine Fuerst was born in Zurich in 1922, and lived in Austria as a child. She was a tall, very slender girl with large hands and feet and wavy black hair. Because she was Jewish, she was forced to leave her school in Bad Vöslau, near Vienna, when Hitler annexed Austria in 1938. A childhood friend of hers, now living in a caravan in Berkshire, told the police that Ruth had always wanted to be a nurse.

A Quaker refugee organisation helped Ruth to flee to Britain in 1939, leaving her parents and two brothers in Austria. She at first lived in a house in Golders Green, north London, where her landlady complained that she was 'very difficult to manage' and 'very keen on the company of men'. At work, in a hotel in South Kensington, she was more subdued: she was a solitary girl, according to a colleague, who spent all her free time reading books about medicine and nursing. She found a placement that summer as a student nurse in Westgate-on-Sea, Kent, where the moral welfare officer remembered her as intelligent and alert.

When war broke out in September, a government tribunal classified Ruth as a medium-risk 'enemy alien'. She could remain at liberty but had to report regularly to the authorities and was prohibited from living near the coast. The refugee council moved her in October from Westgate-on-Sea to the house of a Congregationalist minister in Lancashire.

Ruth was morose in her new home, said the minister's wife, and reluctant to help with domestic work. 'She seemed to be in a mental fog and did not seem to be happy,' her landlady observed. 'The reason for this behaviour was no doubt due to her unfortunate experiences in her own country at the commencement of the war in 1939. She did not seem to take any interest in her appearance and was dirty and slovenly.' It was not surprising that Ruth felt so low: she missed her home, feared for her family and had been forced to abandon her training as a nurse. The minister's wife arranged for her to be assessed by a specialist, who concluded that she was mentally ill. He recommended that she return to London, where she could be supervised by the refugee council.

In January 1940, when Ruth was living at a women's refuge in Highgate, she learnt that her parents and youngest brother had escaped Austria and made it to New York. But in May that year Ruth was herself arrested, as one of the 24,000 Germans and Austrians who the British government feared might act as saboteurs if Hitler invaded. Ruth was interned at a camp for women and children on the Isle of Man, in a village enclosed with barbed wire. Some of the Jewish refugees in the camp were bullied and insulted by German and Austrian internees who were loyal to the Nazis.

Ruth returned to London on her release in December 1940. She found a room in a Paddington boarding house and a job at a Mayfair hotel. Early in 1942 she became pregnant by a Cypriot waiter, and in October that year she gave birth to a daughter in a mother and baby home in West Hampstead. Her child, Sonya, was taken into care in Tunbridge Wells, Kent, where Ruth was sometimes able to visit her. Ruth wrote regularly to her mother in New York with news of the baby. In one letter, she told her mother that she had become friendly with Dr Willi Hoffer, a Viennese psychoanalyst now living in St John's Wood.

Over the next few months Ruth worked as a waitress in Notting Hill and as a lathe operator at a munitions works in Mayfair. She seemed very short of money, said a friend. Some of her colleagues, noticing that she was struggling to complete her shifts, guessed that she was pregnant. She left the munitions factory in June. She was living in a basement in Oxford Gardens, a few streets from Rillington Place, when she went missing in August 1943.

Christie told the police that he met Ruth Fuerst in a snack bar on the corner of Lancaster Road and Ladbroke Grove. He said that she came home with him two or three times while Ethel was visiting her family in Sheffield. She was tall, Christie wrote in his notes for Harry, 'almost as tall as me'. He described her as: 'Very slim through apparent starvation. Very intellectual (obviously unbalanced and depressed).'

One afternoon, Christie claimed in his notes, he offered to treat Ruth's chronic catarrh, and proceeded to gas her with a contraption he had devised. This was the glass jar that the police had found in his garden. It had two rubber pipes fed into holes in the screw-top lid, one to connect to the gas bracket and the other to administer gas; the smell was masked by a pungent Friar's Balsam tincture in the jar itself. Christie then had sex with Ruth, he said, and he strangled her.

On receiving a telegram from Ethel, informing him that she was on her way back to London, he wrapped Ruth's body in her leopard-skin coat and hid it under the floorboards in the front room. The next day, while Ethel was at work in Hammersmith, Christie moved the body to the washhouse. In the night, he dug a hole in the garden and buried the corpse. He raked over the ground and burned Ruth's clothes in a dustbin.

When the Metropolitan Police sent Ruth's death certificate to her mother in New York, Friedl Fuerst refused at first to accept that her daughter was dead. She wrote to Scotland Yard, asking them to explain how they had put a name to the bones they had found: the medical authorities she had consulted said that such an identification was impossible. 'If there is not sufficient proof, you have not the right, to issue a death certificate,' she wrote, 'I will not believe it.' She was in 'desperation', she said. 'I want to know the truth.' Ruth was the second child that Mrs Fuerst had lost during the war – her eldest son, Gottfried, had vanished in Vienna in 1942, probably having been deported to a concentration camp. The London police replied to Friedl Fuerst with an explanation of how they had identified Ruth's remains.

The other skeleton assembled from the bones in Christie's garden was that of Muriel Amelia Eady, a sailor's daughter born near the east London docks in 1912. When her mother died in the flu epidemic of 1918, Muriel was placed in a children's home in east London, and when she was twelve she was sent to Acton to help her mother's invalid sister-in-law run a lodging house for policemen. After the death of this aunt in the mid-1930s, Muriel took a job as a laundress at a hospital in Cambridge.

Muriel was a small, plump, dark-haired woman. During the war she moved back to London to live with her mother's sister, Martha Hooper, in Putney. Muriel's private life was a mystery to Mrs Hooper. 'We got on quite well together,' she said, 'but she was reticent and did not confide in me. I got on to her a few times because she stopped out late, but otherwise there was no unpleasantness between us.' Her father occasionally visited her in Putney, and she sometimes met up with one of her two older brothers, who lived in south London.

Muriel took a job on the assembly line at Ultra Electronics, in Acton, and in the evenings would drink at the Half Moon in Putney with her best friend, Pat. When Pat didn't turn up for work one day in 1944, Muriel went looking for her and was heartbroken to discover that she had been killed overnight in a bombing raid. After that Muriel visited the Half Moon several times with a middle-aged man in a Homburg hat.

Muriel met Reg Christie at Ultra Electronics that year. He was working as a driver for the firm, having left the police force at the end of 1943. She and her gentleman friend used to visit him and Ethel for tea at Rillington Place, and the two couples once went to the pictures together.

Muriel disappeared on Saturday 7 October 1944. Having come home after a half-day at work, said Mrs Hooper, she had set out again at 4 p.m., saying she wouldn't be late. She was wearing a camel-coloured cloche coat and a black frock with a pink collar. Her aunt suspected that she was pregnant. She didn't worry when Muriel failed to return that night, as she was sometimes away for a day or two, but when a birthday card for Muriel was delivered to the house a week later, Mrs Hooper informed the authorities that her niece had gone missing. The police concluded that she must have been killed in one of the doodlebug raids on London.

According to the account that Christie gave to the police, Muriel came to see him alone that Saturday in October. He gassed her with his machine, he said, strangled her as he had sex with her, then buried her in the garden.

Christie said that his dog Judy had dug up Muriel's skull in 1949, at the time of the Evans killings. He had stuffed it under his raincoat, walked round the corner to St Mark's Road, prised open the corrugated iron on the window of a bombed house and thrust it through the opening. He heard the skull hit the floor with a thud. Back at Rillington Place, Judy also dug up a thigh bone, which Christie then stuck in the ground to support a fence in the garden.

After taking Christie's confession, the police learnt that two children had come across a human skull in a derelict house in St Mark's Road in December 1949, soon after Christie claimed to have dumped it there. About this, at least, he seemed to be telling the truth. At the time, the local police had assumed that the skull belonged to a victim of a German bombing raid.

Harry thought that Christie's latest confessions made it all the more probable that he had murdered Beryl Evans and her baby. He had now admitted that he had been killing women since 1943. He had even claimed to have hidden Ruth Fuerst's body in the place that Beryl's and Geraldine's bodies were found. Christie's description of his gassing device also helped to explain how he might have knocked women out without suffering the effects of gas himself.

***

The Queen and the Duke of Edinburgh were driven through west London on Thursday afternoon, passing Rillington Place as they made their way up St Mark's Road. The residents were already decorating the street for their coronation party. 'We are really going to town on our coronation arrangements,' said Fred Styles, a lorry driver whose family lived above the Newmans at No 11, 'and the result will show that this is not the drab place it is made out to be.' He and his wife Bessie had raised the huge sum of £114 from the forty or so families in the street's twenty buildings. 'We want to give the kids the best time of their lives,' one woman told the *Kensington Post*, 'especially since the bad publicity of this street must have had a terrible effect on their little minds.'

Harry visited Rillington Place for the party on 6 June, a bright, cold Saturday. A large picture of Elizabeth II adorned the entrance to the cul-de-sac, along with a banner reading 'Long Live the Queen'. The men had built flower boxes to brighten the window sills, and frames for portraits of the new monarch. The women had made bunting to run along the fronts of the houses, and fancy-dress costumes and paper hats for the children. The lampposts were wrapped in red, white and blue ribbons, the kerbs painted with red, white and blue stripes, the buildings draped with 750 Union Jacks. Even Christie's house was hung with a few flags and a picture of Queen Elizabeth. 'We couldn't leave No 10 out,' said Fred Styles. 'It would have looked so conspicuous.'

George Rogers, a Labour politician who had been MP for Kensington North since 1945, opened the proceedings. 'This street has had some bad publicity lately,' he told the residents, 'but you have made it one of the finest decorated streets in London; certainly I have seen nothing to compare with it.'

Police officers stood guard at No 10 that afternoon, watching the bun-eating and singing contests. For the fancy-dress parade, the Styleses' daughter, Brenda, wore a drummer-girl costume, with a huge drum strapped around her midriff, while another girl was festooned in confectionery wrappers, to celebrate sweets having finally come off the ration in February. The winners included Colin Bailey, dressed as a king, Derek Wilkinson, dressed as a television set, and Beryl Petts, who came as a zebra crossing. At tables set up in the middle of the road, the children sat down to jelly and blancmange, provided by Mr Woods of the Rainbow Café on the corner. Each child was given a cup, saucer and spoon printed with royal insignia, a bag of fruit and sweets, and a 1953 shilling, donated by the newsagent in St Mark's Road.

The residents then gathered to watch a Punch and Judy show on a stage that had been erected at the walled end of the street: the children laughed – and a few cried – to see Mr Punch whack his wife Judy, jettison their baby, run squeaking from a policeman. In the house to the left of the puppet booth, at least seven women and a baby had been murdered in the previous ten years.

After the children's party, the adults danced and sang to a radiogram that had been set up on the stage. The organisers were presented with gifts: fifty cigarettes and ten cigars for each man on the committee; a bunch of flowers and a box of chocolates for each woman.

'It has gone wonderfully well,' said Fred Styles as the festivities wound up, 'better than anybody expected.'

***

By now, Lewis Nickolls of the Scotland Yard laboratory had delivered his findings on Beryl Evans's second post-mortem. The lab had been unable to detect any semen or carbon monoxide in her body, he said. Her pubic hair was similar to one of the bundles in the tin, but it had not been trimmed in the same way. There was nothing to corroborate Christie's account of her death. Perhaps he had been lying when he claimed to have killed Beryl, in an attempt to shore up his insanity defence. Apart from his confession, there was no evidence that he had murdered Beryl Evans, let alone her child.

In June, Harry's colleague Peter Baker of the *Mirror* managed to track down Lucy Endicott, the young woman with whom Tim Evans had had an affair in the summer of 1949. Baker met her at a hotel in Yorkshire.

When she was staying at Rillington Place, Lucy said, Tim and Beryl often quarrelled. One night Tim was furious with Beryl for having gone out to the pictures with Lucy. He told Beryl that her place was with the baby, and started to slap and punch her. Beryl took the bread knife from the table to defend herself and he moved towards her, warning: 'I'll push you through the bloody window.' Lucy stepped forward and tripped him up.

Two neighbours witnessed a fracas in the Evanses' flat at about this time: Jessie Hide, whose house in Lancaster Road overlooked the back of 10 Rillington Place, said she saw two people grappling at the lit window, like puppets in a booth; and Rosie Swan, at No 9, said that she saw struggling figures silhouetted on the back walls of the Lancaster Road terrace.

Tim and his mother, Agnes, fell out badly that summer, said Lucy. He hated Agnes 'like poison' because she always used to take Beryl's side rather than his. When Agnes confronted Tim and Lucy over their affair, the pair left Rillington Place together and stayed with a couple they knew.

A few nights later Lucy moved out, leaving a note: 'Sorry Tim. I have gone home to mother. It wouldn't work.'

Tim's friend asked him: 'What are you going to do now, Tim?'

'I'm going off the track,' Tim replied. 'If I ever get hold of Lucy I'll smash her up or run her over with my lorry.'

Tim's friend advised him to think things over before doing anything rash, and he warned Lucy about Tim's threats. Tim went home to Rillington Place.

***

Christie retracted his claim to have had sex with Beryl Evans at the time of her death. 'Normally I would have done it,' he wrote in his notes for the *Pictorial* in June, 'but my back was too stiff and painful.' He also now said that he had gassed her for only a minute or two. Perhaps he was again changing his story to match the pathologists' findings.

Dr Hobson visited Christie at Brixton on Friday 12 June, ten days before his trial was due to start. Christie told him that he was beginning to remember 'something about the baby', at which Hobson broke off the interview. He informed Derek Curtis-Bennett, Christie's barrister, that he did not want to question him any further. If Christie confessed to killing the child, he said, it would be impossible for him to testify that he was insane. Hobson needed to believe that Christie was a man possessed by a deranged, death-dealing lust, not a man who coolly killed a baby because her cries might get him caught.

Harry was frustrated to hear that the psychiatrist hired by the *Pictorial* was not pushing Christie about Geraldine's death. Both he and Hobson wanted Christie to confess to killing as many women as possible, but on the issue of the child's murder their wishes diverged. Harry could only hope that Curtis-Bennett would raise the matter in court.

At Pear Tree Cottage, Fryn received an irritated note from Sir Norman Birkett, in which he said that he was 'somewhat mortified' to hear from Derek Curtis-Bennett that she had also asked him to get her into the Old Bailey. 'This is the method best calculated to lead to a muddle,' warned Birkett, 'with the result that nobody does anything and the day comes and no seats.' Her frantic efforts to secure a place in court seemed to have backfired.

Having still not heard from the Old Bailey by 17 June, five days before the trial, Fryn wrote to Birkett again. She was 'all of a twitter with suspense', she said, and desperately hoped that with his 'kind interest and assistance' she would be able to attend. On Friday 19 June, Birkett confirmed at last that he had obtained a special pass for Fryn. She thanked him for working this 'miracle'.

Hoping that Joanna could act as her 'eyes' in the courtroom, Fryn wrote at once to the Under-Sheriff of the Central Criminal Court. 'I have a perfectly appalling ankle,' Fryn told the Under-Sheriff, again pretending she had an injury rather than admit to her failing sight. 'So my secretary will be coming with me so as to help me up the stairs. Whether it is possible to get her in to those seats at the back or not I don't know.'

PART TWO

9

That body-ridden house

On Monday 22 June 1953, the first day of Christie's trial, Joanna drove Fryn to the Old Bailey in her Daimler, a four-and-a-half-mile run from St John's Wood. The courthouse, built in the neo-Baroque style in 1907, lay just east of Fleet Street, near St Paul's Cathedral. The road outside was busy with police vans, photographers, reporters and news vendors. A long queue had formed for seats in the public gallery of Court No 1, which had been renovated just in time for the trial. Joan Elton, a 44-year-old vet's receptionist from Stanmore, Middlesex, had been waiting since 11 p.m. the previous evening, with a rug, a camp stool, two flasks of tea and a packet of sandwiches to see her through the night.

To Fryn's horror, she and Joanna were at first refused admission to the court. An official told them that Fryn had been granted access for only a single day, the Wednesday. Joanna explained that there must have been a mix-up: Fryn had applied through her osteopath's friend under her married name, and through Sir Norman Birkett under her professional name: though 'Mrs Harwood' had been granted a ticket for just one day, Birkett had arranged for 'Miss Tennyson Jesse' to attend the whole trial. The officials were annoyed that places had been reserved for Fryn under two names, but agreed to admit her and Joanna. A policeman in the lobby, seeing 'Alibi Alf' on Fryn's ankle, offered to show them to the lift. Fryn was relieved: she had been worried about negotiating the white expanse of the marble staircase.

Fryn and Joanna took their seats in the City Lands benches of Court No 1, which were reserved for about forty special guests.

'Fryn,' said a very thin figure, towering over her against the light.

'Who is it?' she asked, unable to make out his features.

'It's Bob,' said the figure.

Robert Sherwood was an old friend of hers, a moustachioed American, 6ft 5in tall, who had won an Academy Award for his screenplay for *The Best Years of Our Lives* and a Pulitzer prize for his biography of Franklin D. Roosevelt – he had written speeches for the American president during the war. He sat down at the end of Fryn's bench.

Also on their benches were Terence Rattigan, the renowned British playwright, and Margaret Leighton, who had starred in the film of Rattigan's *The Winslow Boy* and in Hitchcock's *Under Capricorn*. Christie's barrister, Derek Curtis-Bennett, had arranged seats for two of Harry's bosses from the *Pictorial*, Reg Payne (the assistant editor) and Fred Redman (the news editor). Two crime novelists had places: Christianna Brand, whose latest detective story was set in the deadly London smog of the previous year, and Anthony Berkeley Cox, whose *Malice Aforethought*, written under the alias Francis Iles, had famously revealed the identity of the murderer from the outset.

A man sitting next to Cox whispered to him that he had been to every Old Bailey murder trial since that of Dr Crippen, hanged in 1910 for the murder of his wife, and he thought this one unlikely to be very satisfying. 'There's no excitement, you see,' he said. 'It's not like not knowing whether he really did it or not; he's confessed; it's just his sanity that's being tried.'

But Cox was eager to see and hear Christie in person – this case, like *Malice Aforethought*, was a kind of inverted murder story, in which the killer was known but his motive and method were mysterious. Nor could anyone be sure whether Christie had killed Geraldine Evans, a crime for which another man had hanged.

For Harry, the chief interest of the trial lay in what it might reveal about the Evans case. He needed to compare the testimony in court to the material that Christie had secretly written for him. He hoped that Christie might yet admit that he had killed the baby as well as Beryl, or at least divulge more about what had happened in November 1949. He also hoped that the defence's insanity plea would be successful. On the previous Thursday, a jury at the Old Bailey had returned a verdict of guilty but insane on the self-confessed strangler John Haskayne, after Brixton's chief medical officer, Dr Matheson, testified that he might have had an epileptic 'blackout' when he killed Grace Barrington. Mr Justice Finnemore, who was due to preside over Christie's trial, had ordered that Haskayne be detained at the Broadmoor hospital for criminal lunatics.

Harry was squeezed on to the press benches next to the dock, in a blue suit and red bow tie, along with Norman Rae of the *News of the World*, Duncan Webb of the *People* and almost forty other crime reporters. At eye level, the room was a dense jigsaw of dark wood: oak panelling, oak boxes and platforms, oak benches abutting oak desks. In the well of the court, Curtis-Bennett and the other lawyers were already sorting through their briefs at a long table stacked with papers. The raised jury box and witness box were to Harry's left, and the City Lands benches, where Fryn was sitting, were beyond the prisoner's dock to his right. The judges' bench was directly ahead of him. In total, about two hundred people were crowded into the chamber.

A flood of light fell on this dark intimate maze from the high windows and the glass ceiling in the dome of the court, as if the room were an elaborate wooden casket with its lid lifted off. The 'white curves went up to meet the white glass roof', wrote Fryn in her novel *A Pin to See the Peepshow*; the light 'welled upon one like water'. Joan Elton and thirty-five other stalwarts of the public queue were perched in a gallery near the roof, looking down on the proceedings.

At 11 a.m., an usher rapped three times with a wooden mallet, at which everyone rose and the Sheriffs of London entered the court through a side door, followed by Mr Justice Finnemore, in a white horsehair wig and ermine-cuffed robe. He sat down at the judges' bench, on a leather chair facing the dock, and placed a pair of gloves and a piece of black cloth on the dais before him. Donald Finnemore was a teetotal Baptist lay preacher and Sunday School teacher, aged sixty-four. He had hooded eyes, down-turned lips, a solemn manner.

'Bring up John Reginald Halliday Christie,' said the clerk of the court.

Christie was escorted directly into the dock from a staircase below. He stood, flanked by Brixton prison officers, as the judge's clerk asked how he pled to the charge of murdering his wife.

'Not guilty,' whispered Christie.

The judge asked him to repeat his plea.

'Not guilty,' he said, slightly raising his voice.

Christie was wearing the blue pin-stripe suit that Harry had bought him, over a pale-blue shirt and a blue tie. The room around him was thick with people, rustling and murmuring, as he stood silent in his raised octagonal enclosure, 16 feet wide and 14 feet deep. He continued to stand, impassive, as nine men and three women filed into the jury box and took their oaths.

From the City Lands benches, a few feet from the dock, Anthony Berkeley Cox could at first see only the back of Christie's bald head, 'and a pair of ears, one just a little higher than the other; and when he slowly turned his head (all his movements were slow), a glimpse of a sharply pointed nose and a forehead positively corrugated with wrinkles'. From the press seats, Duncan Webb saw Christie's 'cold unwavering eyes', watchful as 'a poised snake'.

Briefly, Christie turned his reptilian gaze on the luminaries in the City Lands seats. Fryn could not see him clearly, but Joanna described him to her afterwards: he had a 'tall, bald head', wrote Fryn, a 'trim, mean figure, a ruddy seamed face, the eyes mean and intent behind glasses, the tongue licking out occasionally between thin dry lips that nibbled incessantly at each other'. As Christie scanned the benches, he caught the eye of Terence Rattigan. The playwright felt a chill run through him.

Christie sat down when Sir Lionel Heald QC rose to open the case for the prosecution. Heald, a Conservative MP who had been appointed to Churchill's government as Attorney-General in 1951, outlined the Crown's evidence: the lies that Christie told his neighbours and Ethel's family after her death in December; his alteration of the date on her letter to her sister; his sale of her wedding ring to a shop in Shepherd's Bush; a signature he forged to gain access to her bank account; his confession on being arrested. Heald read out the section of Christie's statement in which he admitted to killing his wife.

Heald cut an authoritative figure, with his thick, arching eyebrows, his crisp upper-class intonation and his schoolmasterly habit of peering over his spectacles. He had spent thirty years at the Bar and had served in both world wars, rising to the rank of air commodore. It was rare for the government's Attorney-General to appear in a murder trial but the Christie case, because of the controversy about Tim Evans's guilt, was politically sensitive.

Heald asked for the jury to be shown plans and photographs of 10 Rillington Place, so that they could imagine themselves into the meagre rooms. They then looked at a bound book in which the police had pasted photographs of Ethel Christie's body. One image showed Ethel's swathed form in a hollow beneath the floorboards, while a portrait of a woman – perhaps her mother or her mother-in-law – gazed serenely from the living-room wall.

When Curtis-Bennett rose to set out the case for the defence, he said that he intended to show that Christie's murders had been impulsive, chaotic and carelessly concealed. 'My case is insanity,' he told the court. In due course, he announced, he would take the unusual step of calling the defendant himself to the witness box. At this news, a hum of excitement ran round the room.

Curtis-Bennett asked that the jury be shown photographs of the other victims found at 10 Rillington Place, and the clerk of the court passed them a third album.

In these pictures, too, the house seemed to have been prised open to reveal its rotten innards. The first photo showed the building from the outside, every curtain drawn, and the next, as if the viewer was advancing on the crime scene, a closer view of the front-room window. Then the jurors were in Christie's kitchen, looking at a covered alcove between a cast-iron range and a filthy sink, and then, as if watching a macabre striptease, they saw first the alcove uncovered, then a view of Hectorina Maclennan's body hunched into the recess, then a closer view still of her waxy back; and then her body was gone, to reveal Kay Maloney's shrouded figure on a floor of earth and ashes; and then this body too had vanished, leaving the swaddled shape of Rita Nelson against the bare bricks of the back wall; the final picture showed the empty cavity.

A separate album contained photographs of the women's bodies at the mortuary. Kathleen Maloney and Rita Nelson were shown wrapped in cloth, then unbound. A dark ligature mark was visible on Hectorina Maclennan's neck.

Heald called more than twenty witnesses to testify to the events surrounding Ethel's death, including her brother and sister, her neighbours, tradesmen with whom she had dealt, the police officers who investigated her murder, the couple who sublet the flat from Reg Christie in March, men who had encountered him when he was on the run.

The court heard evidence from Charles Brown, the landlord of No 10, and from two of his tenants: Franklin Stewart, who described how Reg Christie had sprinkled disinfectant in the hallway in the first weeks of the year, and Franklin's sister Louise, who had seen him pouring Jeyes Fluid in the hall and in the street outside. Louise had been sharing a room with Beresford Brown and their baby at the time of the murders. They were now married, and the baby was six months old. Beresford, dressed in a sharp suit and tie, had accompanied Louise to the Old Bailey.

Derek Curtis-Bennett, in cross-examining the West Indian tenants, tried to suggest that Christie had used disinfectant not to conceal the smell of rotting bodies but to get rid of the smells of the other people in the house. 'As far as the upstairs, first and second floors, are concerned, were they occupied while you were there by four coloured people?' he asked Franklin Stewart. 'Did the passageway get dirty from time to time? Had some of the coloured people spilt water in the hall and left it there?'

'I would not know,' Stewart replied.

At the lunch adjournment, Christie was taken through the opening in the floor of the dock to the cells two storeys below. Everyone else filed out through separate exits. The court was organised to keep the participants apart. Mr Justice Finnemore withdrew from his raised platform to his room; the jurors to the jury room; the barristers to the bar mess; the spectators in the gallery down a staircase that led straight to the street, their places to be taken up after lunch by those waiting in the queue outside. The press and the guests of the court streamed out to the huge lobby, and headed to the staircase across a floor of Italian marble. Above them, a young woman on a ladder was completing the restoration of a mural that had been badly damaged by German bombs in 1941.

The foreign reporters – from France, the United States and Australia – repaired for lunch to the cafeteria in the basement or to restaurants nearby, while Harry and the other British journalists made for the pubs across the road. It was a very warm day. The sun glowed on the Old Bailey building's pale stone and on the gold-leaf statue of Lady Justice that rose from its central dome, a sword in one of her hands and the scales of justice in the other.

Laurence Thompson, who was covering the trial for the *News Chronicle*, reflected as he left the building on how sinister Christie made the outside world now seem. 'There were a dozen of him strolling round Old Bailey in the sunshine in the lunch hour,' he wrote. 'He might be one of your own neighbours, and you wonder what you really know about them.'

***

Back in Court No 1 after lunch, Curtis-Bennett asked the clerk to read out the whole of the statement that Christie had made to the police when he was arrested, including his descriptions of the deaths of Kathleen Maloney, Rita Nelson and Hectorina Maclennan. He then asked Inspector Griffin, who had led the investigation into their murders, to give a rundown of Christie's criminal record. Griffin disclosed that in the 1920s and 1930s Reg Christie had been convicted of Post Office theft, vehicle theft and the theft of money and cigarettes from a cinema, as well as a physical assault on a woman. In this 'topsy-turvy case', as Thompson of the *News Chronicle* described it, Christie's counsel was seeking to blacken his character.

As the evidence was heard, Fryn and Bob Sherwood passed notes back and forth along the City Lands benches, to the irritation of their neighbours.

In his final parry of the afternoon, Curtis-Bennett asked Griffin about the Evans murders of 1949. The inspector confirmed that Tim Evans had accused Christie of having killed Beryl and Geraldine, and that Christie had been the chief witness for the prosecution at his trial. Curtis-Bennett pointed out that Christie had started killing even before those murders. 'When the trial of Evans was going on in this very court,' said Curtis-Bennett, 'there were lying, in all probability, in the garden of 10 Rillington Place two skeletons no one knew anything about?'

'Yes,' said Griffin. 'Quite probably.'

Harry was glad that Curtis-Bennett had managed to introduce evidence about the Evans case before the court adjourned for the day.

***

On Tuesday, another sunny morning, Fryn and Joanna were joined on the City Lands benches by Derek Curtis-Bennett's older daughter, Susan. Some of the relatives of the murdered women were also in court: Rita Nelson's estranged father and her sister; Ina Maclennan's brothers. Harry watched from the press benches as Christie entered the dock from below, made a deep bow to Mr Justice Finnemore and took his seat in a green upholstered chair.

When Derek Curtis-Bennett resumed his cross-examination of Inspector Griffin, he requested that the clerk of the court read out two statements that Christie had made to Griffin at Brixton prison, one describing the murders of Ruth Fuerst and Muriel Eady, and the other describing Beryl Evans's death. Christie leant forward as his words were read to the court.

On behalf of the Crown, the Attorney-General put a few questions about the Evans case to Griffin. He got the inspector to agree that Tim Evans had been tried and hanged for the murder of Geraldine, not Beryl. Heald asked him to confirm that the child had been strangled with Tim Evans's own necktie.

'With a tie,' corrected Griffin. It had not been established whose tie had been found around her neck.

Heald asked the detective if he had any reason to believe that the wrong man had been hanged for the murder of Geraldine Evans.

'None,' said Griffin, firmly.

Curtis-Bennett leapt up. 'I object to that very strongly,' he said. 'Sir Lionel has no business to ask that. It is an improper question.'

Mr Justice Finnemore said that there was no suggestion that Christie had killed Geraldine Evans. To Harry, it seemed obvious that the judge, like the Attorney-General, was determined to rule out the possibility that this court had overseen a miscarriage of justice in 1950. The government and the judicial establishment were doing all they could to uphold the Evans verdict.

Heald called several other witnesses for the prosecution, among them Dr Camps, the pathologist; Dr Nickolls, the director of the Scotland Yard laboratory; and Dr Odess, the Christies' family doctor, who said that Christie had seen him thirty-two times in the first half of 1952, complaining of diarrhoea, flatulence, piles, headaches, pain in his lower back, depression, insomnia and memory loss. Odess produced a letter of referral in which he had described Christie as 'a very decent, quiet-living man, hard working, and very conscientious'.

Curtis-Bennett then made his opening speech for the defence. His delivery was so subdued that Anthony Berkeley Cox could barely hear him. In an English trial, observed Cox, 'drama is bad form. It makes us feel embarrassed. One could imagine the producer warning his cast: "Above all, gentlemen, no drama. Play it down, please. Play everything *down*!" '

But Curtis-Bennett's claims about his client were dramatic. Christie had been 'as mad as a March hare' when he killed Ethel, he said: to prove it, the defence would produce evidence about his attacks on the other women in 'that grim, body-ridden house'. Christie had sexually assaulted several of his victims, he said, and he had showed signs of deviance even with Ethel, whose pubic hair he seemed to have cut off and kept. 'What an extraordinary aberration that must be,' said Curtis-Bennett, 'the collection of pubic hair' – the four clumps in the tin were laid out, he observed, 'like butterflies'.

When Christie emerged from his insane episodes, said Curtis-Bennett, he sometimes behaved rationally in trying to cover up his crimes, but there was none the less only one conclusion to draw from the evidence: 'This man is a raging lunatic,' he said, gesturing at Christie. 'This man is mad – hopelessly and utterly mad.'

Curtis-Bennett was equivocal on the subject of Geraldine Evans. He said that he would not argue that Christie had killed her, since Christie had confessed only to the murder of Beryl; and yet, he said, it was open to the jury to think he might also have murdered the child. This hint at his culpability was as much as Harry could hope for.

There would be just two witnesses for the defence, announced Curtis-Bennett: the prisoner and a psychiatrist who had examined him. He asked the jury to bear with Christie in the witness box: 'I understand that his voice is extremely low, even lower than mine, and you may not be able to hear what he says.' He added: 'You may gain the impression when he gives evidence that when he is talking about these matters he is talking about a third person, and not about himself at all.'

Christie was called to testify at 3 p.m. He walked slowly across the court room from the dock, a hand in his left-hand trouser pocket, and peered at the short flight of steps before climbing up to the witness box in which he had testified against Tim Evans in 1950. When the usher showed him a card, he stared at it for almost half a minute. He mopped his brow, wiped his hands and blew his nose. He took hold of the Bible and, almost inaudibly, read out the oath.

Curtis-Bennett got up from the benches below, ruffled his papers and asked, gently: 'Are you John Reginald Halliday Christie?'

'Yes,' Christie half-whispered. The court fell almost silent as everyone strained to hear the two men. The jurors leant forward, though they were sitting right next to the witness box, some of them cupping their hands to their ears.

'Do your best to speak up, Mr Christie,' said Curtis-Bennett.

He asked Christie to confirm various facts about his early life, to which he muttered, 'Yes.' Christie agreed that he had been gassed in the First World War, and able only to whisper for three and a half years. The doctors at the time had considered this a symptom of shock.

In 1920, he confirmed, he had married Ethel.

'You had no children?' asked his counsel.

'No.'

'You wanted children?'

'Yes.'

Curtis-Bennett asked whether he had been happy with Ethel.

'Very happy,' Christie said. 'I put her to sleep,' he murmured, gripping the witness stand, tears trickling down his cheeks.

Curtis-Bennett asked him about the killings of the other women whose bodies were found at 10 Rillington Place. Christie's accounts were even scrappier and more confused than the statements to the police that had been read to the court. He showed no emotion about the women's deaths.

Why did Ruth Fuerst come back to his house? asked Curtis-Bennett.

Christie was very still. He looked puzzled. After a long pause, he mumbled: 'I don't know.' Nor did he know what had happened when she came inside, he said. 'I strangled her. I must have strangled her.'

'Was that the first person you strangled in your life?'

'I don't know,' said Christie.

'You don't even know that?'

'No,' said Christie, shaking his head.

'Do you remember whether you killed anybody between 1944 and 1949?' asked Curtis-Bennett.

'I don't know,' whispered Christie, shrugging slightly and spreading his left hand in a gesture of helplessness. 'I may have done.'

'Can you tell us what happened?'

'At times I have got something in my mind,' he said, vaguely, 'and I cannot get it out.'

'How long has that gone on?'

'I have had it for years,' said Christie. 'After the first war.'

Asked about the death of Beryl Evans, Christie said that he thought it had been he who strangled her, after gassing her, and Tim Evans who disposed of the body, fearing that he would be held responsible for her death.

'Did you kill the baby Geraldine?' asked Curtis-Bennett.

'No,' said Christie.

'Why did you lie about Mrs Evans?'

'I think it was because I never interfered with or touched the baby,' he said. 'They put both of them together.' He was suggesting that he had denied Beryl's murder for fear of being suspected of assaulting the child as well.

When asked again about Ethel, Christie repeated that he had been trying to put her out of her misery, because she had tried to kill herself, and that he had concealed her death afterwards because 'I could not realise she was gone.'

As the afternoon wore on, wrote the crime novelist Anthony Berkeley Cox, the courtroom 'became tinged with gold from the electric bulbs along the cornices,' and 'the impression of theatrical unreality became more and more strong. Perhaps the parts in the drama were being too much underplayed; perhaps the lighting began to have a hypnotic effect; but it certainly became more and more impossible to believe that this worried little whisperer… could really have killed seven women in circumstances of unrelieved sordidness, and that it was of real crimes that he was so deprecatingly giving us the revolting details.'

'The whole thing was so obviously impossible,' wrote Cox. 'One could not use such a situation even in a detective-story. The man did not even fit any of one's ideas about murderers. It must be just a stage-play that we were watching, with the chief part quite astonishingly miscast.'

Fryn, too, was struck by the 'eerie unreality' of the scene. Christie 'certainly did his best', she wrote, 'to appear insane in the box. His brow was furrowed with the effort to remember. The long pauses between his answers added to the horror of each successive story.' He seemed a bemused spectator of his own atrocities.

Curtis-Bennett asked Christie about the other residents of No 10. It was unclear what he intended with this line of questioning, unless to elicit the jury's sympathy for his client.

'When Mr Brown took over the house,' said Christie, 'he put some odd pieces of furniture which he bought into each room, the four upper rooms, and then let them to coloured people with white girls.'

'Was that unpleasant?' asked Curtis-Bennett.

'It was very unpleasant,' said Christie, 'because one or two were prostitutes.'

'Was your wife upset by that?'

'Very,' said Christie. 'Two black men and one of the white women had assaulted my wife, and a black man had assaulted her while I was in hospital last year, and I had to come out of hospital before I finished treatment on account of that because my wife was alone.'

When the day's proceedings closed at twenty past four, Mr Justice Finnemore reminded the jury not to discuss the case with anyone outside the court. Christie's evidence would continue in the morning.

As Fryn and Joanna left the Old Bailey, they offered a lift to a flower seller they had just met. In the car, the man told them that in late January or early February, Christie had visited his stall outside a tailor's shop in St James's, Piccadilly. 'What a smell of dead bodies here,' Christie remarked. 'Can't *you* smell it?'

'No, I can't,' the flower seller replied. 'I been on this stall thirty years and I never smelt anything like that.'

Fryn wasn't sure whether to believe this story, but she liked it anyway. 'It is pleasing to think of him sniffing at the flowers and making that remark,' she wrote; 'it is macabre and fits in with the picture of Christie that the scent of flowers should awaken that of mortality in his nostrils.' Here was a man so corrupt that he smelt sweetness as rot.

***

Tottie was waiting for Fryn and Joanna at Pear Tree Cottage. He had turned seventy-nine in March, and he rarely went out now, unless to watch the cricket at Lord's, across the road from their house, or the tennis at Wimbledon – Joanna would drive him down to south-west London in her Daimler. His most recent play, *The Thin Line*, had flopped at the Whitehall Theatre in March, but he still drew an income of more than £10,000 a year from his business concerns, and he still cut a powerful figure around the house. Joanna remembered her first meeting with Tottie, in 1950. He had been spreadeagled in a large red armchair, resting a folded copy of *The Times* against his cherry-coloured corduroy slacks. He lazily turned his big head towards her, and asked if she could help him with a crossword clue.

On hot days like this one, Tottie enjoyed sunbathing naked in the garden, with a newspaper at hand to cover himself in an emergency. In the evening he would fix himself a whisky and soda before sharing a light supper with Fryn, the peppery smell of phlox drifting in through the garden door and their beloved poodle, Guido, curled up by a window. Tottie had stocked the cupboard under the stairs with half-bottles of champagne, to discourage Fryn from over-indulging in white port. After supper he would change into a pair of orange, green and red pyjamas, a gift from Fryn, and retire to his bedroom to smoke, drink cocoa and eat sardines.

Fryn slept in a separate bedroom, along the corridor from Tottie. Sometimes they delivered love notes to each other's rooms at night.

10

The rope deckchair

Cecil Beaton, fresh from photographing the Queen, joined Fryn, Joanna and the other guests on the City Lands benches on Wednesday. He cast an eye over Christie as he returned to the witness box. Today he was wearing a spotted red tie with his blue suit. 'In appearance he is meticulous and only slightly ridiculous,' Beaton observed in his diary. 'Probably he is too poor to be prissily neat. His handkerchief a dirty grey crumpled mass, his collar too big for him. The effect is of incredible ordinariness. He is like every other man in the street.' His hands, he noted, 'the hands that had strangled so many women', were 'large, knobbly, knuckly'.

'Now, Mr Christie,' said Derek Curtis-Bennett. 'I think we had got last night to the end of the story of Mrs Christie, had not we?'

He started to question him about Kathleen Maloney, but Christie's answers were so indistinct that Curtis-Bennett stopped him and asked him to speak into the microphone that had been fitted to the witness box overnight. The device was wired to loudspeakers, one placed next to the shorthand writer, sitting below the witness box, and the other next to the clerk of the court, below the judges' bench. Christie adjusted it as he continued.

'I think I wanted to get rid of her, out of the house,' he said, more audible now, 'because she was very repulsive. I believe she got up and, as far as I remember, got hold of a metal pan. I think she meant to strike me with it.' He was reverting to his original story about Kay Maloney's death, rather than the account he had given in his notes for Harry.

'You keep saying you "think",' observed Curtis-Bennett. 'Is this what you remember now or what you remembered at the time?'

'It is all very hazy, you see,' said Christie.

He recalled that Maloney sat down in a chair by the kitchen door. 'While she was in that chair I think I strangled her.'

'What with?' asked his lawyer.

'I think it was a piece of cord,' said Christie.

'Did you get the piece of cord from that?' asked Curtis-Bennett, indicating a deckchair that an usher had brought into the room to show the jury.

'I believe I did,' said Christie.

Most of the evidence before the court had relayed Christie's crimes at one remove: in spoken testimony, written documents, photographs, plans, diagrams. But this deckchair was a brutal, untranslated relic of the murders, a raw chunk of 10 Rillington Place. It made a kind of temporal rupture in the courtroom, as if a solid piece of the past had been thrust into view. The chair had no cover; its frame was lashed with several lengths of rope, forming a crude webbed seat.

This 'strange deck-chair', wrote Fryn, 'instead of canvas, had string threaded across and across in the most erratic manner with knots here and there. Tail ends of string hung down in bedraggled fashion.' For Cecil Beaton, the 'awful old deck chair' conjured up the 'squalor of these poor lives', their 'incredible terrible sordidness'. Christie had apparently tightened one of its cords around Kay Maloney's neck.

Christie did not mention to the court, as he had claimed in his notes for Harry, that he often kept a strangling rope in his pocket when women called round. This, after all, would imply premeditation.

The judge cut in: 'Do you want to tell the jury at all why you strangled her?'

'I do not think I know.'

'Had you any motive against any of these people,' asked Curtis-Bennett, 'or against your wife?'

'No,' said Christie, 'there was no reason. There is no sense.'

Christie continued in this vein, with sparse, disjointed descriptions of the killings of Rita Nelson and Hectorina Maclennan. 'I never hurt anybody,' he claimed at one point, and: 'It must have been me,' at another. Sometimes, as if trying to summon a memory, he paused for a few moments, stroking a hand across his forehead.

Cecil Beaton was repulsed by Christie. 'His eyes are bright, furtive and pained,' he wrote, 'his forehead drawn and fully pained, a furrow that is more like a pool than a frown, his mouth thin and cruel, and a tongue like an adder that keeps flicking out during the forming of his carefully enunciated sentences.' Christie spoke in ready-made 'bank clerk phrases', said Beaton, such as: 'Prior to that I recollect nothing.' The language he used seemed to bear little relation to the violent acts he was acknowledging. His long pauses between answering questions, said Beaton, were 'terrifyingly dramatic'.

Christie gave a muddled account of his meanderings through London while the police were searching for him. After four nights at the Rowton House hostel he had taken to the streets, occasionally resting in a picture house or an all-night café. Several of the public sightings of him in the last week of March – in east London, Battersea, King's Cross, Paddington and Notting Hill – had been accurate. At one point, Christie said, he had heard people in a café talking about the case, and he had seen a newspaper headlined: 'Will the Killer Strike Again?'

Had he tried to hide from the police? asked Curtis-Bennett. On the contrary, said Christie: on his way back to west London he had thanked a policeman who stopped the traffic so that he could cross the road.

Under cross-examination by the Attorney-General, Christie said that he had resigned from his job in December because he was having severe headaches. 'I had been thinking of going away for two and a half years, ever since those blacks came and lived in the house.'

And why did he hide Ethel's body under the floor?

'I did not want to be separated from her. That is why I put her there. She was still in the house.'

Heald questioned Christie closely on his efforts to conceal Ethel's death, and he read out the Christmas card in which Christie had claimed that Ethel was unable to write because of the rheumatism in her fingers.

'That, of course, was a complete invention,' said Heald.

'Not entirely,' said Christie, 'because she had suffered from rheumatism for quite a long time.'

The judge leant over. 'She had not got rheumatism then,' pointed out Mr Justice Finnemore sternly, 'because she was dead.'

Heald asked: 'If on 14th December when you killed your wife in the bedroom there had been a policeman there, you would not have done it, would you?'

'I don't suppose so,' replied Christie. 'That's obvious.'

When Curtis-Bennett rose to ask Christie if he thought that it had been wrong to kill his wife, he replied: 'I do not really think so.'

Heald got to his feet again for a final question about Beryl Evans.

'Mr Christie,' he said, 'you have given evidence twice on oath about Mrs Evans. On one occasion you swore you did not kill her, and on the other occasion you swore you did kill her. That is right, is it not?'

'It can't be right,' said Christie.

'How do you expect the jury to believe you?' asked Heald.

Christie did not reply.

The Attorney-General, Harry noticed, was determined to undermine Christie's claim to have killed Beryl, because it cast doubt on the conviction of her husband for Geraldine's murder.

Christie left the witness box, where he had spent just over an hour and a half that day.

The microphone had transformed Fryn's impression of Christie. Now that everyone could hear him, she said, he was no longer a 'vague little madman' but 'the practical man of business' and 'the man in the limelight'. He had slipped suddenly from one persona to another, from faltering supplicant to puffed-up prima donna. He had seemed to enjoy positioning the device and commanding the court's attention. 'Here was a very wicked and a very cunning man,' said Fryn, 'if indeed he could be called a man and not a monster. The microphone may have allowed the whole Court to hear him, but it also, oddly enough, allowed the whole Court to see him as he really was.'

Curtis-Bennett called his last witness to the box. Dr Hobson testified that Christie's claims not to remember his crimes were sincere: at the time of each killing, Christie had blotted from his mind the knowledge that he was doing wrong. He sometimes lied afterwards, Hobson acknowledged, but at other times he unconsciously suppressed unpleasant facts. 'I believe that these tricks of memory or avoidance of getting down to disturbing topics is to preserve his own self-respect,' explained Hobson, 'to preserve this fictitious aura which he has of himself, rather than to avoid incriminating himself.' If his recall of Ethel's killing was inaccurate, this was because 'as much as Christie can love anyone, he loved his wife'. He could not bear to know that he had murdered her.

Hobson proposed that Christie suffered from severe hysteria, a product of the mustard-gas injuries he sustained in the First World War. His attraction to dead bodies, Hobson suggested, went back to his childhood, when he had been riveted by the sight of his grandfather's corpse. Later, as a policeman patrolling the bombed streets of London, he had been fascinated by the bodies he found in the ruined buildings.

After the murders, Hobson said, 'I think he got some feeling of satisfaction in continuing to live in Rillington Place with the dead bodies near by.'

The doctor believed that Christie's anger towards women stemmed from his first sexual encounter. At the age of sixteen or seventeen, he had paired off with a girl in Halifax, but found himself unable to 'perform'. The next day a friend had sex with the girl, and she told him about her disappointing dalliance with Reg. For a time, said Hobson, Christie had been called 'a nickname which implied that he was not quite a man'.

'You need not give the actual word,' advised Curtis-Bennett.

In his cross-examination, the Attorney-General asked Dr Hobson whether he endorsed Curtis-Bennett's characterisations of Christie as a 'maniac', a 'raving lunatic', 'mad as a March hare' and 'hopelessly and utterly mad'.

'None of these was made on your advice?' Heald asked.

'No,' Hobson said.

'And you would agree that they were wholly unscientific? And calculated to mislead anyone?'

Hobson hesitated.

Curtis-Bennett jumped up: 'I am entitled to conduct this case,' he said, 'without being instructed how to conduct it, even if it is by the Attorney-General.'

Heald rephrased his question. 'Would you agree it would be wholly inappropriate,' he asked, 'to describe him as hopelessly and utterly mad?'

'It would be inappropriate,' said Hobson. Heald had succeeded in getting Curtis-Bennett's own witness to contradict him.

This closed the case for the defence.

As the court broke for lunch, a guard touched Christie on the shoulder to guide him to the stairs. 'Take your bloody hands off me,' hissed Christie, turning on him in fury. In the cells, he was silent and sullen.

***

When the court rose again at two o'clock, Heald called two psychiatrists to rebut the medical evidence presented by the defence.

Dr John Matheson, chief medical officer at Brixton prison, made his way slowly to the witness box – he had lost his left leg during the First World War, along with the sight in his right eye.

In answer to Heald's questions, Matheson described Christie as a physically feeble and sexually immature man, who when faced with difficulties tended to exaggerate and act in a hysterical manner. In the moment of killing, he said, Christie had known that he was acting illegally. 'I think he is sane,' Matheson said, firmly.

Christie stared at the prison doctor as he spoke.

Christie's counsel cross-examined Matheson, trying to get him to agree that the defendant's impulse to have sex with dead women was itself evidence of madness. Matheson would say only that it was very abnormal.

Curtis-Bennett next tried to show that the psychiatrists testifying for the defence and the prosecution were almost in agreement. He put it to Matheson that Dr Hobson thought it 'possible, even probable' that Christie did not know that what he was doing was wrong, whereas Matheson himself thought it 'possible, but not probable'.

'Yes,' agreed Matheson.

'And that is the only issue between us?'

'Yes; put that way, it is.'

Christie ran his tongue over his lips as he watched Matheson leave the box and return to his seat at the lawyers' table.

Dr Desmond Curran, the final witness for the Crown, read from a prepared statement. In prison, he said, Christie had been 'noticeably egocentric and conceited'. He kept a photograph of himself in his cell, cheerfully boasted about the case and admitted in conversation to 'doing some of them in'. His intelligence was above average. He was polite and well behaved. 'He has never said or done anything to suggest he was not in his right mind.'

'I would regard Christie as a highly abnormal character rather than a victim of disease,' said Curran. 'His loss of memory is too patchy to be genuine. He is like other criminals and murderers: he has a remarkable capacity for dismissing the unpleasant from his mind.' He thought Christie had a motive for murder: he 'wanted to have unconscious people to have intercourse with, possibly because he did not want them to know if he was impotent'. He had killed Ethel to clear the way to satisfying this desire.

Christie slipped a note to his legal team in the well below the dock. 'I have run out of fags,' it read. 'Can you get me any?'

After Curran's evidence, the judge adjourned the trial. The court would reconvene the next day to hear the closing speeches for the Crown and the defence, then the judge's summing-up.

As Christie was taken down to the cells, he apologised to the guard at whom he had snapped during the lunch recess. 'I'm very sorry, sir,' he said. 'I just had an outburst of temper.'

Duncan Webb of the *People* felt only disgust at Christie's testimony: 'As an act for an audience it was pitiful,' he wrote.

'It was distressing. It was nauseating. For in all his answers in the witness box Christie consistently overplayed his parts. He would have us accept everything that was to his benefit, and reject that which discredited him. Glibly, he remembered those facts which must indicate insanity, and readily failed to recall the facts that clearly indicated his guilt.' Christie, said Webb, had given 'a sickening exhibition of artifice and cunning stupidity'.

But Cecil Beaton left the courthouse persuaded that, although Christie had shown 'devilish cleverness' in concealing the murders, he was unquestionably crazy. Harry, too, came out of the court still convinced that Christie was mad.

The playwright Terence Rattigan was so disturbed by what he had heard and seen that he decided not to return for the verdict the next day. He would instead watch the cricket at Lord's, where England were due to play Australia. Joan Elton, the receptionist who had queued for the first day of Christie's trial, also planned to watch the Test match. She set up her camping stool outside the cricket ground in St John's Wood that night.

***

In his closing speech on Thursday 25 June, Curtis-Bennett described the 'appalling strain' of conducting this case. He had found it 'long and exhausting', he said, and he hoped that the jurors would forgive him if he had occasionally used the 'language of exaggeration'. But Christie had presented a picture, he said, of utter madness. 'Let us study it quite quietly,' he suggested. 'There is nothing to be gained by being vehement.'

He ran through the evidence, pointing to all the instances of his client's recklessness: he had let out his flat to an Irish couple while bodies were rotting in its walls and floor; he had given his correct name and address at a hostel after leaving the crime scene; he had killed the only person he loved. He encouraged the jury to imagine Christie's feelings after Ethel's death: 'Here is a man whose wife has died at his hands, who makes no friends, and is living in a house where there are coloured creatures.' Curtis-Bennett seemed desperate, and blatantly racist, in this attempt to depict Christie as a grieving widower sent mad by having to share his home with black people.

What sane man could strangle women, Curtis-Bennett asked the jury, in order to have sex with their dead bodies and reap their pubic hair? He thumped the table: 'This man is crazy, isn't he?' He urged the jurors to make their own assessment of Christie. 'You saw him; did you not think he exhibited every sign a layman can see of being mad; the long time before he could answer questions, the pauses, that deadly quiet, almost silent voice?' Christie, he said, should be an object of pity rather than horror. He should be locked up for the rest of his life.

Heald then rose to give the closing speech for the Crown. At this point, said Duncan Webb of the *People*, Christie's 'mask of insanity' slipped: 'he leant forward in his chair in the dock, his eyes bright, with sudden comprehension'.

The Attorney-General commiserated with the jury on the ordeal of the past four days. 'You must really feel like travellers who have been to some strange country,' he said, 'and almost wonder whether the whole thing was not a dream.' They did not have to establish a motive for Ethel's killing in order to convict Christie, he assured them; only to believe that he had known that what he was doing was wrong. Sexual perversion, he said, was not in itself evidence of insanity.

Heald instructed the jurors to disregard the Evans case, except insofar as the murder of Beryl had a bearing on the issue of madness. As a member of the government, he said, it had been especially important for him to ensure that 'nothing avoidable should be said in court that might cast an unjustified reflection on the administration of justice'. Geraldine's murder was not at issue, he reminded the jury: 'no suggestion has been made and there is not the slightest warrant for any suggestion, and no one ought to think for a moment there is any question that Christie killed that child'.

After lunch, Mr Justice Finnemore delivered his summing-up, in which – for more than two hours – he even-handedly recapped the facts of the case. As he spoke, the temperature climbed to the mid-seventies; some in the courtroom found their eyelids drooping and their heads nodding. Derek Curtis-Bennett, having celebrated his closing speech over lunch, was heard snoring.

Christie was attentive, though. He cupped his chin in his hands as he stared at the judge. At one point he passed a note to his legal team. 'I trust you did get a few cigs for me,' it read, 'as I am completely out of stock.' He sent down another note: 'I am not afraid.'

As Finnemore wound up, at four o'clock, he told the jury that they must decide whether it was not just possible but probable that Christie had known, at the moment he killed his wife, that he was doing wrong. This was the legal test for insanity. As for the Evans case, 'I am going to ask you to put it entirely out of your minds.'

The jury retired to deliberate and the rest of the court cleared. Seasoned reporters guessed that it might be midnight before the verdict.

In the cells below the courtroom, Christie was cheerful and chatty. He asked the guards for news of the Test match at Lord's. Australia were 150 for 2, he was told, and Lindsay Hassett was batting well for the Visitors. 'Hassett is going to make a century,' said Christie. 'I wish I was at Lord's watching.'

After less than an hour and a half the signal came that the jury was ready. Christie was led up to the dock, and the spectators hurried back to their seats. The jury filed in, and sat down with set faces. Christie smiled apprehensively at Curtis-Bennett. Mr Justice Finnemore asked the jurors for their verdict.

The foreman rose. 'Guilty of murder,' he said, hoarsely. Christie's smile fell away. His knobbly knuckles whitened, the *Mirror*'s crime correspondent noticed, as he gripped the edge of the dock.

Finnemore waited for his clerk to place the square of black cloth on his wig, and then told Reg Christie that he would be taken to a place of execution where he would be hanged by the neck until he was dead. Christie looked away. 'May the Lord have mercy on your soul,' said Finnemore. 'Amen,' added a chaplain. Christie turned quickly. He raised his hands to his face as he was led to the stairs.

Most of the journalists scrambled for phones or raced back to their offices to report the outcome of the trial, but Harry had until Saturday night to file his copy. He was annoyed that both the judge and the Attorney-General had managed to close down questions about the Evans case, and he was disappointed in the verdict. Now that Christie had been sentenced to death, there was hardly any time left to discover the truth.

Christie took a small parcel of clothes and belongings with him in the van to Pentonville, the north London prison at which executions were performed. As he was driven away from the Old Bailey, he was unsettled to hear the crowd booing and shouting abuse. 'How disgusting people are,' he remarked to a guard.

***

Fryn thought that both barristers had performed well, and that the judge's summing-up had been admirably fair. The jurors, she wrote, had decided that Christie was 'a horrid little man, not only a peculiarly lustful and filthy murderer but a deliberate one who, whatever he said, could not be believed'.

Her friend Bob Sherwood was also impressed by how the trial had been conducted. 'It was all superbly calm and business-like,' he wrote in the *Evening Standard*. The lawyers for both sides 'seemed more interested in presenting the evidence than in making headlines for themselves'. They did not raise their voices or lose their tempers, he observed. 'I could not help imagining what a trial as sensational and as revolting as this one would be like in New York, Chicago or Los Angeles. The lawyers would be striding up and down, often soaring to the heights of forensic extravagance.' As an American, he said, he 'marvelled at the dignity and majesty, the clarity and equity of British justice'.

The crime novelist Anthony Berkeley Cox stopped off after the trial at a café near the courthouse. As the waitress pushed his cup of tea across the counter, he glanced to his side – 'and there was Christie at my elbow, getting a cup of tea himself. I looked round the room. There was Christie, too, sitting at that table just over there. And at that one, close by. And there was Christie, just going out of the wing-doors. I counted them. There were five Christies there, all looking as meek, and as worried, and as insignificant as Christie himself.' He could not shake his sense of Christie's ordinariness, his ubiquity. Where Bob Sherwood had seen the court's restraint as a mark of civilisation, Cox saw that the same British restraint, in a man like Christie, could be a cover for depravity. In the trial, as in Christie's demeanour, appalling cruelty and violence had been dampened down, underplayed, contained by a surface order.

Christie was a grotesque cartoon of the old-fashioned Englishman. Like many of his class and generation, he had seemed to adhere to a rigid moral code: he was emotionally reserved, courteous, disapproving of immigrants, prostitutes, pubs and strong liquor, devoted to his pets and his garden, deferential to his social betters, admiring of the police and the army. Because he appeared in many ways so conventional, some commentators were at pains to define his difference. A doctor who attended the Old Bailey trial on behalf of the *Daily Herald* described him as a 'necrophiliac sado-masochist, a hair-fetishist and a psychopath'.

A 'psychopath', a term popularised by the psychiatrist Hervey Cleckley in 1941, was an individual who appeared normal but was incapable of feeling love, remorse or shame. To label Christie in this way was to identify him as intrinsically alien, and to distance him from the society that had helped forge him, in the same way that calling him a 'monster' or a 'creature' discounted him as an exception.

But the *Herald*'s anonymous doctor seemed to acknowledge that Christie had acted on familiar fantasies. In his article, he reassured readers that it was normal for a man to tell a woman: 'I want to squeeze you to death.' It was wrong, he said, only if he actually strangled her.

Rosalind Wilkinson, the young social researcher who was carrying out a survey of London prostitutes, encountered similar language when she went into a pub alone one evening and was offered a drink by a stranger. 'Within less than five minutes of my accepting,' she said, 'he was saying that he wished to take me outside and "kiss me to death".' She was not immediately troubled by his words. 'I can remember accepting as a matter of course that a man should say such things in such a situation,' she wrote. 'To me at the time there was nothing strange about it.'

Though she declined his invitation, she and the man got talking. He was a divorced merchant seaman, she learnt, who was about to catch a train to join his ship. He proudly showed her the photographs and discharge reports in his wallet. She was touched by the 'almost joyous gratitude' with which he responded to her, a woman who was prepared to laugh and talk with him for fifteen minutes in a dingy pub. It was only later that she felt unnerved by the words he had used when they met. Perhaps his longing to kiss her 'to death' sprang from despair. But the language of desire, the wishes that a man might express to a woman as a matter of course, seemed to have become inflected with violence.

At Pentonville prison, Christie was shown to the cell in which he would stay: a small room, painted green and cream, furnished with a bed, three chairs, a table and a shelf stacked with books and games. Six guards were assigned to watch him round the clock, two for each eight-hour shift. Christie told one of the guards that he was appalled by the suggestion that he had murdered a child. He killed for only 'one reason', he said, implying that his motive was lust. While having a bath at the prison, according to the guard's report, Christie took hold of his penis and boasted: 'You can see why the women came down to Rillington Place.'

11

Gassings

The papers announced at the end of the week that the prime minister was unwell due to overwork, and would be resting for the next month at Chartwell, his country retreat. Churchill had in fact suffered a serious stroke on Tuesday 23 June, the second day of Christie's trial, and was paralysed down his left side. He stayed in post as prime minister only because Sir Anthony Eden, the Foreign Secretary and his likely successor, was also very ill, with complications from an abdominal operation he had undergone in April. The gravity of both men's conditions was concealed from the public. According to a *Pictorial* columnist, Churchill remarked from his sick bed: 'At least I have had the honour of removing that creature Christie from the front pages.'

Christie wasn't kept off the front pages for long. The press had a field day with the Rillington Place story over the weekend, running all the material that they had been holding until after the trial. On Saturday 27 June, under the headline 'Finish Your Confession, Mr Christie', the *Mirror* published a letter to Christie from Tim Evans's mother. 'You were too clever for my poor Tim,' wrote Agnes Probert; 'you killed his wife and baby and got him hung.'

'I know my boy is no murderer, and so do you,' said Agnes. 'But why? Why did you do it?' She asked if he had killed Geraldine because she was 'crying for her Mummy'. She implored him to clear her son's name – now that he had been condemned to death, she said, he had nothing to lose.

Agnes sent her letter to Pentonville prison but it was not shown to Christie, on the grounds that the Home Office thought it wrong to subject him to 'this kind of pressure'. Perhaps the government did not want to encourage Christie to say anything further about the Evans case. Agnes went to the House of Commons to ask her MP, George Rogers, to lobby for an inquiry into her son's conviction.

***

The *Pictorial* still couldn't run any of the material that Christie had written while on remand in Brixton, in case he appealed the verdict, so Harry instead filed a feature about his own encounters with the condemned man. He described how Christie had asked him in 1949 who he thought had killed Beryl and Geraldine Evans. 'He was anxious to try out his story on me,' he wrote. 'He was anxious to know whether I suspected him.' Harry made clear that he now thought Christie guilty of those crimes.

Harry had met many killers, he told his readers – Neville Heath, who strangled and mutilated two women; John Haigh, the acid-bath murderer; Christopher Craig, 'the young yellow thug' who shot down a policeman – but none was as wicked as Christie. 'Heath murdered for passion,' he wrote, 'Haigh for gain, Craig because he hated policemen', but Christie 'showed no other motive than the urge to experience what he thinks is the sheer cold joy of killing'. The forthcoming confession in the *Pictorial*, promised Harry, 'will amaze and shock you'.

That Sunday's *Pictorial* also published an interview with Mary Ballingall, a twenty-year-old Irishwoman who had paid several visits to Christie in Rillington Place in January. 'He usually behaved like a gentleman,' Mary told Harry's colleague Tom Tullett. 'He spoke well and seemed to be very generous. He always seemed kind and gentle and rather sad. I felt sorry for him.' Mary had given her story to the police several weeks earlier.

In the foggy morning of Friday 23 January 1953, Mary was on the platform at Ladbroke Grove Tube station, with her three-week-old daughter, when Reg Christie stepped forward and offered to light her cigarette. She accepted, they got chatting, and he accompanied her to the National Assistance Board office in Hammersmith, where she picked up just over £1 in welfare payments. 'That's not enough to keep you and the baby,' said Christie, handing her another £1 and inviting her to visit him that afternoon.

When Mary arrived at 10 Rillington Place at 2 p.m., Christie showed her into the kitchen, where a strong fire was burning. He gave Mary a glass of port, then a glass of Tizer pop, while he had a ruby wine. As they drank, he told her that his wife had died. He then offered her gifts: a pair of screw-on earrings, with white and blue stones, and a small bottle of whisky. He invited her to come again on Sunday, reminding her not to tell anyone his name or address. By now, Christie had already hidden the bodies of Kathleen Maloney and Rita Nelson in the alcove, and Ethel's body under the floor in the front room.

Mary didn't turn up on Sunday, but Christie sought her out at the National Assistance offices the following Friday, and on Sunday 1 February, she returned to Rillington Place, leaving her boyfriend to look after their baby. Christie led her to the kitchen, lighting the way through the dark hall with a torch, and asked her to sit on his knee. She refused. He then took her, by torchlight, to the other parts of his flat. In the front room he showed her his war medals and pictures of himself in police uniform. He warned her not to walk in front of the window, as she might be seen by his neighbours.

They then went to the bedroom at the back, which was furnished only with a trunk and a mattress. Christie opened the trunk and shone his torch inside. As Mary leant over to see in, he grabbed her, pulled her on to the mattress and put a hand up her skirt. She threatened to scream, at which he stopped, and invited her to choose some clothes from the trunk. She took a flared green coat, a pair of blue suede boots, two old-fashioned petticoats, a long white scarf, two pairs of cotton stockings, two pairs of leather gloves, one of them lined with fur and one with fleece. They returned to the kitchen, where Mary accepted another glass of Tizer and a ruby wine.

Mary visited again at 7 p.m. on Thursday. If she was troubled by Christie's attempted assault, she was also tempted by the treats he provided. In the kitchen, which was hot as a furnace, she sat in the deckchair strung with rope and drank a cup of tea while Christie went next door to No 9 to borrow some money to give her. He locked the kitchen door after him, saying that he didn't want the black people upstairs to know she was there.

While Mary waited, she noticed a smell of gas in the room. She put on her coat, at which Christie's dog, Judy, moved in front of the door, growling. Christie, on his return, explained that he had trained the dog to stop anyone from leaving without his permission. He gave Mary a £1 note, then locked the door from the inside. 'Nobody will miss you,' he said. She asked him what he meant. He said that she had given him nothing in return for all the things he had given her, and he wanted her to stay the night. Nobody would miss her, he repeated. Mary said that she had told a friend his name and address. Christie seemed angry to hear this, but agreed to let her go. She did not visit him again.

In the notes that Christie wrote for Harry in Brixton, he alluded to these encounters with Mary Ballingall. Each time she had called round, he said, he had a rope in his pocket, ready to strangle her. 'She was very lucky,' he observed. 'I was just waiting for the right moment.'

The *News of the World* ran a piece about two of Christie's former girlfriends. In the late 1920s, while separated from Ethel, he had shared a flat in Battersea with a woman called Maud Cole, who in 1929 told him to move out as he was not paying his way. He whacked her round the head with her son's cricket bat, then stuck his fingers in her mouth to stifle her screams. She pulled away and fled to another apartment. 'Don't let him get to me,' she begged her neighbour. 'He's trying to murder me.' Christie was sentenced to six months in prison for the assault.

In 1943 Christie was forced to leave the police force because his bosses had learnt that he was 'immorally consorting' with Gladys Jones, an auxiliary policewoman at the Harrow Road station. Two years later, Gladys's husband returned from the Mediterranean, where he had been serving with the RAF, and exchanged blows with Christie in Gladys's room in Ladbroke Grove. Christie was summoned to court as co-respondent in the Joneses' divorce case in 1947. 'Liar!' he shouted at Mr Jones when he accused him of sleeping with his wife. 'He's telling lies!' Christie was ordered to pay costs in the case.

***

Other women's accounts of their experiences with Christie did not reach the pages of the press. Their stories, like Mary Ballingall, depicted his overtures as direct and persistent, nothing like the bewildered, accidental entanglements he had described in the Old Bailey.

When Christie was on the run in March 1953, a woman wrote to the police, under the name Helen Sunderland, to report a frightening encounter with him. She gave no date for the incident, but it seemed to have taken place after he murdered Ethel.

For many weeks, Helen said, she had seen Christie pacing up and down Piccadilly, staring at her and the other streetwalkers. Most of the women who solicited in the area knew him by sight, and agreed that they didn't like the look of him.

One night Helen was standing on the corner of Half Moon Street and Piccadilly when Christie suddenly appeared and offered her a cigarette. He was being so nice that she accepted a lift home to Kilburn in a taxi, and in the cab he invited her to stop off at his flat for a cup of tea. He was feeling lonely, he said, and he had a dozen pairs of nylon stockings that she could have. Before she could answer, he had directed the driver towards Lancaster Gate. She got out with him somewhere in Notting Hill, and they walked until they reached 'a dirty little House next to a brick wall'.

Inside his flat, Helen said, Christie kept putting his cold, damp hands against her face and neck, and then told her to undress. She refused, saying she had to get home to her baby. He told her it was impossible for her to leave, and he had something to show her that might give her a shock.

Christie left her in the front room for a few minutes, locking the door as he went, and then returned with a heavy-looking blanket over his arm. He secured the door behind him. What was he going to do? she asked. He told her to wait and see. She grabbed the blanket and it fell to reveal a length of cord. He stared hard at her and ordered her to take off all her clothes because he was ready to show her what he had brought her to see. She asked why he could not show her when she was dressed. Because when he showed her, he said, she would be sure to scream and run away. At this, she became really scared. She darted to the door, banged at it, kicked it. Christie took the rope off his arm and held one end in each hand.

Helen lurched forward and gave Christie a powerful kick in the groin. His glasses and trilby fell off as he dropped to the ground. She dashed for the front window, opened it and scrambled out, then ran and ran until she reached Bayswater Road. A man came to her aid, and offered to return to Rillington Place with her to confront her attacker. She said she was too scared. She just wanted to go home.

When she saw Christie's photo in the paper at the end of March 1953, she told the police, she had recognised him at once.

The details in the letter suggested that it was genuine, but the police were unable to trace 'Helen Sunderland'. The letter-writer, perhaps afraid of being charged with soliciting, had disguised her identity and falsified her address.

In the run-up to the trial Sir Lionel Heald, the Attorney-General, had received a telephone call from a man who said that Christie had been responsible for an attack on his wife, Judy, more than a decade earlier.

One day in 1940, Judy Bacon, a 24-year-old actress who worked for the Auxiliary Territorial Service, had just parked her car in Whitehall when a policeman knocked on her window. It was pouring with rain. 'Come and have a coffee in the blockhouse,' he said. 'There are other War Office staff there.' Not wanting to seem snooty, she agreed, locked her car and ran the hundred yards to the blockhouse through the downpour.

Judy entered a small doorway surrounded by sandbags, and walked along a narrow passage. Hearing a noise behind her, she turned to see the policeman staring at her from the entrance.

'I came in here for a coffee,' she warned him, 'and nothing else. If you put a finger on me, I'll give such a scream I'll bring the whole War Office in here.'

He came forward and dived at her, knocking her against the back of the passageway, grabbed her throat with one hand and pinched her nose with the other so that she could barely breathe. She kicked him in the groin with all her strength, and as he staggered back she rushed for the entrance, ran to her car and drove away.

Once she was home, Judy rang her father and asked him what to do. He was sympathetic, but discouraged her from reporting the assault. 'Who would believe the word of an ATS girl,' he said, 'against that of a policeman?'

After the war Judy married an actor – Charles Cameron-Wilson – and had three sons. In March 1953, when she saw Christie's photo in a newspaper, she immediately showed her husband, telling him that this was the man who had assaulted her in the blockhouse. 'Nonsense,' said Charles, but on reading the story he realised that Christie had been working as a war reserve police officer in 1940. He rang 999 and was put in touch with Heald, who was leading the prosecution case.

When the Attorney-General learnt that the Cameron-Wilsons had three little boys, he advised against taking Judy's report any further. 'I don't want to call your wife,' he said to Charles. 'It is the most appalling case and we have enough evidence to hang Christie a hundred times.' Heald may have been trying to protect a respectable family from scandal. But it meant that Judy's story, for a second time, went unheard.

After the trial another woman wrote to the Metropolitan Police to say that she had encountered Christie just before the war. Faith Wallis had been in charge of recruitment for Air Raid Precautions in Paddington when Christie applied for a job as a warden in the summer of 1939. He explained to her that he had not sought a post in his own area because he didn't want his neighbours to know that the war was coming. This was a very odd claim – perhaps the truth was that he wanted to avoid the district in which he was known. Faith did not take to him, she said: 'He was so plausible and smarmy. He tried to ooze charm and made me feel so sick that I decided that he was not the type of man who should be put on duty in a post with women.' She turned him down, suggesting that he apply to the police instead.

Faith came across Christie again during the Blitz, when she was chief warden at the Westbourne Grove air-raid shelter and he was serving as a policeman for the Harrow Road force. He used to drop in at her shelter, and she occasionally saw him in the streets when she was sweeping up broken glass or helping the walking wounded to safety. She and another ARP officer discussed why Christie strayed off his beat and 'floated around' so much. They agreed that he might have been more shaken up by the bombings than he cared to admit – 'as we all were from time to time', said Faith.

Christie sometimes came to Faith's shelter looking for one of its regulars, a glamorous Irish woman with olive skin, tawny hair and hazel eyes who was known to the staff as 'Miss Spain'. She worked at the Windmill Theatre in Soho, which evaded the obscenity laws by having its nude dancing girls pose as motionless 'living statues', and which famously kept its doors open throughout the war. Faith had the impression that Miss Spain had lost touch with her family in Ireland.

In December 1940 Faith bumped into Miss Spain near her home in Paddington. The young woman looked shocked and upset, said Faith. She told Faith that she had just been out for something to eat with Christie and he had become furious when she refused to go into an empty house with him afterwards. Until now he had been kind to her, she said, and she had been intrigued by him, but his behaviour that evening had scared her stiff. Faith advised her to avoid him: he didn't seem a 'nice type', she said.

Later that year Faith noticed that Miss Spain was no longer visiting the shelter. She asked after her in a pub in Paddington, but no one seemed to know where she had gone. When Christie came into the shelter again in February 1941, quite affable and 'full of smooze', Faith asked him if he knew where Miss Spain was. 'He just pounced on me,' she said, 'what did I mean, what was I suggesting, he wasn't that kind of a man, I should be careful, if his wife heard me say things like that she would tear me to pieces etc.' She replied that she couldn't care less what he got up to; she had only asked after Miss Spain because she was hoping that she would sing 'Lily of Laguna' at the Valentine's Day old people's party.

Christie glared at her, pushed his hand repeatedly over the top of his head and took a seat, shaking. Faith, seeing that he was in a rage, left him to cool down. After drinking a cup of tea, he got up to go, telling her: 'Please don't discuss this woman with me again, she was nothing to me, my wife is the only woman in my life.'

'Say you!' retorted Faith, at which Christie, still glaring, went up the steps to the street.

In 1953, when Faith Wallis learnt that Reg Christie had murdered several women, she wondered again whether he had something to do with Miss Spain's disappearance.

Perhaps Faith was also right to wonder whether Christie had been unbalanced by the bombing of London. He had been struck dumb with shock in 1918 after a mustard-gas attack, and he began to murder women in the early 1940s after two further shocks – he was knocked down by a bomb during the Blitz, and then overcome by gas from a blown-up main. By gassing and strangling women, he seemed to restage his own collapse on the Western Front: he watched as his victims choked and fell silent.

Christie's injury in the First World War may have had other consequences. Some victims of mustard gas were plagued, like him, by headaches, insomnia, irritability, gastric disorders.

Some suffered bouts of amnesia, or passed into dissociated mental states.

***

The most revealing of the interviews to run after Christie's trial was with Joan Howard, a Yorkshire woman who had lived at 10 Rillington Place for three months in 1951, when she was twenty-three. Her piece appeared on 28 June in the *Sunday Dispatch*, the paper that had almost stolen Harry's scoop.

Joan met Charles Brown, the landlord of No 10, in a pub in Tottenham Court Road in April 1951, and arranged to rent the first-floor back room at £2 a week. When she moved in, two of the other rooms on the upper floors were occupied by black men living with white women, and one by a single black man. Joan's boyfriend, a corporal in the RAF, came to stay with her when he was on leave.

One afternoon Ethel Christie approached Joan in the back yard and told her that a woman and a baby had been murdered in the house a year and a half ago. She pointed out the wash-house in which Beryl and Geraldine's bodies had been found. Joan was shocked: she had known nothing about the murders. Ethel invited her into the kitchen, where she pulled a big album and a bundle of photographs from a cupboard behind the door. She showed Joan pictures of Beryl and Geraldine, which Reg had taken, and a newspaper cutting about the trial at the Old Bailey. Reg walked in while they were looking at the photos and angrily told Ethel to put them away: he had heard and seen enough about the case, he said.

Ethel invited Joan into her flat again three days later. This time she told the younger woman that her husband was mean and cruel to her, and she didn't know why she stayed with him. She added that Reg had been behaving strangely ever since the murders of Beryl and Geraldine, and she felt certain that he had 'done it'. Joan didn't take this accusation seriously, assuming that Ethel was lashing out at Reg in spite.

Ethel called Joan down from her room later that day to say that her husband wanted to take her picture. Reg photographed Joan in the garden with his cat and dog. He promised that he would give her copies of the photos.

From her bedroom window, Joan used to see Reg in the garden, playing with his pets or tending to his plants. Ethel invited her to hang her washing on their clothesline, but warned her not to go into the area beyond the paved yard.

Over the next few weeks Ethel and Joan regularly met for a cup of tea in the ground-floor kitchen when Reg was at work. Ethel complained to Joan about her marriage, saying that Reg was 'not sexy' and they had not been physically intimate at all since the Evans murders. She told Joan how sad she was not to have had a baby. She seemed anxious and depressed, Joan said, often taking pills from an array on the counter, but she did not repeat her suspicions about the Evans killings.

In the hallway of No 10 one day, Joan saw a young woman who looked so pale and faint that she offered her a cup of tea in her room. The woman, who would not give Joan her name, told her that she had just had an 'illegal operation' in the flat below. Joan suspected that the other women she had seen calling at the Christies' place had come for the same reason.

Joan often smelt gas in the hall when she came home late at night, and would turn off the opened tap at the foot of the stairs. Reg occasionally came out of his bedroom to shine a torch on her as she climbed the steps to her room. She sometimes heard arguments from the Christies' bedroom, directly beneath hers at the back of the house, shouts and screams that would last into the early hours. She did not mention this to Ethel or anyone else, thinking it none of her business.

One afternoon Ethel was having tea with Joan in the kitchen when Reg came in. He said to his wife: 'Tell her what we have discussed.' Ethel asked Joan if she would come to their bedroom to be photographed in the nude. 'I don't do that sort of thing,' replied Joan. Reg laughed.

After this, the Christies turned on Joan. Reg accosted her in the hall one day as she came down the stairs, and accused her of being a prostitute. Joan retorted that she had taken no one upstairs but her boyfriend. Perhaps Reg suspected her of having sex with the black men in the house. 'The only place for women like you,' he said, 'is dead. If I had my way I would do it.' Ethel then joined them, and repeated Reg's accusation that Joan was a prostitute. Joan threatened to smack her in the face, at which Ethel ran out of the house and took refuge next door with Rosie Swan, while Reg headed off to call a policeman.

By the time Reg came back with an officer, his landlord, Charles Brown, had turned up at the house. Brown encouraged Joan to file a complaint with a solicitor about the Christies' insults to her, for which he offered to pay the 10 shilling fee. Brown doubtless wanted rid of the racist old couple on the ground floor, so that he could let out their rooms to more congenial tenants at a higher rate.

When Joan returned to No 10 after filing her complaint, Reg came out of his living room. 'Remember what I said,' he told her. 'I'll still do you in.'

Joan left Rillington Place in the middle of July 1951. According to the *Dispatch*, she even now remembered Reg Christie's staring eyes: 'I seemed to feel them.'

Joan had told her story to the police in April 1953, but she had not been called to repeat it in court, despite her information about the relationship between Reg and Ethel Christie. Perhaps the Attorney-General had not wanted to publicise her references to the Evans murders.

***

The Australian newspaper *Truth* decried the 'howling orgy' of articles about the Christie case in the British press. 'The most unpleasant feature,' it said, 'was the digging up of the girls who had been visitors to Christie's house and who were now willing to tell their stories.'

But the *News Chronicle*, a liberal paper, believed that such stories had helped to tear apart the nation's 'veil of apathy', giving 'a brief but vivid glimpse of a strange and sordid half-life that most of us never see'. Christie's trial, it said, had revealed 'a shabby underworld of bleak lodgings and even bleaker homes through which shadowy figures flit without permanence or purpose'.

'This is the life that the Welfare State with all its aspirations and all its humanity has never reached,' said the *Chronicle*. 'There are still too many of our fellow citizens to whom we have not brought the sun and air.'

The *Daily Worker*, the British Communist Party paper, also focused on the social dimension of Christie's crimes. 'When we read the account of the Christie case,' it observed, 'we smell, not only the odour of decaying flesh, but the stench of corruption of a whole form of society. We see, not only a man accused of murder, but we note the status and mode of life of those who are said to be his victims. How could such crimes have remained for so long undiscovered had they not been human debris ruthlessly ground between the upper and nether millstones of capitalist society?' Nearly all of Christie's victims were poor and desperate, as the *Daily Worker* pointed out. They were also all women, a class particularly vulnerable to the social and economic power that men like Christie could exert, and to the dehumanising fantasies they might entertain.

On Sunday 28 June, three days after sentencing Reg Christie to death, Mr Justice Finnemore delivered a lay sermon in a Baptist chapel in Birmingham. He implored his congregation to examine their own consciences when they read about crimes like this one. 'Have you ever stopped to ask yourself,' he asked the churchgoers: 'Am I partly responsible? Have I any part of that guilt to bear myself?'

***

As the last constable cycled away from 10 Rillington Place that Sunday, ending a ninety-nine-day police vigil, the residents of the street cheered and shouted their goodbyes. Charles Brown turned up to reclaim his house, in the company of his wife, a cousin, a nephew and a few friends. One of these was Beresford Brown, who was now living with his wife Louise and their baby in Charles Brown's home in Silchester Terrace, a few minutes' walk away.

Charles Brown said that No 10 was up for sale at £1,500. 'Do you want to buy it?' he asked a *Daily Herald* reporter. Brown's cousin chipped in: 'We have had some offers already from people who want to make an exhibition of the house. Anyone could make millions from it, as a showpiece. The lease still has twelve years to run.' Christie's address had become a byword for depravity, as notorious a crime scene as any in British history.

Brown applied to the police for £10 to repair the damage to his property, and £50 in compensation for lost rental. He fitted a new lock to the front door, and hammered a nail into the frame of the bay window to stop intruders from pushing it open.

Someone stole the black door knocker from 10 Rillington Place later that week, and on Friday the police were called to the house to see off a group of women who were trying to break in through the window that Brown had nailed shut. Perhaps their raid on Christie's house was an act of defiance. Like Bluebeard's wife, the trespassers wanted to enter the killer's lair. They wanted to see for themselves the scene of domestic horror in which Ethel Christie had been trapped, and into which those young women had stumbled. Christie's acts were as irresolvable as a dream or a fairy tale, difficult either to assimilate or to dispel.

***

As Cecil Beaton was weeding the flower beds outside his house in Wiltshire, his charlady asked him if it was true that he had attended the trial of 'that terrible man' in London. He confirmed that he had.

'What made you do such a thing?'

Beaton felt briefly embarrassed. 'It was very dramatic and interesting,' he offered, 'and I have never been to a trial at the Old Bailey before.' (To a journalist who had phoned to ask him the same question, he had replied, lamely: 'I'm interested in human nature.')

'Well,' said the charlady, 'aren't you haunted by the man?'

'Yes,' said Beaton. 'I think I've thought a lot about him during the last few nights.'

'Well, he's soon got it coming to him,' she said as she headed back to the house, 'what he deserves.'

12

Into the fall

On Saturday 27 June, Ambrose Appelbe and his clerk, Roy Arthur, visited Christie in Pentonville prison. They advised him not to appeal the jury's verdict but instead to make a plea for mercy. If a medical panel were to deem him insane, they told him, the Queen might yet commute his death sentence. Christie accepted their advice. Appelbe applied for a medical review, and the Home Office agreed to appoint three doctors to assess Christie's mental state by 15 July, the date scheduled for the execution.

On Wednesday, the *News Chronicle* reported that Christie had told a prison official that he had killed Geraldine Evans, though the paper warned its readers that: 'Christie has been proved, many times, to be unreliable.' When Roy Arthur asked Christie about the article, he denied making any such statement.

Harry was frustrated that he could not visit Christie in Pentonville – he felt sure that he could persuade him to confess to the baby's murder. Francis Ross, who had sold Christie's photographs to Harry, was also refused access to the jail. Ross wrote to his MP, perhaps at Harry's suggestion, to complain: 'If he has anything to say about the Evans Case, he will say it to me, his friend, not to officials,' Ross argued. 'Why, then deny me a last visit to him? Perhaps they don't want the truth!'

Since Christie was not appealing the verdict, the *Pictorial* was finally free to launch its exclusive. Harry's scoop was advertised in rival publications and on posters all over the country. 'My Urge to Kill Ten Women', ran the headline of the first instalment on Sunday 5 July. 'In writing this story of my life,' it began, 'I am going to try to explain why I have flagrantly broken one of God's foremost laws, and why I have always succumbed to a black, sinister force which has never allowed me to be at peace. "Thou Shalt Not Kill" is the Commandment that has haunted me all my life. I have broken this Commandment many times, so many times that I cannot be sure of the number of women who have died by my hands.' Harry had heavily adapted the statement that Christie had composed in Brixton: this preoccupation with the Sixth Commandment did not appear in his notes.

Harry also imagined the voyeuristic delight that Christie had felt when he murdered Ruth Fuerst: 'She looked more beautiful in death than life,' wrote Harry. 'I remember as I gazed on the still form of my first victim experiencing a strange, peaceful thrill.' A large photograph of Ruth accompanied the story.

On the front page, the paper published a picture of Ethel Christie, posing in her bathing costume in the garden of 10 Rillington Place. Inside, under the heading 'Christie – the Photographer', it ran three more pictures that Christie had given to Francis Ross: Ethel lying on a beach, Ethel standing in a park, Ethel smiling beneath a plane on a day trip to London Airport.

***

The calls to reopen the Evans case grew so strong that on 6 July the Home Secretary, David Maxwell Fyfe, announced to the House of Commons that he had appointed J. Scott Henderson QC to conduct an immediate private inquiry into whether a miscarriage of justice had taken place. George Rogers, the MP for Kensington North, asked why the inquiry could not be held in public, but Maxwell Fyfe insisted that a private investigation was the best way to ensure that all the evidence was heard.

Another Labour politician asked whether the *Pictorial* had funded Christie's defence, and how it had obtained the 'confession' published on Sunday. He was not given an answer, though the government had received a confidential memo on the subject from Brixton prison: 'It is virtually certain that a contract for this article was passed out through Cliftons,' said the governor. 'It is impossible for us to do anything about it or even to voice our suspicions.'

Scott Henderson called about twenty witnesses to his inquiry, held between 8 and 12 July in a gloomy jury room in the Law Courts on the Strand. He interviewed the police, doctors and lawyers who had been involved in the two trials, members of Tim Evans's family and the builders who had been working at 10 Rillington Place when Beryl and Geraldine were killed. The *Pictorial* supplied him with the 7,000-word statement that Christie had written for Harry in Brixton.

Scott Henderson went to Pentonville to interview Christie himself. Christie told him that he had been 'very fogged' throughout the investigations. In his confessions, he said, he had described 'not what I could remember so much as what I was picturing, because right away through the whole lot I have been picturing a load of things'.

When asked if he had killed Beryl and Geraldine, Christie said: 'I only wish I could find out. I want to know the truth about it as much as you do.' He explained that he was even now not sure that he had committed any of the murders. 'Thank you,' he said when Scott Henderson finished questioning him. 'Is there anything else I can help you with?'

In his cell at Pentonville, Christie played cards and dominoes with the guards. He retained his smooth, smiling demeanour, they reported, though he told them that he had started to suffer from headaches and was finding it difficult to sleep. He was pleased with the quantity and quality of the prison food, and the plentiful supply of cigarettes. His only requests were that the prison replace a damaged domino in the set in his cell, and serve him tea and milk at bedtime instead of cocoa. Christie received a letter from a man with whom he had served in the First World War, and had not seen since. 'I am in good health and quite happy,' he wrote back, 'and am being looked after very well in these unfortunate circumstances.'

In the second part of the *Pictorial*'s exclusive, on 12 July, Harry described Christie's murder of Muriel Eady. Christie had made little comment on this killing in the notes he had written in Brixton, so Harry again put words in his mouth. 'My second murder was a really clever murder,' he wrote, 'much cleverer than the first one. I planned it all out very carefully.' He had lured Muriel to his home, gassed her with his contraption and then had sex with her. In Harry's words: 'She was too dazed to resist me.' Afterwards he strangled her. 'For the second time in my life,' wrote Harry, 'I looked down upon the still, lifeless form of an attractive woman who had died at my hands. Once again I experienced a quiet, peaceful thrill.' The paper ran a photograph of Muriel.

Harry also recounted Christie's humiliation on the 'Monkey Run', a lane along which Halifax boys and girls met on Sunday nights to 'cuddle and kiss'. As Dr Hobson had testified in the Old Bailey, Reg had picked up a 'mill girl' one Sunday, and she afterwards told his friend that he had been unable to have sex with her. He became known as 'No-Dick Reggie' or 'Can't Get It Up Reggie', the nicknames that Curtis-Bennett had discouraged Hobson from repeating in court. Christie developed a 'burning hatred' of the girl who had subjected him to his friends' laughter and scorn, wrote Harry.

The rage that female laughter could trigger in men was a staple of B-movie melodrama. In the British film *The Woman in Question*, released in 1950, a detective investigating the murder of a prostitute guesses that she was strangled because she mocked a man. 'Suddenly she laughs at him,' imagines the detective. 'The whole thing goes smash.'

In *Empire News* on 12 July, a former inmate of Brixton prison said that Christie had talked to him about women. 'They dress up and paint up and give you the come-on,' Christie apparently told him, 'and you can't help thinking they wouldn't look nearly so cheeky nor so saucy if they were helpless, and dead.'

***

The conclusions, though not the contents, of the private inquiry were published on Monday 13 July, only a week after it had begun. There was no evidence, said Scott Henderson, to support the allegations that Christie had carried out abortions, nor to support his claim to have killed Beryl Evans. Christie's account of her death was not only 'unreliable' but 'untrue': he must have claimed her murder only to bolster his insanity defence. The evidence against Tim Evans, on the other hand, was 'overwhelming'. Scott Henderson concluded that Evans had been correctly convicted for his daughter's murder.

On the same day, a panel of three doctors reported to the Home Office that Christie was sane. He was 'conceited, cool, cunning, alert, bad tempered and vicious', they said. 'Christie's lies are purposive, intended to be gainful, to deceive and lead away from facts and truth.' The Home Secretary ruled that he should hang on Wednesday 15 July, as planned.

Christie sent Harry a request to see his sister Dorothy before he died. Harry passed on the message to Dolly Clarke in

Liverpool, promising that he would keep her visit a secret, and the next night she came to Pentonville prison.

Dolly told Harry afterwards that she had found Reg in good spirits. 'Don't worry about the morning,' he told her. 'They won't hurt me. They'll take my glasses off before they hang me, so I won't see much.' To demonstrate, Christie had removed his horn-rimmed spectacles, and then put them on again. It was a strange gesture. He seemed to be suggesting that the blurring of his vision would blunt his pain, as if he would not feel what he could not see.

Reg Christie made a will in which he left his marriage certificate and his photographs of Ethel to her sister Lily in Sheffield, with an 'apology for any trouble I may have brought about'. He had already given his half-moon reading glasses to his solicitor, Ambrose Appelbe. He bequeathed his remaining possessions to Dolly.

Shortly before 9 a.m. on 15 July, Christie was taken through the door of his cell to the execution chamber, where the hangman, Albert Pierrepoint, was waiting for him. Pierrepoint had hanged scores of men in the previous decade, among them Neville Heath, William Joyce, John Haigh, Timothy Evans, Derek Bentley and more than two hundred Nazi war criminals. He had already gauged Christie's height and build by observing him through a peephole in the cell door.

Pierrepoint tied Christie's wrists to a belt. He reached up to remove his spectacles, meeting his eyes as he did so, and laid the glasses carefully on a scrubbed bone table. Christie blinked, screwed up his eyes, then fixed his gaze on the door. A white hood was placed over his head, a rope around his neck, and he shuffled towards the trapdoor in the floor – 'drifting forwards', said Pierrepoint, 'his legs stumbling. I thought he was going to faint.' Pierrepoint pulled the lever to open the trapdoor, and pushed Christie into the fall.

Dr Francis Camps carried out a post-mortem on Christie's body, which was then buried in the grounds of Pentonville prison, twenty paces from Tim Evans's grave. Within an hour of Christie's death, his wax effigy was on display in the Chamber of Horrors at Madame Tussauds in Baker Street.

The RSPCA shelter at Kensal Green destroyed Christie's cat a week later. They had been deluged with offers to adopt Tommy, but the vets had found him impossible to tame. The cat was 'wild', said the *Mirror*: 'not civilised'.

Because the English courts tried a defendant for only one murder at a time, no one was convicted of the killings of Ruth Fuerst, Muriel Eady, Kathleen Maloney, Rita Nelson or Hectorina Maclennan. They were interred at Gunnersbury cemetery in Acton, near the twice-buried bodies of Beryl and Geraldine Evans.

Rita's mother had no idea what had become of her daughter's remains. 'Could you please let me know if my girl is buried yet,' she wrote to the Metropolitan Police from Belfast. 'What kind of turn out was there. And where is she Buried. I am here I know nothing and there is nobody to tell me anything. I had no way of getting over to see the last of her.'

***

On 19 July, four days after Christie's death, the *Sunday People* ran an interview with his friend Francis Ross. During the war, Ross said, he had seen Christie, in police uniform, chase off two Canadian soldiers who seemed to be attacking a woman in the Edgware Road. She turned on him, shouted: 'Mind your own business!' and then spat in his face. Christie, said Ross, was left trembling with rage.

In the early days of his marriage, Christie had told Ross, he had been uncertain about whether he was performing adequately in the bedroom: he became obsessed with the thought that he was not a 'real man'. One afternoon, he had come home early from work and overheard Ethel laughing as she discussed their sex life with a friend. 'I could have strangled them,' he said to Ross. These stories seemed to confirm that Christie's murderous fury sprang from humiliation.

Some of the psychiatrists who interviewed Christie thought that he was driven by fear. 'He would appear to have a dread of women,' observed Dr Stephen Coates, who examined Christie in Brixton in June 1953: 'There is little to explain Mr Christie's criminal acts: except the suggestion that they were committed to ward off acute feelings of fear produced in him by women.'

At the Springfield Mental Hospital in south London the previous July, Dr Dinshaw Petit had diagnosed Christie's back pain and diarrhoea as symptoms of 'psychological trauma', describing Christie in his notes as 'an insignificant, old womanish, city man. Girlish voice and manner, mincing walk. Latent homosexual, though not overt.'

Dr Petit's language showed his scorn for homosexual men (and for women): Christie was 'girlish' (weak, submissive), 'old womanish' (peevish, fussy), an ineffectual figure with a 'mincing', prissy gait. The doctor's prejudices were widely held in Britain, where sexual relationships between men were illegal. In March 1952 the computer scientist Alan Turing had been convicted of 'gross indecency' with another man, and in May the *Pictorial* had run a series on the 'homosexual problem', headlined 'Evil Men'.

As the psychiatrists saw it, Christie's extravagant stagings of manliness were covers for a self that he perceived as weak and effeminate, emasculated by the gas attack of 1918. At the photographic studio in Marylebone, he had put on a performance of sexual dominance, asking Kay Maloney to photograph him as he pretended to penetrate Maureen Riggs. In Brixton prison, he had boasted about his murders, as if his violence was proof of his virility.

In his notes for Harry, Christie had expressed the hope that a 'course of treatment' at Broadmoor – electro shock therapy, perhaps, or injection with hormones – might transform him into 'a decent and respected citizen, who could move about freely without any evil thoughts or tendencies'. Whatever aberrant impulses he detected in himself, he had believed that doctors might free him of them.

***

The final part of the *Pictorial*'s ghost-written confession – 'How Mrs Evans Died' – kept much closer to Reg Christie's original words than the previous instalments. Harry was careful not to take liberties with material about the Evans murders. The piece repeated Christie's claim to have killed Beryl at her request, and his denial of having had any part in Geraldine's death.

Harry composed a sidebar in which Christie – posthumously – stated his opposition to capital punishment. Christie had complained in his notes for Harry that during the war 'people were applauded and decorated with medals for killing a lot of other people and the Government say that *is good*, the man was a hero for his part in killing people. Now that the fear is over they say that the law and the Government take a serious view of a person killing people and that rather, that *he* should be *killed* not decorated.' Either Christie's wartime experiences had created a profound confusion in him about the morality of taking another person's life, or he was yet again finding justifications for the murders.

Harry's last pieces on Christie were marked up by Fred Redman, the news editor, before being funnelled through a network of riveted pipes to the typesetters upstairs and then to the printers in the basement. The *Pictorial* offices were strewn with the day's debris: coffee cups, gin and beer bottles, ashtrays packed with butts, wire waste-bins stuffed with crumpled sheets of paper. The building shuddered and hummed as the presses rolled.

When Harry left Geraldine House in the early hours of Sunday morning, vans emblazoned 'DAILY MIRROR' and 'SUNDAY PICTORIAL' were swinging out of the parking lot. The pubs and cafés around Fleet Street were still open, and a news vendor was calling out the headlines of the first editions stacked on his stall.

In 1939, when Harry first set foot in Fleet Street, he had stood in awe at a memorial to the journalist Edgar Wallace and silently pledged to follow his example: 'To Fleet Street he gave his heart,' read the plaque. In those days, Harry recalled, he had been full of zeal, a healthy, good-looking lad, 'trained to the hilt, as a solid, all-round reporter; trained to write straight-forward, simple English, to report the truth – and only the truth – accurately, swiftly, certainly'. He had been 'the happiest and proudest young man in the world', he said. 'Fleet Street represented the beginning of all things, the end of all things, the meaning of all things.' He laughed now at his naivety.

***

Several prominent figures spoke out against the newspaper coverage of Christie's trial. The publisher Victor Gollancz complained that the tabloid press, 'with the vilest of motives, to increase profit', had 'gone all out to titillate those sadistic and lascivious instincts that lie dormant in almost everyone'. Some newspapers had teased their readers with descriptions of the victims' 'well-developed' and 'scantily clad' bodies, as if inviting them to indulge in the fantasies that Christie made real.

The Conservative MP Christopher Hollis told the *Sunday Express* that he found it 'incredible' that the papers gave their readers every detail of such a case. 'So long as the Press continue to grab at these stories with an hysterical enthusiasm, they must take a considerable share of the responsibility if from time to time other sordid and horrible crimes of the same kind are committed.' By this logic, the tabloid press also bore some responsibility for Christie's crimes: by disseminating sensational stories about sex and violence, the newspapers had fostered fantasies of sex and violence.

The *Mirror* ran a series of articles in defence of its coverage: 'There is no good saying there is too much crime published in the Press or that the newspapers make too much of horrors like the Christie case,' the paper insisted. 'The world is as it is. The newspapers are bound to reflect it or give a false picture.'

Harry's exclusive had been a triumph for the *Pictorial*, dominating the news-stands for weeks. But Harry, now, felt tainted by what he had done. He had colluded with a serial killer, acted as his ventriloquist, and failed to secure a confession to Geraldine Evans's murder. His quest for justice had ended with the most lurid and lucrative account of sexual violence in his newspaper's history. His scoop had replayed Christie's peep-show, making a spectacle again of his victims' deaths. Perhaps his crusade to clear Tim Evans's name had only ever been an attempt to justify the underhand tactics and the shocking copy.

Harry begged his editors not to assign him to any more crime stories.

***

In a stormy session in the House of Commons on 29 July, more than twenty Members of Parliament raised objections to the findings of the Scott Henderson inquiry into the conviction of Tim Evans. Several Labour MPs condemned the inquiry's conclusions and the government's decision to keep its workings secret.

Geoffrey Bing, the Member for Hornchurch, said that the inquiry had ignored the evidence of tradesmen who had been working at 10 Rillington Place in the week of the Evans murders. If the labourers' testimony was accurate, said Bing, Tim Evans's so-called confession to murder made no sense. The builders had been storing materials in the washhouse for several days after Evans claimed to have placed his wife and child's bodies there.

Bing also called attention to irregularities in the way the police had conducted the case, including their loss of one of the builders' timesheets. He pointed out that the most compelling evidence against Evans was his confession in Notting Hill, which allegedly contained facts that only the killer could have known. But it had been established during Evans's trial that most or all of the information had already been given to him by the officers who interviewed him – he had been told how his wife and daughter had died, and where they had been found; he had been shown the tie with which Geraldine had been strangled.

Reg Christie had lied during Evans's trial, said Bing. He had claimed to have been suffering from severe back pain at the time of the murders in 1949, but he had gone to the doctor with this symptom only afterwards – it might even have been brought on by the strain of shifting Beryl's body.

Bing complained that the government was still withholding the transcript of Evans's trial, as well as refusing to publish Scott Henderson's report in full.

Sydney Silverman, the Labour MP for Nelson and Colne, urged the government to set up a public inquiry. A miscarriage of justice was bad enough, he said, but 'if we allow people to believe that, having made the error, all the resources of the community are being employed to hush it up and deny it, then indeed confidence in the administration of justice will be undermined in such a way that it can never recover'. Many Labour MPs suspected that the Tory government was keen to uphold the verdict not only to protect the reputation of the justice system but also because they didn't want to give succour to those who opposed capital punishment.

The controversy about the Evans case was becoming so intense that Fryn Tennyson Jesse's editor decided to publish a joint volume containing the transcripts of both the Evans and Christie trials. Jim Hodge told Fryn that her introductory essay would need to make a judgement about which man had killed Beryl and Geraldine Evans. He warned her that he was struggling to obtain the shorthand notes of either trial from the Home Office. It was going to take 'every vestige of reputation and prestige' to get hold of them, he said: 'At present they have quite eluded me. Getting in to the Old Bailey is as nothing!! There is very obvious reluctance to let us have them, and it may be some time yet before I can lay my hands on them – if ever.'

After making further efforts to get the trial transcripts, Hodge wrote to Fryn: 'The thing sticks out a mile that they don't want us to have the Notes, and the only reason that I can see is that they want to close the Evans and Christie incident without a further stink being aroused.' But having read the conclusions of Scott Henderson's inquiry, Hodge was convinced that there had been no miscarriage of justice in the Evans case. He forwarded the summary to Fryn: 'The Evidence is to me quite conclusive that Christie had nothing to do with the murder of Mrs Evans and her daughter,' he wrote, 'and the Findings are sound and logical.' Hodge thought that Tim Evans was guilty.

PART THREE

13

The back room

Each morning Fryn would slowly climb the stairs to her attic study in Pear Tree Cottage, panting gently, with Joanna following behind her. Fryn still used morphine and barbiturates – 'pinkies' (Soneryl) and the stronger 'blues' (Medinal) – and she occasionally drank heavily, but she kept to a strict working routine. She and Joanna took their places in the study: Fryn at a gate-legged table, Joanna at a typewriter on a desk overlooking the garden. The window was surrounded by shelves of poetry, the wall to its right packed with history books, the wall behind with a collection that Fryn described as 'the finest true-crime library in London'. 'The room was a little factory in its way,' said Joanna, 'both sanctuary and arsenal.' Below them, the long sitting room on the ground floor was lined with volumes of mythology, religion and fairy tales, and the first-floor rooms with biographies, novels and plays.

Fryn lit her single cigarette of the day – 'she smoked as if she were learning', said Joanna, 'and didn't much like it' – and then started to dictate. She could reel off her thoughts for a straight hour, having already composed her ideas in her head and made a few scrawled notes to guide her. She dictated letters, passages for her latest novel, reflections on the Rillington Place murders.

The Christie and Evans essay was the most important that she had yet tackled. As part of the Notable British Trials series, it might change the consensus on the Evans verdict, even on the death penalty. Since she did not yet have the transcript of Evans's trial, she began by considering Christie.

Fryn thought that Reg Christie was motivated by 'lust, monstrous and uncontrolled'. He was 'a thwarted little man, a sexually unsatisfied little man', she wrote, whose 'sexual incapacity grew to fill his whole mind. He needed complete submission – a submission that might be as complete as that of death.'

She believed it significant that Christie had offered women abortions, even though the lawyers in both trials and at the Scott Henderson inquiry had dismissed the possibility that he performed such operations. Like other social problems raised by the case – prostitution, domestic violence, sexual assault, the trade in pornographic photographs – abortion was a contentious, almost taboo subject. A group of women had been campaigning since the 1930s to legalise terminations when a woman's psychological or physical health was at risk, but successive governments had ignored their calls.

The left-wing paper *Reynolds News* reported in December 1952 that 500 women a year were dying after illegal operations: 'If the misery and suffering that is a consequence of backstreet surgery is to be driven out of our social life,' the paper argued, 'the law of the country must be changed.' For a start, it said: 'The conspiracy of silence surrounding this problem of abortion must be ended.'

In her novel *A Pin to See the Peepshow*, Fryn described the danger and indignity of back-street abortion. The novel's heroine, Julia, visits a seedy newsagent's shop by a railway arch to undergo an illegal operation. She is frightened, having read stories in the *News of the World* about girls who have died after such procedures. In a yellow-papered, red-curtained parlour behind the shop, she hands £10 to the abortionist, Mrs Humble, who scrubs up with carbolic soap, boils her instruments and starts work. 'This was degradation indeed,' thinks Julia. At home that night she vomits, then succumbs to 'the pains' that Mrs Humble warned her would come. She is in agony for three days, in bed for two weeks. A friend tells her to go to hospital to get 'tidied up', but she refuses. 'I'm over it,' she says, 'and never want to think of it again.'

Even before the war, an estimated 44,000 to 60,000 illegal abortions were carried out each year in England and Wales. A back-street abortionist typically pushed the nozzle of a syringe into a woman's cervix, and then squeezed a bulb to squirt a solution of soap or disinfectant into her uterus. The tube was left in place for a while, along with gauze packed into the vagina to staunch the bleeding. The foetus usually 'came away' after a few hours or days. There could be complications, such as excessive bleeding, or sepsis if the instruments were not properly sterilised, or an embolism if air was accidentally pumped in.

It may have been by carrying out such a procedure that Christie first experienced the feeling of power over a woman. He 'assaults his subjects in a defenceless condition', Fryn observed: 'his sexual excitement is intensified by their helplessness'. Pregnancies, or rumoured pregnancies, linked nearly all the women Christie was accused of killing. Ruth Fuerst and Muriel Eady had been thought to be pregnant when they went missing. Rita Nelson and Beryl Evans were carrying babies when they died. The post-mortems on Kathleen Maloney and Hectorina Maclennan revealed that both had recently been pregnant. After Christie's arrest, several women told the police that he had offered them abortions. No one came forward to say that he had carried out such an operation on her, but then to do so would have meant admitting to a crime.

Long before Christie was charged, it was widely rumoured that abortions were performed at 10 Rillington Place. Joan Howard, who lived in the house in 1951, had claimed to have met a girl who had undergone an illegal operation in the Christies' flat. Len Trevallion, a Notting Hill policeman, said that it was common knowledge that Westbourne Grove prostitutes went to the Christies to end their pregnancies. His colleague Herbert Strait said that a plainclothes squad had kept a watch on No 10 because of these rumours. Peter McKay, who collected clothing subscriptions from the Christies, had heard the rumours too. Lucy Endicott, the young woman with whom Tim Evans had an affair, said that Tim had told her that Beryl was thinking of getting an abortion from Christie, and Jessie Hide, whose garden backed on to 10 Rillington Place, had asked Ethel directly whether her husband had offered to end Beryl's pregnancy. 'Fancy asking my Reg such a thing,' Ethel replied.

When Ethel went missing in 1952, customers in the tobacconist's shop next to the Rainbow Café discussed whether Reg might have sent her away because she had threatened to go to the police about his illegal practices. Three months after that, when women's bodies were found in No 10, several neighbours assumed that they were casualties of abortions. When Christie was arrested at the end of March, someone Fryn knew in Notting Hill remarked: 'Oh, I see they have got the abortionist.'

In 1949, the police searching Christie's flat had found an old Higginson syringe, a device marketed as an aid to vaginal douches and rectal enemas, but also used to induce miscarriages. The gassing jar they found in his garden in 1953 might have been used to knock women out before such operations. The abortions may have been performed in the back bedroom, away from the street and close to the water supply in the kitchen and washhouse.

Ethel must have known about Reg's procedures. If she took part in them – because she wanted the money, because she wanted to help desperate young women, because she dared not disobey her husband – her collusion would have bound her all the more tightly to him. The punishment for conspiring to bring on a miscarriage was usually two or three years in jail, and the maximum sentence was life.

This illicit activity may have contributed to Ethel's anxiety in the early 1950s, but she was also troubled, as she told Joan Howard, by the suspicion that her husband had murdered Beryl and Geraldine Evans. 'Such knowledge as she had may creep into the consciousness of a wife,' Fryn wrote, 'until at some point she comes to the realisation that she has known it all the time.' Fryn may have been recalling her own dawning awareness, in the early days of her marriage, that Tottie was having an affair with the mother of his son.

Ethel was in such a nervous state in May 1951 that her doctor prescribed phenobarbital, potassium bromide and chloral hydrate to calm her down and help her to sleep. At about this time Joan Howard heard shouts and screams from the Christies' bedroom.

After Joan moved out, Ethel's condition worsened. By 1952, according to Reg, she was such a 'bundle of nerves' that she would start at any noise in the hallway. In April that year, she quarrelled with Sylvia Edwards, who lived on the first floor, about whether the front door should be left ajar. Ethel tried to shut the door and Sylvia stopped her, insisting that she needed to listen out for her baby daughter, who was outside in a pram. The two women tussled over the door and Ethel called the police to report an assault. When Reg got home from work, he was livid with his wife for phoning the police switchboard. He would have called a sergeant he knew, he said; he didn't want strangers looking into their business.

Christie spent three weeks in the St Charles Hospital in North Kensington that summer, with acute back pain and diarrhoea, but he turned down the offer of in-patient treatment at a psychiatric hospital in south London, on the grounds that his wife mustn't be left alone with the black men. Perhaps he was scared of leaving Ethel alone at all, in case she confided to anyone her suspicions of him. In August, Christie was declared unfit for work, being two stone underweight, tremulous and anxious. He returned to British Road Services in September, as an accounts clerk in their Hampstead depot, but he couldn't concentrate: 'My head was just splitting day after day,' he said, 'knowing what might happen while I was away.' He may have sensed that Ethel's hatred of the black tenants was a proxy for her fear of him – what he might have done, what he might yet do – just as his paranoia about the tenants channelled his own dread. For years Reg and Ethel had adhered to a pact of silence, but now they were both breaking down, and the pact was unravelling.

During the very cold November of 1952, Ethel wrote to her elderly aunt in Sheffield to ask if she and Reg could come to stay: he had recently been in hospital, she explained, and the change would do him good. Her aunt replied that this was not possible, instead inviting them to visit for a few days at Christmas. Reg asked Ethel's brother Henry to find them a room in one of the properties he owned in Sheffield, but he too turned them down. Ethel was desperate to leave the house. 'I wish we could get out of here,' she wrote to her sister Lily. 'It is awful with these "people" here.'

Reg Christie gave in his notice at British Road Services on Monday 1 December 1952, pretending that he had new employment in the north. By Saturday, his last day of work in the Hampstead depot, a foul, claggy blanket of coal smoke and diesel fumes had descended on London. The yellow smog thickened, growing so dense and dark that by Sunday it was impossible to see more than a few yards ahead, and difficult to breathe. The sulphurous air seeped into the houses of Rillington Place, with a stink of burnt matches and rotten eggs, leaving a greasy film and a sprinkling of smuts on every surface. It seared the residents' throats, pricked at their eyes, like the sulphurous yellow gases that had overcome British soldiers at Ypres in 1918.

'It was really dreadful here at the week-end with the fog,' Ethel wrote to her sister in Sheffield on Friday; 'it made us feel quite ill.' Reg strangled her to death in their bed that Sunday.

***

Joanna drove Fryn to the Christies' former home in September 1955. Fryn sat in the car while Joanna knocked at the front door of No 10, which was eventually opened by a 'black gent' from one of the upper floors. He spoke hardly any English, Joanna said (perhaps she could not understand his accent), but he was able to convey that he didn't know when the tenant of the ground floor would be back. The curtains of the house were tightly drawn. To Fryn, it seemed that the windows were blank memorials to Christie's victims. 'Through those tombstones one cannot see,' she wrote, 'one can only stare at them and wonder.'

At the end of 1953, Charles Brown had rented out 10 Rillington Place, at £5 a week, to George Lawrence, a 25-year-old boxer from Jamaica. Lawrence's white wife, Elsie, told a reporter from the *Sunday People* that they were delighted with their new home. Their daughter and nieces romped about the house, she said. 'They are certainly not frightened.' George was papering and painting the rooms, and he planned to put up a plaque in the kitchen to commemorate the murders. 'After all,' said Mrs Lawrence, 'it's historic.'

One day in the spring of 1954, George Lawrence and a young white woman were stopped and searched by a policeman in the

West End. On finding marijuana roll-ups in the woman's handbag, the officer charged Lawrence with possession.

The magistrate at Lawrence's hearing asked how he had met his female companion, and Lawrence explained that she had come to see his house. 'It's the house where Christie lived,' he said. 'Everybody comes to look at it.'

The magistrate was disgusted: 'You showed her where the bodies were stored, I suppose,' he said, as he sentenced Lawrence to six months in jail. 'You are a foul beast. It's a pity we can not deport you. Very often people like you get hold of these fools of little white girls and supply them with Indian Hemp. Then the girls become the sluts you see in the court from time to time, and later on some of you live on their immoral earnings.' All this because his female companion – who faced no charges – had reefers in her handbag.

Christie had made similar assumptions about the relationships between the black men and white women in his house. But the social researcher Rosalind Wilkinson, in her study of London prostitutes, explained why migrants and sex workers might seek out each other's company. Many prostitutes enjoyed being with men who did not look down on them, she said, and the men, having arrived 'in a new and bewildering culture, find that they are not wanted by white people and are often forced to form associations with the class who will associate with them'. A black man who lived with a prostitute was often vilified as a 'pimp' or a 'ponce', Wilkinson wrote, but he rarely lived off his girlfriend's earnings. If she did financially support him, it might be because she wanted him to be at home when she got in from work, or to mind their baby while she was out – since the woman earned more money, the man in effect played the part of a wife.

In 1954 Rillington Place was renamed Ruston Close, at the residents' request, and Charles Brown rented out No 10 to Eric

Lloyd Sanchez, a Jamaican who described himself as an 'acrobatic dancer'. Sanchez and Brown had been arrested in 1950 when police found thirty-five packets of marijuana in Sanchez's home in Bayswater. Brown, who had been playing cards with Sanchez, protested his innocence. 'I don't live here,' he said. 'I don't even smoke.'

Sanchez had since become the kingpin of Notting Hill's marijuana scene. The local press described him as a flashy, debonair figure, who dealt drugs from 'Hashish Hall', a dilapidated twenty-room mansion in Ladbroke Grove. When the police raided the building in August 1954, Sanchez climbed out of a fourth-floor window, slid down two drainpipes and fractured his spine as he hit the ground. A stash of drugs was found on the premises and Sanchez was sent to prison. He let out the rooms at 10 Ruston Close while he was in jail.

Fryn and Joanna returned to No 10 towards the end of September 1955. This time they were greeted by Sanchez, who had completed his prison sentence. He would be happy to show them round, he said. He took them to the upstairs rooms, where they saw the tenants coming and going, and out to the washhouse. Fryn and Joanna inspected the 'sordid little garden' and the ground-floor flat. Sanchez told them that his white wife had moved out of the house while he was imprisoned, but the police hadn't believed him when he said that he didn't now know where she was. He invited Fryn and Joanna to see for themselves that she wasn't in the alcove in which Christie had hidden his victims.

Fryn was horrified by the house. She wondered whether this degraded place had cast a malevolent spell over Christie and Evans, driving them both to murder. She was unsettled by the district, too. 'North Kensington is the ugliest and the most unsafe and the most negro-populated part of London,' she wrote to an acquaintance, 'a ghastly part of the world, quite stiff with blacks.' Her language carried an ugly echo of the phrase 'stiff with dirt', as if she equated dark skin with filth.

Fryn prided herself on her progressive views on race – she was an outspoken opponent of segregation in the American South, and a friend of the famous singer and black activist Paul Robeson. The first time that she and Tottie took Paul and Essie Robeson out to dinner in London, she recalled, Paul flung his arm out and Essie admonished: 'Paul, Paul, you mustn't do that.' He reassured his wife: 'Yes, I can,' he said. 'I am free here.' Fryn told him that it made her proud to be English that he should feel that way. She was shocked when the Robesons' 'dear little boy' had to leave his kindergarten in north London because other mothers objected to the presence of a black child. But, for all her principles, Fryn recoiled from the black residents of Notting Hill.

Outside No 10, white women in slippers and curlers were sitting on rickety chairs by their houses or perching on the kerb, chatting to neighbours. The cul-de-sac formed a 'natural playground', said Fryn, and children 'of all colours' were playing in the street with empty tins and other cast-offs.

Fryn and Joanna introduced themselves to a young white woman who was walking her dog. She told them that she lived at No 8, and when she was thirteen had earned pocket money at weekends by taking Geraldine Evans out in a pushcart. Tim and Beryl were a nice couple, she said, and she was sure that Mr Evans had not killed his wife or child: Tim 'thought a lot' of the baby, Beryl was 'a really lovely girl', and the couple didn't quarrel 'so as you'd notice'. (Fryn commented afterwards that working-class couples could probably 'yell each other's heads off without anybody noticing much'.)

According to this young woman, Ethel Christie had been a pleasant person, who kept to herself and did not sit out on the street like her neighbours; she just said good morning and good evening quietly as she went by. Fryn asked what Reg Christie had done with his dog when he went on the run. The woman told her that he had taken Judy to the vet to be put down on the day before he disappeared: 'He was very fond of that dog.'

Fryn was taken aback to hear that Christie had been an animal lover. 'Well well!!' she wrote. 'I give up ever trying to disentangle the mixture that is known as human nature.' She was so devoted to her own pets that in 1935 she had written a whole book about the cats and dogs at her holiday home in the south of France.

That autumn Fryn and Tottie's poodle, Guido, suffered a series of fits – twisting and falling, banging into furniture as if he were blind – and a vet came to Pear Tree Cottage to inject him with a fatal dose of barbiturates. As the needle went in, Guido screamed, wrote Fryn, and then fell silent. Fryn grieved for her 'affectionate, gentle, brilliant' little dog. 'I can't ever have another,' she told a friend. 'It was a dreadful day.'

Fryn and Tottie's own health was deteriorating. Tottie had become very deaf and was unable to get about without the aid of two walking sticks. Fryn's legs were so swollen and tender that she too found it difficult to walk, and she had lost a stone in weight over the summer. Her consultant, after performing a series of blood tests and X-rays, told Tottie that she was suffering from pernicious anaemia and degeneration of the spinal cord. She would need regularly to be injected with liver and B12, in addition to the morphine she was already prescribed. 'I am living at the end of a syringe,' Fryn told a friend.

***

Rosalind Wilkinson's survey of prostitutes in London was published anonymously in 1955, with only the name of the editor on the title page. Wilkinson had fallen out with the British

Social Biology Council, which had commissioned her survey, and which now insisted on cutting large sections of her report.

Wilkinson had disobeyed several of the council's instructions. Though told to work undercover, she had found this ineffective as well as unethical. Instead, she had decided to be open with her interviewees about her identity and her purpose. In this way, she said, 'I was at ease and could give my attention to the girl instead of being afraid of being found out, and she talked freely about prostitution because that was the reason for our relationship.' Nor did she make detailed inquiries about her subjects' early lives, as the council had asked, instead accepting the women's explanations for why they had taken up prostitution.

In his introduction to *Women of the Streets: a Sociological Study of the Common Prostitute*, the former police inspector C. H. Rolph distanced himself from the anonymous researcher's findings. While he praised her 'perceptive feminine subjectiveness' and her 'readable' style, he described her fieldwork as 'incomplete and inconclusive'. The council, he said, could offer no recommendations based on her report.

The mission of the British Social Biology Council was to preserve and strengthen the family unit, and it had hoped that this study would enable it to recommend measures to curb the sex trade. But Wilkinson's report suggested that social or legal reforms would make little difference. The women she interviewed knew how to find other work if they wanted it, she said; they were undeterred by the threat of fines or imprisonment; and they were rarely recruited or controlled by pimps. She questioned whether the women were really the problem at all, suggesting that it might be worth considering their customers instead: 'It was interesting to ask myself,' she wrote: '"Who are these men?"'

14

A dear little baby

It had taken Jim Hodge a year to get the transcript of Tim Evans's trial out of the Home Office. When he sent it on to Fryn, he admitted that reading it had only confused him further. 'The more one thinks of it,' he wrote, 'the more hopeless it seems to find the true story.'

Early in 1956, having read both transcripts, Fryn issued lunch invitations to the men who had been involved in the cases. In her letters to them, she strove both to flatter and to impress, adopting the assured, confiding air of a grande dame of British crime writing. She breezily referred to Scotland Yard as 'the Yard', the House of Commons as 'the House', the Old Bailey as 'the Bailey'. 'I rather gather my ideas and yours are the same,' she told Sir Lionel Heald, the Conservative MP who had prosecuted Christie, 'but you speak naturally with much greater knowledge.'

Over lunch at Pear Tree Cottage, Heald told Fryn that he was sure that Christie had not killed Beryl Evans, as she was a 'different type' to most of his victims, nor the baby, whose murder was 'entirely out of keeping with his whole make-up'. He warned Fryn that the Evans case had become highly political. Some Labour MPs were characterising the Scott Henderson inquiry as a government cover-up, devised by 'the wicked Tories' to thwart the campaign to abolish the death penalty.

Inspector Griffin, who led the Christie investigation, came to lunch, as did Colin Sleeman, who was Derek Curtis-Bennett's junior in the trial, and Geoffrey Freeborough, the solicitor appointed to represent Tim Evans in 1949 (Freeborough was 'a nasty bit of work', Fryn told Hodge). Fryn liked having people to lunch so that she didn't have to venture half-seeing into the world. She could hold court in the dining room with Tottie and Joanna at her side, while the Dutch maid served them a meal prepared by the Dutch cook – sometimes a roast, sometimes a curry or an omelette.

Superintendent Jennings, who had built the case against Evans, 'came at a quarter-to-one', said Fryn, 'and stayed till half-past-five gently trickling things out. He brought all his documents with him to refer to, and read from them in answer to my questions while Joanna took down what he said.' Jennings told them that he was convinced that Tim Evans's confession to the murders was truthful: Evans 'was frank and he could not tell us the story fast enough', he said. 'It was so forthright and not as though he was thinking up a story.' Jennings had to keep asking Evans to 'go steady' to give Inspector Black time to write his words down. He said that he was amazed when Evans claimed in court that he had made the confession only because he was afraid that the police would otherwise take him downstairs and beat him up.

Fryn and Joanna visited Inspector Black at Hammersmith police station, and found him friendly and relaxed. He, too, assured them that Tim Evans's statement at Notting Hill had been spontaneous. On the train journey from Wales to London, he said, Evans had been sullen and tearful, perking up only when they got talking about Queens Park Rangers football club, but at the police station he had launched into his confession, speaking at great speed. Black had been thunderstruck by the change in his demeanour. He insisted that he and Jennings had applied no pressure, and that he had taken down Evans's words verbatim. On the journey to the magistrates' court, Tim had again told Black that he had killed his wife and daughter, adding that he had removed the wedding ring from Beryl's finger after her death, then sold it to a jeweller in Merthyr Tydfil. The sale of the ring was confirmed by the Welsh police.

A few of Evans's defenders had pointed out that he was unlikely to have used some of the language in the Notting Hill confession: his statement described Beryl as 'incurring' debt, for example, which was not a word used in ordinary conversation. But Fryn thought that Black had only adapted what Evans told him: 'It is second nature for a police officer to use the official phraseology,' she observed. Evans, by all accounts, had warmed to Black: he had described him to his mother as 'a gentleman'. At no point had he accused the police of falsifying his statement. Nor did Fryn think that the police had suppressed the statements of the builders who had been at No 10 in November 1949. The builders' evidence was not decisive in any case: though it undermined Evans's claim to have put the bodies in the washhouse on 8 and 10 November, it remained possible that he had placed them there after 11 November, when the building work was complete.

Malcolm Morris, who had led the defence of Tim Evans in 1950, came twice to lunch. He told Fryn that Evans was not a brutish-looking lout, as he had been portrayed, but an ordinary, mild-mannered, fresh-faced young working man. Morris had believed that Evans was innocent, he said, but his client's many lies had made it difficult to persuade the jury of this. He impressed on Fryn how hostile to Evans the trial judge had been. The judge's summing-up had been 'deadly' to the defence.

Desmond Curran, the psychiatrist who had examined both Evans and Christie on behalf of the Crown, said to Fryn that he should check with the Home Office before accepting her invitation. 'Never ask the Home Office!' cautioned Fryn. 'I never do, and I have edited five trials, and nobody has ever objected to anything I have said yet. I have a very fine nose for libel, or for saying the incorrect thing. The HO is bound to say No as a matter of course, and then you wouldn't be able to come to me and I shouldn't be able to invite you, and what I want is merely your personal opinions and thoughts, which I should not quote as yours.' Curran agreed to meet, inviting her to his consulting room in Marylebone so that he could, confidentially, show her his papers on the two cases.

Fryn's favourite lunch guest was the pathologist Dr Francis Camps, who had already published his own account of the Christie investigation. 'He roared and burbled with laughter,' she said, 'and not only at his own jokes.' Camps told Fryn that Christie was one of the few murderers he had met who he had strongly disliked as a person. He described Evans as 'stupid, primitive, pathetic, but not so bad, and not mentally defective'.

Camps and Fryn swapped stories about other crimes. He invited her and Joanna to watch him give evidence at the Old Bailey, where he was appearing in the trial of a clerk charged with killing a prostitute in Paddington, a murder apparently inspired by a story in the crime magazine *True Detective*.

Fryn read the publications that were already appearing about Evans and Christie, among them Camps's *Medical & Scientific Investigations in the Christie Case*, Duncan Webb's *Deadline for Crime*, Lord Altrincham and Ian Gilmour's *The Case of Timothy Evans: an Appeal to Reason*, R. T. Paget and Sydney Silverman's *Hanged – and Innocent?* and Michael Eddowes's *The Man on Your Conscience*. She had lunch with Eddowes, a solicitor who believed passionately in Evans's innocence. He was 'delightful to meet', said Fryn, 'full of enthusiasm and a little bit mad – particularly on this subject'. She met the barrister Jeremy Hutchinson, who had written a strong defence of Evans in the *Observer* and who lived nearby with the actress Peggy Ashcroft. 'How difficult it is to pin down the facts of the case,' Hutchinson remarked, 'and not let one's convictions push them about!'

Fryn told Jim Hodge that her friend Joe Jackson, now an assistant commissioner at Scotland Yard, had congratulated her on persuading so many people to speak to her: 'He said that absolutely no one on earth but I would have got so many people to come and see me and tell me things, which is true and shows there is something in being a woman after all, which is a nice feeling. I haven't met too many, believe me.'

Scotland Yard continued to defend the Evans verdict. Sir Harold Scott, who had been the Commissioner of the Metropolitan Police at the time of Evans's trial, insisted in his memoir of 1954 that 'the risk of an innocent man being executed is so remote that it can be disregarded'. But James Chuter Ede, who as Home Secretary had authorised Evans's execution, was having doubts: 'I think Evans's case shows that a mistake was possible,' he told the House of Commons in 1955, 'and that, in the form in which the verdict was actually given on a particular case, a mistake was made.'

***

Fryn laboured on her essay in the attic study every weekday until 7 p.m., stopping only for lunch. Her eyesight was becoming so poor that Joanna had to read almost everything to her. The material was extremely confusing as it was. 'This has been the most difficult thing I have ever attempted,' wrote Fryn: 'everything must remain supposition and one has to think of every possible supposition.'

Tim Evans's and Reg Christie's contradictory statements were particularly perplexing. 'I must admit,' Fryn said, 'that that terrible series of so-called confessions shakes me badly.'

If Christie had killed Beryl and then shown Tim her body on the bed, could Tim really have believed that she had died during an abortion? How had he accounted for her swollen and bloodied face? Had he not noticed that she had been strangled? Why had he then taken the blame for his wife and baby's murders in the long statement that he made to the Notting Hill police? Why had he changed his story so many times?

But if Tim had killed Beryl, why had he at first falsely claimed to have put her down a drain? Why had he later said he had put the bodies of his wife and child in the washhouse on 8 and 10 November, when the builders were still working there? How had no one noticed him hiding them? When he accused his neighbour of accidentally killing Beryl during an abortion, had he really just happened to blame a man who turned out to have a habit of strangling women to death and concealing them on his premises?

The slew of stories and counter-stories made it impossible to be sure of what had happened inside Rillington Place in November 1949. The answer must lie in the detail, and yet the detail pointed one way and then another. It was like the moment in which the heroine of Fryn's novel gazed into the home-made peepshow, and was dazzled by the distorting perspectives: in 'that space of some ten inches by five, she was lost in a fourth dimension of which she had never heard'. Its tiny objects seemed to loom out and then fall away, leaving the whole unsteady and unknowable.

***

In April 1956 Fryn tried to arrange a meeting with Tim Evans's mother, who was still living at 11 St Mark's Road, and had reverted to her previous surname, Evans, after the death of her second husband in 1953.

'I wish to present the case for your son in the best possible manner,' Fryn wrote to Agnes, 'and I think only you and your daughters can help me. May I come to see you with my secretary at half past eleven next Thursday morning?'

Agnes turned down Fryn's request. 'I am a widow,' she explained in her reply, 'I go out to work at 645 in the morning and I dont come home till 645 in the evening then I am to tired to see anyone.' She said she was very sorry if she seemed rude, 'but to be quite frank with you I am getting a bit sick of people using me and my Daughter to make money at our expense if not getting my son more cleared and what is more I am not geting nothing out of it but seeing my name Mrs Evans splashed all over the papers and people pointing me and my daughter out in the streets I don't like it all I want us to be left in peace.'

'I will not see any one again,' wrote Agnes; 'that is my last word on the matter.'

To discover what Tim's family might know, Fryn instead wrote to Bernard Gillis QC, the barrister who had represented Agnes and her daughters at the Scott Henderson inquiry. Could he come to lunch next week? she asked. 'So much more gets said at the relaxation of lunch than by interviewing people.'

Gillis came the next Friday, 29 June, bringing along Morley Lawson, a Brylcreemed, moustachioed City solicitor who had appeared alongside him at the private inquiry. They filled Fryn in on the case, complaining about the limited role that Scott Henderson had allowed the Evans family.

On 25 July, Jim Hodge wrote to Fryn with news of Derek Curtis-Bennett, who had represented Christie at the Old Bailey. Curtis-Bennett had sunk into dissipation after the trial. In the summer of 1955, at the age of fifty-one, he took a second wife, a 25-year-old cabaret singer he had met in a cocktail bar. Nine months later she died of a drugs overdose in their Earl's

Court flat. Curtis-Bennett resigned his posts, stayed briefly in a convalescent home and by early July was wandering the streets of South Kensington. 'He looked so utterly tired, forsaken and lonely,' said a hotel manager who had sold him a bottle of champagne. 'He said he could not bear to go back to his flat.'

Curtis-Bennett returned to his apartment on 23 July, bleeding from the forehead, and was so unsteady that he had to be helped up the steps by the block's caretaker. He collapsed, drunk, and suffocated to death in the same room in which his young wife had died.

Hodge said to Fryn that he felt very sorry for Curtis-Bennett's children, two of whom had come to Court No 1 to watch him defend Christie. Fryn responded to Hodge's news only by remarking that she had of course not invited Curtis-Bennett to lunch. She had finished her introduction to the two trials, she told Hodge: 'The bloody thing is done at last.'

At this moment, when she thought the essay was complete, Fryn received a letter from Morley Lawson, the solicitor for Tim Evans's family. He had managed to change Mrs Evans's mind, he told Fryn. Agnes had agreed to meet her.

***

Joanna drove Fryn to 11 St Mark's Road in the last days of July 1956. Agnes's older daughter, Eileen Ashby, opened the door to them, saying that her mother was out but would be back soon. Fryn presented Tim's sister with a bunch of flowers, and Eileen invited the visitors to sit down while they waited. The place was neat as a pin, said Fryn, the perfect opposite of the house round the corner at 10 Ruston Close.

'Excuse me a moment,' said Eileen, 'I must go upstairs and fetch baby down and put him to sleep.' She returned, said Fryn, 'with a beautiful little baby with a ruffle of russet hair on his head. He smelt as clean as a flower.' As Eileen settled him into his pram, she confided: 'He's adopted, you know; my husband and I adopted him on our sixth anniversary.' She said that they had been unable to have their own child. 'We are hoping to save enough money to adopt another,' she added, 'so that John isn't the only one.'

Fryn, having suffered the grief of several miscarriages, was touched by Eileen's quiet resolve in overcoming the problem of her childlessness. She wondered whether the perambulator in the 'spotless little sitting-room' had once belonged to Geraldine Evans, whose pram had been abandoned at Rillington Place.

When Agnes came home, Fryn and Joanna stood up to shake her hand. The baby, delighted to see his grandmother, held out his arms, crying: 'Nanny, nanny.' Agnes apologised to Fryn for the letter she had sent her, saying that she hadn't understood what she wanted. Fryn said it didn't matter at all.

Agnes and her daughter told Fryn that they had been worried about Beryl and Geraldine's whereabouts in the weeks after they disappeared. On Sunday 27 November 1949, Eileen had called at Rillington Place with her brother's newspapers (the *Sunday Pictorial* and the *News of the World*), which she had picked up from the newsagent on St Mark's Road. She knocked three times for the top floor, but no one came to the door, so she knocked once, for the Christies' flat.

When Ethel appeared, Eileen asked if Beryl was at home. Ethel told her that she had gone away to Brighton, having quarrelled with Tim. She said that she had helped Beryl down the road because she was struggling to manage the baby and her luggage. Eileen remarked that it was very mean of Beryl not to have taken Geraldine round to see her grandmother before she went. Reg then came to the door and told Eileen: 'They've had a row. Best leave young couples alone.'

The next day Tim's half-sister Maureen called at No 10. At first there was no reply when she knocked, but Ethel eventually peered out of the curtain and then opened the door. When Ethel repeated that Beryl had left on Tuesday 8 November, saying that she would write soon, Maureen replied: 'We have not heard from her. The least she could do is write to my mother and tell her about the baby.' Ethel said that Beryl was 'not as nice' as Maureen thought she was: she had once left the baby alone in the house, she claimed, and returned smelling of gin.

Reg Christie then came down the street. 'What do you want?' he asked Maureen. He told her that Beryl had gone to Brighton and Tim to Bristol. When Maureen asked why Beryl had not written to them, he said: 'Your mother interfered too much.' He added that Beryl had left without saying goodbye to them either.

'Well, one of you is telling lies,' Maureen countered, 'as Mrs Christie just said Beryl said goodbye and would write.'

Ethel started to speak but Reg interrupted her: 'You shut your mouth.' He refused to let Maureen into the house to collect Tim's post, and when she threatened to go to the police he flew at her, warning her that he 'knew more about it than I thought he did'. He said that Tim wouldn't thank her if she brought the police into it.

Eileen told Fryn that she and her sister had informed the police about their visits to Rillington Place, but Inspector Jennings had decided their information was not relevant.

Eileen added that she had seen Reg silence Ethel before. If he didn't want his wife speaking to visitors to the house, he would jerk his head at their door and snap 'In', at which she would shrink back into the flat.

Agnes repeated to Fryn what Tim had told her in Brixton: Christie killed Beryl and Geraldine, and Christie was the only person who could explain what had happened. She insisted that her son was incapable of the crime for which he had hanged. 'That wasn't the sort of thing Timothy could have done,' she said; 'he hadn't the courage.'

As Fryn and Joanna left the house in St Mark's Road, Agnes noticed Fryn cautiously tap her foot on the ground outside the front door. 'It's all right dear,' said Agnes, taking Fryn by the arm to guide her out; 'there's no step.'

Fryn was moved by her encounter with Tim Evans's mother and sister. They had been so calm, earnest and kind. And their recollections cast doubt on the honesty of Ethel as well as Reg Christie. Ethel must have been lying if she said that she had seen Beryl and the baby leave the house in the second week of November. Perhaps Reg had told her to say that they had gone away, and she had taken it too far. He, realising her mistake, told her to shut her mouth.

Reg may also have instructed Ethel to claim to have heard a bump upstairs on 8 November: they both visited the Notting Hill police station to report this noise on 5 December, four days after their original interviews. 'I have remembered one or two points,' Ethel told the detectives, 'which I think I ought to mention to you.' If Ethel was covering for Reg, she must have known even before Tim Evans's trial that her husband had been involved in Beryl and Geraldine's disappearance – but then she had been protecting him, or turning a blind eye to his business, ever since he hid the stolen post-office sacks in their rooms in Halifax in 1921.

Fryn was baffled that Tim's solicitor, Geoffrey Freeborough, had not suggested that his barrister call Agnes, Eileen or Maureen to the witness box to discredit the Christies' testimony. 'I can't help feeling that a mistake was made by the instructing solicitor at Evans's defence,' she told Bernard Gillis, who had represented the family at the inquiry. She said to Hodge, more frankly, that Freeborough had made a hash of the Evans case.

Seeing the 'dear little baby' in St Mark's Road reminded Fryn of the little girl who had been killed at 10 Rillington Place.

For Agnes and her daughters, she realised, the deaths of Beryl and Geraldine Evans were not an intellectual puzzle but a lasting grief.

Fryn told Jim Hodge that she needed to make changes to the introduction. She inserted two new paragraphs, amended her conclusions and sent the revised manuscript to Edinburgh.

***

In her essay, Fryn said that she found it hard to believe that Christie had inflicted the injuries to Beryl Evans's eye, cheek and lip that Dr Teare had noticed at the post-mortem: Christie had not hit any of his other victims. Teare, assuming that the injuries were part of the murderous attack, had suggested that Beryl was punched twenty minutes before she was strangled, but this was a minimum time for the swelling to develop. Fryn proposed that she had been beaten up the night before she was killed.

By his own admission, Tim had violent rows with his wife in the days before her death. He was angry that Beryl was behind on the rent and the hire-purchase payments, was keeping him from seeing other women, turning his family against him. 'It has become the custom for people to think that Evans was a weak and simple little man,' Fryn wrote. 'Weak he was, but he was unfaithful, insensitive, quarrelsome and given to violent impulses.' She believed that he had assaulted his wife on Monday 7 November.

Yet Fryn thought that it was Christie who murdered Beryl the next day. 'Taking everything into account,' she wrote, 'I think it more likely that Christie killed Mrs Evans than that Evans did.' He had probably murdered her 'under the guise of performing an abortion', she wrote, and 'for the satisfaction of his usual necrophiliac lust'. He must have then killed Geraldine to cover his tracks: 'Whoever murdered the baby, murdered her because her presence was a danger and would lead to the discovery of her mother's death.'

Fryn guessed that Christie told Tim that Beryl had died during the abortion to which he had agreed, persuaded him to help conceal the body and assured him that Geraldine was being looked after by a couple in East Acton. 'Christie was smooth-tongued and had a nice way with him,' said Fryn. 'He had been brought up respectably. He was, in Evans's eyes, well educated; he earned by his brain and not his hands.' She thought that Tim had not known when he surrendered himself in Wales that his child had died. She could only imagine why he had confessed to his wife and baby's murders two days later: pathological mendacity ('he lied as he breathed', she observed), guilt about his part in the supposed abortion and in the hiding of Beryl's body, fear of Christie, fear of the police, confusion, stupidity, shame, sorrow.

'There are objections to this conclusion,' Fryn admitted; 'it does not satisfy all the conditions or resolve all doubts. No explanation that I have thought of does this; each one leaves something unaccountable. I have arrived at it because it offers less obstruction to my mind than do the others, but I am fully conscious that it is not the only one.'

***

Hodge told Fryn that her essay was 'a marvellous piece of work' and sent her a payment of £500, double the usual fee. He had at first been convinced that Tim Evans was guilty, he said, but her analysis had changed his mind. 'I agree with your ultimate conclusion,' he said: 'it could *not* have been Evans.'

Fryn said afterwards that she had not written anything quite so 'appallingly difficult' in her life as this essay, partly because of her failing sight, and partly because of the grimness and complexity of the material. 'Joanna has been so marvellous that without her of course I couldn't have done it at all. We are both almost unconscious.' And yet her immersion in the task had fended off her darkest moods. For two years she had been 'taut as a piece of stretched elastic', she said. 'The very arduousness of it saved me.'

15

With these dirty hands

Occasionally, in the years after the Christie case, Harry Procter covered the light-hearted stories that he enjoyed. At London Airport in 1956, he rescued Marilyn Monroe from a horde of photographers by ushering her to safety behind an ice-cream counter, along with her husband, Arthur Miller, and their travelling companions, Laurence Olivier and Vivien Leigh. The grateful Marilyn, who was about to shoot *The Prince and the Showgirl* with Olivier at Pinewood Studios, gave Harry an interview, which ran in *Paris Match* with a photograph of the two of them together.

But Harry's bosses refused to take him off exposés and crime stories. 'What do you want to do, then?' sneered Reg Payne. 'Edit the "What the Stars Foretell" column?'

The *Pictorial*'s editor, Colin Valdar, was a trim, well-spoken chap, who looked more like an RAF squadron leader than a tabloid boss, but he was determined that his paper should be the raciest in Fleet Street. Valdar, said Harry, wanted stories of 'sex, scandal, surprise, sensation, exposure, murder. And as many pictures of half-dressed, big-bosomed damsels in distress as possible.' The circulation wars were becoming more intense than ever. Though the daily and Sunday papers still sold millions of copies, many readers were also getting their news and entertainment from the television, especially after the launch in 1955 of ITV, a commercial channel that was less high-minded than the BBC.

In the *Pictorial* conference one morning, Valdar asked for ideas for a centre-page picture feature. 'We're going for six million this week,' he said, in shirtsleeves, braces and bow tie. 'Cudlipp's on my back. I need a great spread with sex, violence, and religion.'

'What about a sexy nun, Colin?' suggested the photographer Frank Charman, Harry's favourite sidekick.

'Okay, Frank, where's the violence?'

Charman thought for a moment. 'Got it!' he said. 'I know of a convent in the Midlands where the nuns go pigeon shooting.' He suggested that the *Pic* could pay one of the sisters to climb on to the roof with a gun, as if to shoot a roosting pigeon, and he would take a picture from below, making sure her skirt was 'hitched up to her bum'. 'I'll try and get her to wear stockings and suspenders,' said Charman. 'The Mother Superior won't know until we publish.'

'Christ!' yelled Valdar, nearly biting through the stem of his pipe in excitement. 'That's it.' He seized a layout pad and slashed at it with a red pencil, sketching out a huge picture beneath a glaring headline: 'Nun with a Gun'.

Some of Harry's assignments were harmless enough. In one piece, he revealed that a 'Hollywood beauty expert' who had appeared on television was in fact a Salisbury market-stall trader known to his customers as 'Bugwhiskers'. The make-up salesman was annoyed that Harry had caught up with him. He explained that it was only by impersonating an American that he had been able to get the BBC to take him seriously as a cosmetics expert. 'Still,' he said. 'I've made a thousand nicker out of it.'

Other stories were more disturbing. One February evening in 1955, Harry drove north in his grey Humber Hawk saloon to try to secure an exclusive interview with Anne Hughes, a young woman who had just discovered that her husband, by whom she had two sons, was in fact her long-lost brother. Harry sneaked Anne and her older child out of a hotel in the Midlands, past a gaggle of journalists who were bidding for her story. He sped out of town with Anne and the two-year-old, chased by a fleet of angry hacks. One of Harry's rivals reported him to the police for kidnapping them.

When he had shaken off their pursuers, Harry checked into a hotel in a neighbouring town with Anne and her son. Anne told him how heartbroken she and her husband had been to learn, upon seeing their birth certificates, that they were siblings who had been separated as babies. Harry drove Anne to London the next day and found a room for her and her boy in an army hostel. He filed the story to the *Pictorial*, where it ran on the front page on Sunday under the headline 'The Girl Who Married Her Brother'.

Within days, Anne told Harry that she had fallen in love with a young corporal who was staying in the hostel, and they had decided to marry. Harry was disconcerted by the speed of this courtship, but he agreed to help; as her first marriage was not valid, she was free to take a new husband. He bought Anne a bridal outfit, arranged venues for the wedding and reception, and asked his eighteen-year-old daughter Phyllis to act as Anne's bridesmaid and to make sure that no other reporters spoke to her before the wedding.

When the ceremony was under way, on Thursday 3 March, Harry was told that his bosses at the *Pictorial* had secretly invited Anne's brother to the reception in Knightsbridge. Harry alerted the newly-weds to their unexpected guest just before he arrived. An image printed in the *Pic* on Sunday showed Anne staring at the camera with a fixed, slightly manic grin, while her brother gazed down at her fondly, and her new husband smiled warily at him. It was 'the best, the newsiest, the most story-telling picture of the year', said Harry. But he felt unsettled by the events he had helped to engineer. 'Get me a pint of nice clean beer,' he said to the colleague who had traced Anne's brother. 'I've got a nasty taste in my mouth.'

In 1955 Harry's wife Doreen gave birth to a sixth child, and later that year she suffered a nervous collapse. ('Journalists' wives!' wrote Philip Gibbs in *The Street of Adventure*. 'Those tragedies have not been written down.') Once Doreen had recovered, she begged Harry to quit the *Pictorial*. 'If you get a job sweeping leaves we can be proud of you,' she said. She told him that his mother, who had encouraged his ambitions, no longer approved of his work either. Harry flushed angrily: 'I've got to live,' he said. 'I've got to think of you and the children.' He bought a twin-tub washing machine for Doreen, who hated housework, and a Hoover carpet sweeper.

In May 1956, Harry was despatched to South Benfleet, in Essex, to befriend a woman whose two-year-old twins had died in a fire on a houseboat. It was rumoured that Violet Wright had started the fire herself, so that she could run away to Australia with her married lover, but Harry pretended to believe in her innocence. She signed a contract with him, promising an exclusive of her story in return for £100. The *Pictorial* photographer Frank Charman took a picture of Violet and her boyfriend. In the piece that Harry ghost-wrote on her behalf, Violet said that the deaths of her babies would always haunt her, and denied the rumours that she had set the fire. 'It is a lie,' she said. 'As a woman, I may have been weak and foolish, but no mother made of flesh and blood could stand by and watch her little ones burn.'

Fred Redman, the news editor, congratulated Harry. 'You see why I can't take you off crime?' he said. 'You are the only man in Fleet Street who could do a job like that.'

Harry bought Violet Wright an outfit for her twins' funeral, and on the morning of the ceremony he accompanied her to the church. But as the tiny white coffins were carried in, he was overcome with horror and self-disgust. He walked out of the building, pushing through a crowd of reporters. 'If you can't take it, Harry,' said a friend from the *Mail*, 'it must be tough.' 'I can't take it, Laurie,' Harry replied. He climbed into his Humber and downed a flask of brandy before driving home.

In the same month as Harry's pieces about the houseboat twins, the *Pictorial* ran a series of stories about the strange goings-on at Madame Tussauds. Several men had become obsessed with the museum's wax figures of women, said the paper, among them a night watchman who had damaged an effigy of the French tennis star Suzanne Lenglen by repeatedly kissing its face after dark. A bank official had written to tell the museum that he was consumed with desire for its statue of the Sleeping Beauty. 'My passion is hopeless and fantastic,' he wrote, 'but my job is suffering and I am losing weight. I am stupidly in love with a waxen figure. Every moment of my spare time I spend gazing at her. This is a cry from the heart. Can you help me? Give me a job as a porter or commissionaire, so that I can at least be near the thing I adore.' An Indian maharajah ordered a waxwork woman of his own. 'This is to be perfect in all proportions,' his secretary informed the museum, 'and bust, waist and legs should all conform to Hollywood standards.' The maharajah required a seated figure, his secretary said, so she could join him at meals. 'In this way His Highness hopes to enjoy a woman's beauty without suffering her idle prattle.' The maharajah paid £700, plus shipping, for the waxwork, and when he was next in London he invited its sculptor to dine with him. 'Thank you,' he said, 'for the most perfect female companion a man ever had – beautiful, undemanding and silent!' The *Pictorial* published photographs of the wax women at Madame Tussauds, alongside an image of the effigy of Reg Christie in the Chamber of Horrors. Christie, too, had liked his women still and silent. He stood in a simulacrum of his tiny kitchen, holding the brush with which he was about to paint over the boarded-up hole in his wall.

One night Harry was drinking in the Printer's Devil, opposite Geraldine House, when Reg Payne, the *Pictorial*'s assistant editor, strolled in with some colleagues. 'Heard you'd just come out of jail, Procter,' he called to Harry. 'What was it, drunk in charge of a motor car?' Harry had been convicted more than once of drink-driving. 'That's right, Reg,' returned Harry. 'But, unlike you, I've never been drunk in charge of a newspaper.' Payne stormed out with his posse. The remaining reporters and subeditors cheered Harry for his impertinence, stuffing £1 notes into his pockets as tokens of their appreciation.

Harry had yearned as a boy to be part of the exciting world depicted in Philip Gibbs's *The Street of Adventure*. But Gibbs's novel detailed the humiliations of Fleet Street as well as its pleasures. Journalism, he wrote, 'produces something of the same symptoms as the drug habit. The victim loathes the poison but craves for it. He knows that he is yielding to a habit of life which will inevitably drag him down, and he is filled with self-pity and remorse... He knows that the temporary thrill of excitement will be followed by deadly depression and by the degradation of his intellect and imagination.' A newspaperman endured 'insults and absurdities, and loss of self-respect', wrote Gibbs, 'and mental irritation, and hours of futile work, and articles never published, and articles chopped down, and nights of dreadful doubt, and mornings of blank pessimism, and days of infinite fatigue'.

Harry told his editors that he refused to cover any more crime stories: his health and his nerves would not take it. Later that year he had a breakdown, and the *Pictorial* fired him.

***

In September 1956, within weeks of finishing her essay for Notable British Trials, Fryn was admitted to hospital for an operation on one of her cataracts. She spent a month on the ward, blindfolded. Tottie sent her a daily love letter, which a nurse read aloud to her in her hospital bed.

Once she was back at Pear Tree Cottage, Fryn corresponded with Jim Hodge about his plans for the Evans and Christie volume. 'I don't think your list of illustrations is *very* exciting,' she told him. 'I suppose you have to have the faces of each of the murderees, but after all one murdered woman, especially if a prostitute, looks much like another!' She suggested that he include a 'really nasty' picture of Beryl and Geraldine, perhaps of their bodies in the washhouse.

Even Hodge, the doyen of true-crime publishing, could be shocked by Fryn's indifference to the murder victims. 'I cannot possibly use more bodies as illustrations,' he told her firmly in April 1957. Images of these 'horrid parcels' would be 'merely morbid', he said, and 'carry us no further'.

That month, Fryn discovered that their live-in cook had been entertaining men in her room in Pear Tree Cottage. The 'blonde angel' from Holland, Fryn wrote to a friend in America, had turned out to be a 'practising prostitute' who 'only liked Indians or even a Negro or two'.

When Fryn ordered her to leave, the cook called the police. Fryn explained to a plain clothes officer that a stream of Indians had been coming to her back door. 'Disgusting,' he agreed. The cook left that night in the company of two Indian men. Fryn also sacked the housemaid, who had been covering for her colleague, and joked to a friend that she was thinking of renaming her house 'Black Brothel Cottage'. The cook, she predicted, 'will come to a very sticky end, because Indians are men of violent passions and she is a cheat and a slut and violent too, and she will either be throttled or stabbed'. Fryn's words revealed the panic, as well as the bigotry, that had been aroused in her by the secret sexual activity under her roof. The truth behind the 'Black Brothel' episode may simply have been that Fryn's cook had an Indian boyfriend. Within weeks of leaving Pear Tree Cottage, Dirkje Van Haren married Sujan Singh Patheja in Hampstead.

Fryn's ninety-four-page essay appeared in the Christie and Evans volume of Notable British Trials in the summer of 1957. Sir Norman Birkett, who had secured Fryn's seat in the Old Bailey, wrote to congratulate her on 'the first-class quality of the writing, the grasp of facts, and the judicial presentation of a complex and emotion-exciting topic'. Fryn's contributions to Notable British Trials had taken true-crime writing into new territory, in which an account of a murder was not just a whodunit but a study of a killer's psyche.

Soon after the book was published, Tottie was rushed to hospital with a brain haemorrhage and Fryn was admitted to the same hospital for emergency surgery to her eye. She caught flu over the winter, then returned to hospital for another eye operation.

Back in Pear Tree Cottage, Fryn and Tottie struggled to recover. In the evenings Fryn would feel her way along the corridor to Tottie's bedroom to sit with him and hold his hand.

Fryn suffered a fatal heart attack in the night of 6 August 1958. Their housekeeper found her in the morning and called Tottie to the bedroom. Sobbing, Tottie lifted the husk of Fryn's body from the bed and rocked it high against his chest.

***

Fighting broke out in the streets of Notting Hill at the end of August 1958, when a group of Teddy Boys attacked black residents with sticks and iron bars. The young white men threw milk bottles, bricks and flaming torches at houses occupied by black families in Bramley Road and Oxford Gardens. Outside Latimer Road station, they shouted abuse at a Swedish woman who was married to a Jamaican man. 'Nigger lover!' they called out. 'Kill her!' Crowds of white residents gathered to gawp at the violence. 'They just stood by, these English people did,' wrote the novelist Colin MacInnes, 'and *watched*. Just like at home at evening, with their Ovaltine and slippers, at the telly.'

The attacks continued into the next month. George Lawrence, who had rented 10 Rillington Place from Charles Brown in the early 1950s, was one of dozens of black men chased down Westbourne Park Road by a group of about 150 white men on Thursday 11 September. 'Get back to the jungle, you black ——', shouted one pursuer. 'Hold those niggers!' cried another. The local newspaper that reported this abuse censored the sexual expletives but not the racial slurs.

One black man shouted back: 'You yellow ——, you are frightened of the nigger lovers!' Another pushed a white woman out of his way, crying: 'Get back to your brothel,' and a third exclaimed: 'There is no justice in this country!'

The police arrested sixty-three people caught up in the violence, George Lawrence among them. The Marylebone magistrate said that he would be lenient with the black men who had been carrying offensive weapons – not on the grounds that they had been defending themselves against racist assaults, but because he considered them inherently unstable. 'Some of these coloured men have been so disturbed by what has happened,' he said, 'that they have become more or less irresponsible. They are not as well balanced as white men and some allowance should be made for them.' Lawrence, who had been armed with an iron bar, was fined £20.

The Labour MP for Kensington North, George Rogers, suggested that the black residents were to blame for the disturbance. 'It was wrong to say this trouble had been started by hooligans,' said Rogers. 'It was the reaction of people very sorely tried by some sections of the coloured people.'

The sociologist Ruth Glass, in a study published in 1960, observed that the violence in Notting Hill was driven partly by frictions between black and white people. Because of the housing shortage, she wrote, 'the coloured are most likely to be thought of collectively – as intruders, competitors and "invaders"'. The black residents also aroused anger and resentment, she said, in matters of sexual relations. But Glass argued that the attacks were primarily an outlet for other social discontents. 'All the current unrests are rolled into one on these streets,' she wrote. 'It is the newcomer who is made the scapegoat for physical and social claustrophobia, especially if he is coloured.' Just as unspoken anxieties had emerged as racial hatred in 10 Rillington Place earlier in the decade – and in Pear Tree Cottage earlier that year – they were now being played out on the streets of west London.

***

After being fired from his job at the *Pictorial*, Harry was unable to keep up with the mortgage payments on his house in Kent. He moved north with his family, taking on work at the *Daily Mail*'s Manchester bureau.

Harry could be a kind and funny husband and father. He sometimes cooked for the family: spaghetti bolognaise, to which he had been introduced on an assignment in Italy; roast lamb rubbed with garlic; meat and potato pie. He took his youngest daughters to the pictures and to the library, where he would pick out books for them. He also started to write the story of his life in Fleet Street, giving it the provisional title 'With These Dirty Hands'.

Harry's eighteen-year-old daughter Val typed up the draft, and Harry posted it to Philip Gibbs, the author of *The Street of Adventure*, who had become a publisher after a prolific career as a journalist and novelist. Gibbs wrote back to say that he had read the manuscript with 'very great interest and admiration'. 'I cannot plead guilty to leading you astray by my old novel,' said Gibbs, 'for you have done magnificently as a journalist.' Gibbs sent the draft to the *Sunday Pictorial* for their comments, and received in return a threat of six libel suits. He made substantial excisions, then brought out Harry's memoir in 1958 under the title *The Street of Disillusion: Confessions of a Journalist*.

Harry's book was in part an act of repentance, in part a chronicle of triumph, swerving from shame to exhilaration and back again. He revelled in his scoops and escapades, and spoke admiringly, even warmly, about some of his editors. But he also condemned them and himself for the pain they had caused. 'Exposure of poverty, injustice, crime, is a good thing,' he wrote, 'but if this weapon is used carelessly and ordinary innocent people become its victims, then this is a terrible thing indeed.' To be damned in bold headlines, he said, is 'far worse than any prison sentence. By it, lives are completely ruined – not only the life of the subject of the exposure – but of his wife, his children, his parents, his friends.'

Harry was defensive about some of the methods he had used to get his stories. At one point, he turned on the reader, who he imagined censuring him for how he had obtained the Christie exclusive: 'Sit down there, you, that man in the back row,' he admonished. 'I'll have no hypocritical comment! How many murderers' stories have you read, sir, in the Sunday papers? If you've never read one, then I'll listen to you. If you have read one, then shut up! We poor slaves are your servants, sir, not your masters. We give you what you want because you want it! Let me tell you, sir, before you throw your back-row seat at me, it was tougher for me to do than it is for you to read about it. But you, sir, you were the boss.'

Harry had been forced to remove the most trenchant criticisms of his actual bosses from the book, but it was they who had more directly controlled him. Perhaps his passion for the causes of Derek Bentley and Tim Evans stemmed in part from a desire to stand up for the little guy, the man screwed over by the system. He felt he had been manipulated by his editors in Fleet Street as he thought that Evans had been manipulated by Reg Christie, and Bentley by Christopher Craig.

Harry continued to insist that Christie was guilty of the Evans murders. To Christie, wrote Harry, killing a woman represented a sexual triumph: 'He was proud of the unfortunate women he murdered, like a seducer is proud of his conquests.' It was this, Harry believed, that had stopped him from confessing to the murder of Geraldine: hers was the one killing that shamed him.

Harry did not repeat the details of the murders, and nor did he describe Christie's death by hanging on 15 July 1953. 'I know nothing of that morning,' he wrote. But he chastised himself for the great mistake he had made in 1949. When he first met Christie, he said, he had not thought to suspect him: 'I ought never to be forgiven for my failure on that night.'

After the Christie case, Harry recalled, his fellow journalists had noticed that he was losing his edge – 'Procter's getting soft,' they said. 'Perhaps I was,' he wrote. 'I did not like some of the stories I was writing. Though I was big-time in Fleet Street I was unhappy.'

Harry had 'exposed and exposed and exposed' on behalf of the *Mirror* and the *Pictorial*. Now he was exposing the newspapers themselves. His memoir reversed the peephole, turning his readers' gaze on himself and the publications for which he had worked, even on the readers themselves. His most important legacy as a reporter was not to be the Christie case after all, but this rollicking, remorseful denunciation of the trade to which he had devoted his life. He dedicated his book to Doreen – 'who gave me the courage to tell this tale'.

Hannen Swaffer, the well-known journalist, drama critic and opponent of capital punishment, hailed *The Street of Disillusion* as 'a brave book' by 'the angry young man of crime reporting'. Though most of the Fleet Street papers had ignored its publication, Swaffer urged every newspaper man to read it. 'It may shock you,' he said. 'Some parts will give offence. But it is all part of an extraordinary revelation.'

16

Dust and rubble

In 1958 the *Daily Express* reported that a newly released convict had made fresh claims about Tim Evans. Donald Hume had met Evans in Brixton prison in January 1950, when they were both awaiting trials for murder at the Old Bailey. Tim was a 'flash boy', Hume recalled, who wore high buckled shoes and a camel-hair coat. They got talking, and Hume told Tim that he was an idiot for having confessed to killing Beryl and Geraldine. He advised him to formulate a single story and to stick to it in court: 'Blame everyone but yourself.'

Hume assumed that Tim was guilty. 'I suppose you knocked the missus off,' he said to him. 'I suppose yours is the same kind of innocence as anyone in here.'

To his surprise, Evans denied it: 'No, I didn't knock the wife off.' It was Reg Christie, he said, who had killed her. As for the baby's death: 'It was because the kid kept on crying.'

'So you did it?' asked Hume. 'No,' said Evans, 'but I was there while it was done.' Evans claimed that he would be all right when his case came to trial because 'a policeman' was going to provide him with an alibi.

Immediately after Evans's conviction, Donald Hume was acquitted of the murder of Stanley 'the Spiv' Setty, whose body parts had been discovered in the Essex Marshes, but sentenced to eight years as an accessory to the crime. The supposed killers – who Hume identified as three gangsters known as Greeny, Mac and 'The Boy' – were never found.

In 1950 Hume told a prison officer about his conversations with Tim Evans, and after Christie's trial three years later, this officer urged him to give his evidence to the Scott Henderson inquiry. Hume refused. 'What do I get out of it,' he said, 'other than a bad name with the rest of the chaps here because I'll be helping the police with what I say?' But when he was released in February 1958, Hume was able to get something out of it: payment for his story.

Hume told the *Express* that he hadn't believed all of Tim's claims, particularly the bit about Christie strangling the baby. But now, he said, he was convinced that Evans and Christie had arranged together to murder the child.

Though Hume was hardly a trustworthy source, his recollections sounded credible – he supplied the name of the prison officer to whom he had spoken in 1950 and 1953. But his account raised as many questions as answers. He seemed not to have asked Tim Evans why Christie had killed Beryl, nor why Tim had claimed to have committed the crimes himself.

Later in 1958, Hume – in return for a fat fee of £2,000 – told the *Sunday Pictorial* that it was he who had murdered Stanley Setty after all: he had invented the figures of Greeny, Mac and The Boy. The paper held the piece until Hume had fled to Switzerland, then ran it on the front page under the headline 'I Killed Setty – and Got Away with Murder'. Hume described how he had stabbed Setty in a fight – 'I plunged the blade into his ribs. I know; I heard them crack' – and then sawed up the body in his Golders Green flat, wrapped up the pieces and dropped them into the North Sea from a light aircraft.

Though the press was not allowed to make payments to those suspected of serious crimes, the *Pictorial* was exploiting a loophole in the law: under the double jeopardy rule, Hume could not be charged with Setty's murder again. This was the paper's most outrageous collusion with a killer yet.

***

In 1960, Harry Procter heard that the well-known radio and television presenter Ludovic Kennedy was researching a book about the Rillington Place murders, and he wrote to tell him that Christie had personally admitted to him that he had killed Beryl Evans. He urged Kennedy to look at Christie's written statements, which were still stored in the *Pictorial*'s safe – he may have hoped that Kennedy would quote Christie from these, rather than from the ghost-written version that Harry had composed for the paper. Kennedy, who had already interviewed Joanna Colenbrander about the research that she had carried out with Fryn, thanked Harry for his letter.

Kennedy's wife, the ballet dancer and actress Moira Shearer, appeared that year in Michael Powell's *Peeping Tom*, a British feature film about a cameraman who kills women with a dagger that springs out of his tripod. In one scene, the cameraman murders Shearer's character after persuading her to visit the film studios for a secret screen test late at night. Powell's film traced the killer's violence to his childhood, showing in flashbacks how his father liked to scare him and to film his terrified reactions. It also rooted the murders in a world that demeaned women and eroticised violence against them. *Peeping Tom* included scenes of a man buying nude 'girlie' pictures from a tobacconist's shop, young actresses complaining of being 'pinched' in cars and 'squeezed' on buses, a director on set repeatedly filming an actress as she simulates a faint, women soliciting for custom in

Soho alleys and stripping off in photographers' studios, newspapers splashing lurid stories about murdered girls.

Powell implied that he, as a filmmaker, and we, as the audience, were complicit in a culture that made morbid entertainment of women's bodies. His film turned its gaze on the watchers. It showed how horror might emerge from pornography, how transforming women into erotic objects might be a precondition for murders such as Christie's, as well as their purpose.

Alfred Hitchcock's *Psycho*, another movie about a voyeuristic serial killer released that year, was nominated for four Academy Awards. *Peeping Tom* was so reviled by critics that it was withdrawn from British cinemas. The film destroyed Powell's career.

***

Ludovic Kennedy's *10 Rillington Place*, which appeared in 1961, argued that Tim Evans's conviction had been a travesty of justice. Like Fryn and Harry, Kennedy believed that Christie had tricked Tim Evans into thinking that Beryl had died during an abortion, persuaded him that he would be blamed for her death and told him that Geraldine had been taken in by a foster family. Evans, he argued, was a vulnerable, gullible man with 'the mind of a child' who had been set up by his much cleverer neighbour. Kennedy's crusading book conferred moral purpose on the suspect genre of true-crime writing, and reignited the debate on the death penalty.

Harry had another breakdown in the early 1960s, but he afterwards got back to work, firing off ideas to television producers, writing plays, articles, a novel, a soap opera. The family moved from Manchester to the outskirts of a town in Hertfordshire, then to the Holloway Road in north London, then to a council house in Dagenham, Essex. Harry and Doreen's daughter Valerie became a reporter for a paper in south London, where she learnt that Iris Bentley was still campaigning to overturn her brother Derek's conviction for murder. When Val met her, Iris said that her family had always been grateful for Harry Procter's kindness to them.

In 1965 Ludovic Kennedy helped form the 'Timothy Evans Committee', enlisting supporters such as the psychiatrist Jack Hobson, who had testified at Christie's trial, and the solicitor Michael Eddowes, who Fryn had described as 'a little bit mad' on the subject of Evans's innocence. Eddowes went so far as to buy 10 Ruston Close for £2,000, to preserve the crime scene. Charles Brown, the previous owner, returned to his home town in Jamaica.

That summer, members of the Timothy Evans Committee visited Notting Hill to inspect No 10. Five West Indian women and their babies were occupying the first and second floors, and a Jamaican-born former RAF corporal was living in the ground-floor front room, in which he had burnt frankincense and myrrh to 'smudge' the malign energy.

One of the upstairs tenants grudgingly opened the door to the campaigners, but she lost patience when more than twenty journalists trooped in after them. As Kennedy was showing the party the washhouse in the back yard, she blocked the front door so no one else could enter. The committee and their entourage couldn't get out either. 'All these murders were a long time ago,' she said. 'You've no right to come snooping around and I live here now.' They were trapped inside the house for half an hour before the police arrived.

***

Harry was diagnosed with lung cancer in 1965, and he died on 10 August that year, aged forty-seven.

In October, Harold Wilson's Labour government temporarily

suspended the death penalty for murder, in large part because of the doubts raised by the executions of Tim Evans and Derek Bentley. In November it appointed Daniel Brabin, a High Court judge, to conduct another inquiry into the murder of Geraldine Evans. The inquiry of 1953 had been held in private over a few days. This one was held in public and lasted for many weeks. A group of lawyers presented Brabin with different theories about what had happened at 10 Rillington Place in November 1949, and cross-examined dozens of witnesses.

Brabin had to consider 800,000 words of testimony and another 800,000 words of paperwork. 'I am trying to look at it from all sides,' he remarked at one point, 'but there seems to be no end to the sides.' It had been so long since the crimes that many witnesses could not remember exactly what they had done and seen. There were so many documents that the lawyers got confused about which was which. The witnesses and the lawyers apologised to the judge for their errors. 'Everyone feels guilty, you see,' he joked.

Late in 1966 Brabin published his findings. He did not accept that Evans was a child-like innocent: the psychiatrists who interviewed him, he noted, attributed his low IQ score to poor schooling rather than intellectual deficiency. Nor did he find any evidence that he had been bullied or brainwashed by the police.

Brabin concluded, to the surprise of many involved in the inquiry, that 'it was more probable than not' that Tim Evans had beaten and strangled Beryl on 8 November 1949, that Christie had helped him to conceal the corpse – perhaps because he did not want a police investigation that might uncover the bodies in the garden – and that Christie then killed the baby. In effect, Brabin argued that Tim Evans had been hanged for the wrong murder. Since Evans had been convicted of Geraldine's killing, the Queen granted him a posthumous free pardon in October 1966.

The Labour government made several social reforms over the next few years: in 1967 it decriminalised abortion, as well as consensual sex between men over the age of twenty-one; in 1968 it banned racial discrimination in employment and housing; and in 1969 it finally abolished the death penalty for murder. The Rillington Place murders had helped bring an end to capital punishment in Britain, making Reg Christie the last serial killer to be put to death by the state.

In May 1970 a camera crew visited Ruston Close to make a feature film about the murders. They had arranged to shoot the street scenes outside No 7, as the tenants of No 10 were worried that they would not be allowed back into their house if they moved to a hotel.

The actor Richard Attenborough, who was playing Christie, and John Hurt and Judy Geeson, who were playing Tim and Beryl Evans, drew up in two dark-green Rolls-Royces. As Attenborough emerged from his car, he looked around him with a 'sinister, private smile', reported Oliver Pritchett in the *Guardian*. 'His spectacles were round and his bald head like a monument.' He was dressed in a grey double-breasted suit like the one that Christie had been wearing when he went on the run. One resident of Ruston Close was startled by the actor's resemblance to Reg Christie: 'That didn't half give me a chill,' she remarked. Another woman was less impressed. 'Quite good,' she said, 'but Christie was much taller and slimmer, and thinner in the face.'

In October that year, as part of a slum-clearance programme, demolition work began at Ruston Close. Men in polo shirts and flat caps climbed on to the roofs of the left-hand terrace and swung their pickaxes into No 10 and the neighbouring buildings, smashing the plaster and bricks into dust and rubble. The wrecking crew set fire to the front rooms and hurled wood into the blaze.

Maud Allen of No 19 watched the houses opposite her own start to come down. She didn't want to leave her home, she told a reporter from the *Kensington Post*, even though it was in a terrible state. 'I like the street,' she said. 'It will be quite an upheaval moving away from all my friends and relations and I don't want to be put into one of those tall blocks of flats.' Fred and Jennie Grimes were still living above Maud's family at No 19, and Fred and Bessie Styles were at No 2.

In November 1970, forty tourists paid five shillings each to see the murder house at Ruston Close. Since Christie's building had been destroyed, the tour guide had put a sign reading 'No 10' on the door of No 2. He showed the visitors round, opening a cupboard door to reveal three bodies wrapped in blankets (he had hired assistants to impersonate the victims), and pointing out a chalk outline that he had drawn on the living-room floor.

Maud Allen was angry to find sightseers back on the street. She stuck furious notices on No 19: 'Would you like to live here – it's murder!'; 'Five shillings to see this hell-hole'; 'Four human bodies live in Murder Alley'. By the end of 1971, the whole road had been obliterated, and building work had begun on a new estate.

***

Richard Fleischer's film *10 Rillington Place*, which dramatised Ludovic Kennedy's theory that Christie had framed Tim Evans, was released in 1971 to critical acclaim. Most works inspired by the case adopted the same narrative, from Howard Brenton's play *Christie in Love* in 1969 to the BBC series *Rillington Place* in 2016. This became the standard version of the Rillington Place murders. Evans's wrongful conviction was held up as a cautionary tale about the way that the justice system might fail, and how, under capital punishment, it might condemn the innocent to death. Reg Christie's story passed into modern folklore, a dark fable about a man who liked to kill women, and the serial killer became a recurring figure in popular culture – from Patricia Highsmith's suave sociopath Tom Ripley, who made his first appearance in print in 1955, to Thomas Harris's whispering cannibal, Hannibal Lecter.

Tim's mother and sisters continued to campaign on his behalf. In 2004 the Criminal Cases Review Commission accepted that Evans was innocent of killing either his wife or his child, though it decided not to recommend the case for re-examination.

But several authors have argued that Evans might have been guilty after all, among them Molly Lefebure in *Murder with a Difference* (1958), John Newton Chance in *The Crimes at Rillington Place: a Novelist's Reconstruction* (1961), John Eddowes (the son of Michael) in *The Two Killers of Rillington Place* (1994), Jonathan Oates in *John Christie of Rillington Place: Biography of a Serial Killer* (2012) and John Curnow in *The Murders, Myths and Reality of 10 Rillington Place* (2020). Beryl Evans's youngest brother, Peter Thorley, also believed that Evans was guilty. In his memoir, *Inside 10 Rillington Place: John Christie and Me* (2020), Peter recalled how unhappy his sister had been in the autumn of 1949. Beryl had showed her fifteen-year-old brother the bruises that Tim inflicted on her. 'Every time I went to visit her and my sweet niece,' wrote Peter, 'I could sense the hatred in the house.'

In the first week of November 1949, Peter's father despatched him to New Zealand on a child emigration scheme. Peter learnt in January 1950 that his sister and his niece had died within days of his departure. He had no proof, but he was convinced that Tim had killed both Beryl and the baby.

***

In the vast repository of material on the Evans and Christie cases at the National Archives in London, I came across a document that suggested a different solution to the mystery of Beryl and Geraldine's murders. I also found a handful of other papers in the archive – an exchange of letters between the Attorney-General and a senior civil servant – that showed how this document had been suppressed.

On Sunday 28 June 1953, Sir Lionel Heald, who just that week had successfully prosecuted Christie, received a phone call at his house in the country from his old friend Stanley Bishop, with whom he had served in the RAF during the war. Bishop was an experienced crime reporter who had been recalled from retirement to cover the Christie case for the *News Chronicle*.

Bishop told Heald that a rumour was circulating in Fleet Street that Christie had confessed to a prison guard that he had killed Geraldine Evans. Bishop said he had advised his editor to be wary of the rumour: he suspected that Christie's solicitors, in league with the *Pictorial*, had 'cooked up' the story. But he warned Heald that his paper would have to publish if they could substantiate it.

Heald was very worried. As Attorney-General, he was responsible for the government's legal affairs, and during the trial at the Old Bailey he had done his best to rule out any connection between Reg Christie and the Evans case. He knew that for Christie to admit to the child's murder would be political dynamite, enabling his opponents in the Labour Party to renew their calls for a public inquiry into Evans's conviction and to advance their case for the abolition of capital punishment. A group of Labour MPs had already tabled a bill to suspend the death penalty for five years. Heald agreed with Bishop that the rumour sounded highly dubious, and discouraged him from publishing anything about it.

On Wednesday 1 July 1953, the day of the debate on the bill, Heald was horrified to see a report of the alleged confession in the *News Chronicle*. The article was restrained: Stanley Bishop warned readers that Christie's statements were not to be trusted.

But Heald knew that even this might be enough to blow open the Evans case. He immediately telephoned the editor of the *Evening News*, a London paper that, like the *News Chronicle*, sold more than a million copies a day, and asked him to ignore the story. John N. Marshall agreed to 'damp down' any references to a confession, and to encourage other Fleet Street editors to do the same.

The same morning Heald wrote confidentially to Sir Frank Newsam, the Permanent Under-Secretary of State at the Home Office, to warn how dangerous this rumour might be. The Tory government was already in crisis: both the prime minister and the Foreign Secretary were seriously ill, a situation that was still being kept secret from the public. The last thing Heald and his colleagues needed was a scandal about a miscarriage of justice, a new controversy about the death penalty and a suggestion that the Christie case had been mishandled. 'I am profoundly disturbed by what has happened,' Heald told Newsam. 'I am greatly concerned as to whether anything can possibly be done.' He was desperate to hush up the story.

The two men met that afternoon. Newsam informed Heald that the Home Secretary, Sir David Maxwell Fyfe, had received the prison guard's report alluded to in the *Chronicle*. But Newsam thought that for the time being they were entitled to ignore the memo, as the government was about to announce a private inquiry into the Evans case. It 'would not be right' for the Home Office to investigate, he said, nor for ministers to make any comment.

Later that day in the House of Commons, during the debate on the bill to suspend the death penalty, the government refused to confirm receipt of a report from a prison officer. The bill was defeated by 256 votes to 195. The death penalty remained in force.

The prison guard's memo was supplied to Scott Henderson in his private inquiry the next week, but he made no reference to it in his findings. He may have thought Christie's latest statement just another of his lies and misdirections; he may have realised the trouble it could cause. The existence of the memo was not divulged to the press. Those who were researching the case, such as Fryn Tennyson Jesse and Harry Procter, did not see it. Heald's bid to close down the story had been successful.

But the guard's memo, along with Heald and Newsam's correspondence about it, was preserved in the Home Office archives. At the public inquiry of 1965, the guard – Joseph Albert Roberts – appeared before Mr Justice Brabin to confirm the accuracy of his report. When the forty-year embargo on the Christie files was lifted in 1993, the memo was transferred to the Public Record Office, among many thousands of other documents. It told another tale of collusion.

Joseph Roberts, a medically trained warder at Brixton prison, explained in his memo that he had accompanied Christie to the Old Bailey on the Tuesday and Thursday of his trial. He was with Christie in the dock when the death sentence was passed on him on 25 June 1953. He then led him down to the cells beneath the courts.

As Christie waited for the van to take him to Pentonville, he congratulated himself on having retained his composure in the courtroom. 'The newspapers cannot say that I fainted,' he said, 'or made a scene in the dock.' He offered to tell Roberts something that might be important and could be of value to him. 'If the police only knew,' he said, 'they could also charge me with the murder of Evans's baby girl.'

Roberts asked if he had killed her. Christie responded at first with his usual vagueness – 'More or less as far as I remember but they can't do anything about it now' – but then gave a brusque, perfunctory account of the events of that week in 1949.

Christie said that Tim Evans had asked him to 'do in' Beryl Evans because she was 'in the way', so he had killed her while Tim was at work. Since the little girl was crying, he said, he had to do her in as well, again while Tim was out.

Roberts warned Christie that he would pass this information on to his superiors.

'Why don't you tell the newspapers,' said Christie, 'and make some money out of me?'

Roberts did not sell the story to the press, but on Friday he sent a memo detailing his conversation with Christie to Dr Matheson, Brixton prison's chief medical officer, and Matheson forwarded it to the Home Secretary.

Lionel Heald was wrong if he thought that Cliftons solicitors or the *Sunday Pictorial* had encouraged Christie to make his statement to Roberts – Harry Procter, Ambrose Appelbe and Roy Arthur knew nothing about it.

Arthur went to Pentonville on Wednesday 1 July to ask Christie whether the story of a confession in that morning's *News Chronicle* was true. But by now Christie had learnt that a medical panel was deciding whether to recommend his reprieve on the grounds of insanity. He knew that to admit that he had killed the child, or had killed Beryl on Tim's instructions, would destroy his chances of escaping the noose. He flatly denied to Arthur that he had made a confession to a guard. 'I should like to know who spread the rumour around,' he said indignantly.

Ambrose Appelbe of Cliftons told the press that Christie had not confessed anything. 'He wishes the rumours to this effect to be denied,' said Appelbe, 'as they might prejudice his position.'

But in his statement to Joseph Roberts – so careless, indifferent, matter-of-fact – Christie may at last have been telling the truth. At the moment that he believed his fate was sealed, he had for the first time provided a story about the Evans murders that did not serve his interests. In his previous accounts of Beryl's murder, he had been seeking to show that he was not rational. Now he was describing a contract killing, and claiming to have murdered a baby to save his own skin.

***

The story that Christie told Roberts at first seems improbable – what would have prompted Tim to ask his fastidious, sickly neighbour to kill his wife? But we know that Tim had hit Beryl before, and that the couple had been quarrelling fiercely in the days before her death. Perhaps it was Tim, as Fryn guessed, who had punched Beryl in the face in the evening of Monday 7 November. Perhaps, still drunk and furious, he told Christie that he wanted rid of her. Perhaps Christie offered to do her in for him, under cover of performing the abortion that she wanted. He was probably unable to resist the opportunity that had presented itself.

When Tim got back from work on Tuesday, he may have been shocked to find that Christie had gone through with the murder. He did not know that his neighbour had killed before, nor that he took sexual pleasure in killing. As Tim understood it, Christie had done him a terrible favour. He was as trapped as the protagonist of *Strangers on a Train*, Patricia Highsmith's novel of 1950, who discovers that a casual acquaintance has made good on an offer to kill his wife. Tim Evans felt complicit in Beryl's murder, as if the violence had issued from him, and bound to Christie by their secret.

The two men put Beryl's body in the empty first-floor room, and Christie said that he would dispose of it in a drain. Tim went to work on Wednesday and Thursday, and Christie probably killed Geraldine on Thursday, because her crying threatened to give them away. He may afterwards have told Tim that she had been taken in by a couple in East Acton – or Tim may have known that his neighbour had killed her, as he apparently told Donald Hume while he was on remand in Brixton. Christie advised Tim to sell his furniture and to get out of town.

If this, or something like it, was how the murders unfolded, Tim Evans's conflicting statements make more sense. He panicked when he received his mother's letter in Merthyr Vale on 30 November. Believing that he had caused Beryl's death, and that the net was closing on him, he turned himself in to the Welsh police. He claimed that he had 'disposed of' his wife, having found her dead after she had taken a drug that he had given her. Later that day in Wales, when the police told him that no body had been found in the drain, he made an attempt to explain his error, and to share the blame: he said that Beryl had in fact died while his neighbour was performing an abortion. Both stories were designed to show that Beryl's death was accidental.

Once he was back in Notting Hill, Tim learnt that the strangled bodies of his wife and his daughter had been found, and that Christie was denying any involvement. Realising that the abortion story could not account for both deaths, and believing that Christie had carried out the murders on his behalf, Tim instead told the police that he had himself killed Beryl and Geraldine. He may have been in despair at what he had set in motion, and he knew that Christie would not be a credible suspect in murders for which he had no motive.

Perhaps Christie had promised to come to Tim's rescue if the worst came to the worst. 'Tell Christie I want to see him,' Tim said to his mother when he was awaiting trial in Brixton. 'He is the only one who can help me now.' He told Donald Hume that 'a policeman' was going to give him an alibi – maybe he believed that Christie would enlist a former colleague. When Tim realised that Christie was not going to intervene, he made a last, desperate bid to save himself: 'Christie done it,' he told his family and his lawyers. This was the truth, if not the whole truth.

In the Old Bailey, Tim maintained that Christie had killed Beryl and Geraldine, but he could not, without incriminating himself, explain why he might have done so. If he were to describe exactly what had happened, both he and Christie might hang.

Tim was confused about his own culpability, torn between guilt at his part in the murders and horror at Christie for having carried them out. He didn't know whose fault it really was.

***

Beryl Evans's brother, Peter, said that the killings of his sister and his niece had cast a shadow over his life. He had never stopped thinking about how and why they died. In 2020, at the age of eighty-five, he was still haunted by the thought that Geraldine might have witnessed her mother's murder.

Ruth Fuerst, Muriel Eady, Ethel Christie, Kay Maloney, Rita Nelson and Ina Maclennan were also mourned – by sisters, brothers, mothers, fathers, friends, lovers. Most of them were survived by children, too. Kay left three daughters and two sons in Southampton, Ina left two daughters in Scotland, Rita left a son in Northern Ireland, and Ruth a daughter in Kent. These children had barely known their mothers – Ina's older daughter was only five at the time of her death, Ruth's baby just nine months old – but they will have learnt what became of them.

In December 2023, I got in touch with a niece of one of the women who Reg Christie had killed, to ask if she would talk to me about her aunt. She replied that she was very sorry, but she could not speak to me: it would cause too much hurt to others in her family. I was reminded that even now, more than seventy years after Christie's death, there were people in private pain because of the things that he had done.

NOTES

A NOTE ON MONEY

xx Comparison based on the Retail Price Index, 1953 to 2022, measuringworth.com.

PREFACE

xxi **At about 8 o'clock one foggy night in March:** MEPO 2/9535, the Metropolitan Police files on the Christie case at The National Archives, London. The officer who took Christina Maloney's statement on 30 March recorded the date on which she met the man as Saturday 21 March, but her statement specifies that they met on a Wednesday, probably 18 March, when Christie was still resident at Rillington Place. Weather conditions from weatherspark.com.

PART ONE

CHAPTER ONE: IN THE WALLS

3 **In the evening of Tuesday 24 March:** Harry Procter, *The Street of Disillusion: Confessions of a Journalist*, Allan Wingate, London, 1958.

3 **Harry turned into Rillington Place:** Description of Rillington Place and the early stages of the investigation from photographs and reports in MEPO 2/9535 and in the *Daily Mirror*, *News Chronicle*, *Daily Telegraph*, *Daily Herald*, *Manchester Guardian*, *Evening Standard*, *Sunday Pictorial*, *News of the World*, 26 to 31 March 1953; Jonathan Oates, *John Christie of Rillington*

Place: Biography of a Serial Killer, Wharncliffe True Crime, Barnsley, South Yorkshire, 2012; Conrad Phillips, *Murderer's Moon: Being Studies of Heath, Haigh, Christie and Chesney*, Barker, London, 1956; weather from weatherspark.com.

4 **Camps was dining:** Francis Camps, *Medical & Scientific Investigations in the Christie Case*, Loretta Lay Books, London, 1953.

5 **Harry realised, with a shock:** Procter, *The Street of Disillusion*; *Daily Mail*, 3 December 1949; *Sunday Pictorial*, 28 June 1953.

7 **Harry had been inspired:** Details of Procter's life from Procter, *The Street of Disillusion*; Val Lewis, *Come Fly With Me*, Nauticalia Ltd, London, 2023; and conversations and email exchanges with Procter's daughters Val Lewis and Madeline Clark.

8 **The novelist Keith Waterhouse:** *Gentlemen Ranters*, No 155, https://www.gentlemenranters.com/16_july_2010_244/.

9 **The *Daily Mirror* was pitched:** Adrian Bingham, *Family Newspapers?: Sex, Private Life, and the British Popular Press*, Oxford University Press, Oxford, 2009; Ruth Dudley Edwards, *Newspapermen: Hugh Cudlipp, Cecil Harmsworth King and the Glory Days of Fleet Street*, Secker & Warburg, London, 2003.

10 **Eighty per cent of the 50 million people in Britain:** Colin Seymour-Ure, *The British Press and Broadcasting Since 1945*, Wiley & Sons, Hoboken, NJ, 1996.

10 **'One minute a reporter':** Peter Wildeblood, *Against the Law*, Weidenfeld & Nicolson, London, 1955.

10 **Shortly before Philip Mountbatten's marriage:** 'Prince Philip Took This Picture', *World's Press News*, 27 November 1947; Madeline Clark, 'Remembering when Fleet Street's journalists blagged their way into Prince Philip's stag do', *Press Gazette*, 16 April 2021.

11 **Redman told new recruits:** Tom Mangold, *Splashed!: a Life from Print to Panorama*, Biteback Publishing, London, 2016.

11 **'Though most English men and women':** Geoffrey Gorer, *Exploring English Character*, The Cresset Press, London, 1955.

11 **The war had nearly bankrupted Britain:** See David Kynaston, *Austerity Britain, 1945–51*, Bloomsbury, London, 2007; Kynaston, *Family Britain: 1951–57*, Bloomsbury, London, 2009. Figures on prostitution from B. Seebohm Rowntree & G. R. Lavers, *English Life and Leisure: a Social Study*,

Longmans, Green & Co, London, 1951. Other figures from the Office for National Statistics.

12 **Harry's secret, wrote a fellow journalist:** Mangold, 'Procter-Land Paradise', *British Journalism Review*, Vol 21, No 1, 2010.

12 **'everything in life is but a peep-show':** Philip Gibbs, *The Street of Adventure*, William Heinemann, London, 1909.

12 **Sales of the *Pictorial*:** Hugh Cudlipp, *Publish and be Damned!: the Astonishing Story of the 'Daily Mirror'*, Andrew Dakers Ltd, London, 1953.

12 **In the Scotland Yard press room:** Details of the early stages of the investigation from MEPO 2/9535 and the *Daily Mirror*, *News Chronicle*, *Daily Telegraph*, *Daily Herald*, *Manchester Guardian*, *Evening Standard*, *Kensington Post*, *Sunday Pictorial* and *News of the World*, 26 to 31 March 1953.

14 **The police interviewed:** Tenants' statements in MEPO 2/9535 and HO 291/228, at The National Archives, London. Other details from UK and Ireland, Incoming Passenger Lists, 1878–1960, Kensington North Electoral Register, 1951–1953; England & Wales, Civil Registration Marriage Index, 1916–2005.

15 **the heavyweight champion:** *Daily Mirror*, 19 July 1949.

15 **equipped with a bed:** TS 58/865, The National Archives, London.

16 **Reg Christie had hated:** MEPO 2/9535.

16 **In 1951 the Notting Hill police:** *Kensington News & West London Times*, 16 February 1951; CAB 143/9, papers from the Brabin inquiry at The National Archives, London.

18 **That week's *Kensington Post*:** 27 March 1953. For experiences of West Indian migrants in west London in the 1950s, see Samuel Selvon, *The Lonely Londoners*, Allan Wingate, London, 1956; Selvon, *The Housing Lark*, MacGibbon & Kee, London, 1965; Clair Wills, *Lovers and Strangers: an Immigrant History of Post-War Britain*, Penguin Books, London, 2017.

18 **'Mr Beresford Brown (coloured)':** MEPO 2/9535.

19 **a crowd of more than two hundred:** *News Chronicle*, 30 March 1953.

19 **By now the Rillington Place story:** *Daily Mirror*, 26 March 1953; *News Chronicle*, 28 March 1953; *Sunday Pictorial*, 29 March 1953.

20 **The police continued to scour London:** *Evening Standard*, 28 March 1953.

20 **Christie's house:** *Daily Mirror*, 27 March 1953; *Sunday Dispatch*, 29 March 1953; *News Chronicle*, 31 March 1953.

20 **Harry Procter's great rival:** *News of the World*, 29 March 1953; Bingham, *Family Newspapers?*; Procter, *The Street of Disillusion.*

CHAPTER TWO: THE MAN OF A THOUSAND DOUBLES

21 **Harry headed to the north:** Procter, *The Street of Disillusion*; *Sunday Pictorial*, 28 June & 5 July 1953. Details of Christie's early life also from HO 291/228; MEPO 2/9535; PCOM 9/1668, at The National Archives, London; Oates, *John Christie of Rillington Place*; *Daily Express*, 26 June 1953.

22 **Near Ypres in June:** Details of Christie's war record and injuries from PCOM 9/1668; MEPO 2/9535; G. J. Fitzgerald, 'Chemical Warfare and Medical Response During World War I', *American Journal of Public Health*, April 2008.

23 **The small, dapper Appelbe:** *Sunday Pictorial*, 29 June 1952; *Daily Telegraph*, 20 March 1999.

23 **Appelbe's chief clerk:** Procter, *The Street of Disillusion.*

24 **The newspapers 'zithered with excitement':** Molly Lefebure, *Murder with a Difference: the Cases of Haigh and Christie*, William Heinemann, London, 1958.

24 **Hundreds of real and phantom Christies:** MEPO 2/9535.

28 **'Race Against Time':** *Daily Mirror*, 31 March 1953.

29 **A man who knew Christie:** *Kensington Post*, 3 April 1953.

29 **Later in the morning two brothers:** Account of Christie's arrest from MEPO 2/9535; *Evening Standard*, 31 March 1953; *Daily Mirror*, 1 April 1953; *Daily Herald*, 1 April 1953; *Daily Telegraph*, 1 April 1953.

29 **'She woke me up':** MEPO 2/9535.

30 **As the van from Putney:** J. G. Ballard, *Miracles of Life: Shanghai to Shepperton*, Fourth Estate, London, 2008.

30 **At nine the next morning:** Procter, *The Street of Disillusion.*

30 **The streets around the courthouse:** *Evening Standard*, 1 April 1953; *Daily Herald*, 2 April 1953; *West London Observer*, 3 April 1953.

33 **In Pear Tree Cottage:** F. Tennyson Jesse papers, Tennyson Research Centre, Lincoln.

33 **Mrs Speelman thought:** MEPO 2/9535.

33 **Fryn was part of a golden generation:** Jesse's life from Joanna Colenbrander, *A Portrait of Fryn: a Biography of F. Tennyson Jesse*, André Deutsch, London, 1984; Victoria Stewart, *Crime*

Writing in Interwar Britain: Fact and Fiction in the Golden Age, Cambridge University Press, Cambridge, 2017.

CHAPTER THREE: DREAMS OF DOMINANCE

37 **The police gave Harry:** MEPO 2/9535.

37 **Henry Waddington:** MEPO 2/9535. Ethel's brother had changed his surname from Simpson to Waddington by deed poll in 1938, replacing the name of his father (who was given his mother's maiden name because he was born just before his parents' marriage) with that of his father's father.

37 **Christie claimed:** MEPO 2/9535.

41 **Kathleen, known to her friends as Maloney:** Details of Maloney's life from MEPO 2/9535; HO 291/228; CAB 143/9; CAB 143/50; Oates, *John Christie of Rillington Place*; Camps, *Medical & Scientific Investigations in the Christie Case*.

43 **In Soho, streetwalkers wore:** C. H. Rolph (ed), *Women of the Streets: a Sociological Study of the Common Prostitute*, Secker & Warburg, London, 1955.

48 **'wretched girls':** Keith Simpson, *Forty Years of Murder*, HarperCollins, London, 1978.

48 **The capital's prostitutes:** Rolph (ed), *Women of the Streets*; Robert Fabian, *London After Dark: an Intimate Record of Night Life in London, and a Selection of Crime Stories from the Case Book of Ex-Superintendent Robert Fabian*, The Naldrett Press, London, 1954.

49 **Churchill's government feared:** Frank Mort, *Capital Affairs: the Making of the Permissive Society*, Yale University Press, London, 2010.

49 **Harry Procter urged the police:** *Sunday Pictorial*, 8 March 1953.

49 **The war had been a boom time:** Julia Laite, *Common Prostitutes and Ordinary Citizens: Commercial Sex in London, 1885–1960*, Palgrave Macmillan, London, 2011; Stefan Anthony Slater, 'Containment: Managing Street Prostitution in London, 1918–1959', *Journal of British Studies*, Vol 49, No 2, 2010.

49 **In 1949 the British Social Biology Council:** Account of Wilkinson's work from Rolph (ed), *Women of the Streets*; Laite, *Common Prostitutes and Ordinary Citizens*; *Daily Mirror*, 17 September 1957; *The Bookseller*, 2 April 1955.

51 **If a man wanted:** In *Exploring English Character*, Geoffrey Gorer notes that 'the habit of the man paying all the expenses when a couple go out is almost universal in England'.

51 **Early in March 1953:** *Sunday Pictorial*, 8 & 15 March 1953; Procter, *The Street of Disillusion.*

53 **'We're fighting vice':** Murray Sayle, *A Crooked Sixpence*, MacGibbon & Kee, London, 1960.

53 **A Mass Observation survey:** *Sunday Pictorial*, 3, 10, 17, 24 & 31 July 1949.

54 **'a general slackening':** Harold Scott, *Scotland Yard*, André Deutsch, London, 1954.

54 **In *The Unfair Sex:*** *Sunday Pictorial*, 10 & 17 May 1953; Nina Farewell, *The Unfair Sex: an Exposé of the Human Male for Women of Most Ages*, Frederick Mueller Ltd, London, 1953.

54 **Dr Doris Odlum:** *Daily Mirror*, 9 April 1953.

55 **In *Woman's Own* in 1950:** John Coldstream, *Dirk Bogarde: the Authorised Biography*, Orion, London, 2004; Kynaston, *Austerity Britain.*

CHAPTER FOUR: THE WASHHOUSE

57 **the *Pictorial* and *Mirror* office:** Photographs of Geraldine House in 1953 by Charles Hewitt, Hulton Archive/Getty Images.

57 **Ruby Crocket:** *Sunday Pictorial*, 5 April 1953.

57 **given a transcript:** CAB 143/45.

58 **Beryl Susanna Evans:** Details from MEPO 3/3147, the Metropolitan Police files on the Evans case at The National Archives, London; CAB 143 and TS 58/843–864 at The National Archives, London; F. Tennyson Jesse, *Trials of Timothy John Evans and John Reginald Halliday Christie*, William Hodge & Co, Edinburgh, 1957; Peter Thorley, *Inside 10 Rillington Place: John Christie and Me, the Untold Truth*, Mirror Books, London, 2020; Ludovic Kennedy, *Ten Rillington Place*, Victor Gollancz, London, 1961; Thomas Grant, *Court No. 1: the Trials and Scandals that Shocked Modern Britain*, John Murray, London, 2019; Procter, *The Street of Disillusion.*

64 **George Stonier:** G. W. Stonier, *Pictures on the Pavement*, Michael Joseph, London, 1955.

65 **The residents of Rillington Place:** Testimony of Christie's neighbours and colleagues from MEPO 2/9535; HO 291/228; *Kensington Post*, 27 March, 10 & 24 April 1953; *News of the World*, 26 June 1953; Oates, *John Christie of Rillington Place*; John Curnow, *The Murders, Myths and Reality of 10 Rillington Place*, www.10-rillington-place.co.uk, 2020; Kensington North Electoral Register, 1951–1953.

68 **When Ethel Christie disappeared:** MEPO 2/9535; HO 291/228.

69 **Fryn Tennyson Jesse wondered:** Jesse papers, Lincoln.

70 **Fryn was married:** Details from Jesse papers, Lincoln; Colenbrander, *A Portrait of Fryn*; Jesse, *The Sword of Deborah: First-Hand Impressions of the Women's Army in France*, George H. Doran Co, New York, NY, 1919; Jesse & H. M. Harwood, *While London Burns*, Constable, London, 1942.

72 **'The heart of a woman':** Jesse, *Trials*.

72 **a married man had contacted the Sheffield police:** MEPO 2/9535.

73 **not had full intercourse:** PCOM 9/1668.

75 **After being ditched:** MEPO 2/9535; Thorley, *Inside 10 Rillington Place*.

CHAPTER FIVE: MY SWEETEST DARLING

77 **Derek Curtis-Bennett QC:** *The Times*, 25 July 1956; *Liverpool Echo*, 1 March 1961; email correspondence with Colin Nicholls KC.

77 **Harry returned to Leeds:** Procter, *The Street of Disillusion*.

77 **At 1.40 p.m. on Thursday:** PCOM 9/1668.

78 **But Roy Arthur:** CAB 143/46; HO 291/227.

79 **'I wish the *Sunday Pictorial* exclusively to have my story':** Procter, *The Street of Disillusion*.

79 **In the first instalment:** CAB 143/21.

80 **The editor of the *Daily Mirror*:** Cudlipp, *Publish and be Damned!*

80 **Harry urged Roy Arthur:** Procter, *The Street of Disillusion*.

80 **The two of them arranged:** CAB 143/9; PCOM 9/1668.

81 **At the prison on Monday:** CAB 143/21; CAB 143/9; PCOM 9/1668.

81 **'brain worked abnormally':** *Daily Mirror*, 20 March 1953.

81 **Harry had been barred:** PCOM 9/1668.

81 **In November 1952:** Craig & Bentley case from Procter, *The Street of Disillusion*; *Sunday Pictorial*, 9 November & 14 December 1952, 1 February 1953; David Yallop, *To Encourage*

the Others: Startling New Facts on the Craig/Bentley Case, W. H. Allen, London, 1971.

83 **In the House of Commons:** *Yorkshire Evening Post*, 28 January 1953.

84 **Maxwell Fyfe assured the public:** House of Commons: New Clause (Suspension of Death Penalty), Vol 449, debated on 14 April 1948.

85 **Lewis Nickolls:** Camps, *Medical & Scientific Investigations in the Christie Case*; MEPO 2/9535; CAB 143/18; CAB 143/7; Ian Burney & Neil Pemberton, *Murder and the Making of English CSI*, John Hopkins University Press, Baltimore, MD, 2016.

86 **In a letter to Rebecca West:** Jesse papers, Lincoln.

87 **'murderees':** Jesse, *Murder and Its Motives*, William Heinemann, London, 1924.

87 **Rita Elizabeth Nelson:** MEPO 2/9535; HO 291/228; *Truth*, 29 March 1953; *Evening Standard*, 27 March 1953; *Daily Herald*, 23 April 1953; *Daily Mirror*, 31 April 1953; England & Wales Civil Registration Death Index 1916–2007.

88 **'Christie, photographer':** *Daily Sketch*, 29 June 1953.

91 **Hectorina Mackay Maclennan:** MEPO 2/9535; HO 291/228; Camps, *Medical & Scientific Investigations in the Christie Case*; London, England, Electoral Registers, 1832–1965; England & Wales Civil Registration Death Index 1916–2007.

95 **'Hello Ina Darling':** MEPO 2/9535; the letters were found among the belongings that Maclennan and Baker left at 10 Rillington Place.

CHAPTER SIX: THE ROOMS UPSTAIRS

97 **Outside the Clerkenwell Magistrates' Court:** Account of proceedings from *Daily Herald*, *Daily Mirror*, *News Chronicle*, 23 April 1953; *Kensington Post*, 24 April 1953; *News of the World*, 26 April 1953; MEPO 2/9535.

98 **In the lunch break:** *Evening Standard*, 22 April 1953; CAB 143/9.

99 **On the advice of the Director of Public Prosecutions:** CAB 143/22.

100 **In the notes that he was writing:** CAB 143/21.

101 **Harry arranged to meet:** Procter, *The Street of Disillusion*.

101 **Agnes's first husband:** Details of Evanses' lives from Jesse, *Trials*; Thorley, *Inside 10 Rillington Place*; MEPO 3/3147; CAB 143/38; CAB 143/19; CAB 143/9; TS 58/851.

105 **Roy Arthur and the defence psychiatrist:** TS 58/851; CAB 143/9; CAB 143/70; MEPO 2/9535.

105 **In his notes for Harry:** CAB 143/21.

106 **Harry told Roy Arthur:** Procter, *The Street of Disillusion*.

106 **'We are the defence':** TS 58/851; CAB 143/9.

107 **Roy Arthur told the police:** MEPO 2/9535; *Daily Mirror*, 25 April 1953.

107 **When Roy Arthur visited Brixton:** CAB 143/9.

108 **In a Leeds pub in 1938:** Procter, *The Street of Disillusion*.

109 **'Get yourself a desk':** John Rodgers, 'The Legend's Dynasty', *Gentlemen Ranters*, No 155, https://www.gentlemenranters.com/16_july_2010_244/.

110 **In his essay:** George Orwell, 'Decline of the English Murder', *Tribune*, 15 February 1946.

111 **'England's fantastic':** Oriana Fallaci, *Limelighters*, Michael Joseph, London, 1967.

CHAPTER SEVEN: AN UNEARTHING

113 **She wrote to Sir Norman Birkett:** Jesse papers, Lincoln.

114 **Fryn decided at least to get a glimpse:** Account of visit from Jesse papers, Lincoln; Colenbrander, *A Portrait of Fryn*; Jesse, 'My Fight Against Blindness', *Woman's Own*, 14 February 1957; Jesse, *Trials*.

114 **In the courtroom:** Account of hearing from *Evening Standard*, 29 April 1953; *Daily Mirror*, *Daily Herald*, *News Chronicle* and *Daily Express*, 30 April 1953; *Kensington Post*, 1 May 1953; *Reveille*, 2 August 1953.

116 **John Haskayne:** *Sunday Pictorial*, 26 April 1953; *News Chronicle*, 27 April 1953; HO 291/227.

116 **The *Pictorial* continued:** *Sunday Pictorial*, 26 April & 3 May 1953.

117 **A Home Office official:** PCOM 9/1668.

117 **In the last session:** Account of hearing from *Evening Standard*, 6 May 1953; *Daily Mirror* & *Daily Herald*, 7 May 1953; *Kensington Post*, 8 May 1953.

118 **Immediately after the hearing:** Procter, *The Street of Disillusion*.

119 **Robert Hookway:** MEPO 2/9535.

119 **The next day, Harry was despatched:** Procter, *The Street of Disillusion*.

120 **Roy Arthur asked the Home Office:** HO 299/18; MEPO 2/9535.
120 **Just before dawn:** HO 299/18; MEPO 2/9535; Camps, *Medical & Scientific Investigations in the Christie Case*; Simpson, *Forty Years of Murder*; *Daily Express*, 7 May 1953; *Sunday Pictorial*, 17 May 1953; *Daily Mirror*, *Evening Standard* and *Daily Herald*, 18 May 1953.
121 **'disgusting surmises':** CAB 143/15–21.
122 **Christie spoke in a low voice:** PCOM 9/1668; CAB 143/9; MEPO 2/9535.
122 **Dr John Matheson:** PCOM 9/1668; MEPO 2/9535.
123 **On the prison ward:** *Empire News*, 12 & 19 July 1953.
124 **He chatted easily:** CAB 143/42.
125 **'an excessively inquisitive creature':** Jesse, *Trials*.
125 **In the film:** *Sunday Pictorial*, 28 June 1953.
126 **Fryn was an inquisitive creature:** Jesse papers, Lincoln; Colenbrander, *A Portrait of Fryn*; Jesse, *A Pin to See the Peepshow*, William Heinemann, London, 1934; Jesse, *The Alabaster Cup*, Evans Brothers, London, 1950.

CHAPTER EIGHT: A SYMBOL RATHER THAN A GIRL

131 **In his latest notes:** CAB 143/21.
134 **'Phoenix-time':** Ben Pimlott, *The Queen: Elizabeth II and the Monarchy*, HarperCollins, London, 2001.
134 **the 'gleaming figure':** *News Chronicle*, 3 June 1953.
134 **In an ice-cold gallery:** Cecil Beaton diaries, GB 275 Beaton, St John's College Library Special Collections, University of Cambridge.
135 **At the Commodore picture house:** *West London Observer*, 5 June 1953.
135 **Fryn was watching:** Jesse papers, Lincoln.
136 **At the request of Scotland Yard:** Camps, *Medical & Scientific Investigations in the Christie Case*.
137 **Ruth Margarete Christine Fuerst:** MEPO 2/9535; CAB 143/8; Germany: Index of Jews Whose German Nationality was Annulled by the Nazi Regime, 1935–1944; HO 396/253; HO 396/173; Rachel Pistol, 'Refugees from National Socialism Arriving in Britain 1933–1945', in *Refugees, Relief and Resettlement: Forced Migration and World War II*, Gale,

2020; Edie Martin, 'Living in Wire: Jewish Women and the British Detention System', The Wiener Holocaust Library, 16 June 2021; England & Wales Civil Registration Birth Index 1916–2007; England & Wales Civil Registration Death Index 1916–2007.

140 **Muriel Amelia Eady:** MEPO 2/9535; England & Wales Civil Registration Birth Index 1916–2007; 1939 England & Wales Register; London, England, Electoral Registers, 1832–1965; England & Wales Civil Registration Death Index 1916–2007.

142 **'We are really going to town':** *Kensington Post*, 24 April & 29 May 1953.

142 **Harry visited Rillington Place:** *Sunday Pictorial*, 7 June 1953. Account of party from *West London Observer*, 29 May 1953; *Kensington Post*, 24 April & 12 June 1953; *Kensington News*, 12 June 1953.

144 **By now, Lewis Nickolls:** HO 299/18; MEPO 2/9535.

144 **In June, Harry's colleague:** CAB 143/9; CAB 143/15; MEPO 3/3147.

145 **Christie retracted his claim:** CAB 143/9; CAB 143/21.

146 **At Pear Tree Cottage:** Jesse papers, Lincoln.

PART TWO

CHAPTER NINE: THAT BODY-RIDDEN HOUSE

149 **On Monday 22 June:** Jesse papers, Lincoln.

149 **A long queue had formed:** *Daily Mail*, 22 June 1953.

149 **To Fryn's horror:** Jesse papers, Lincoln.

150 **Also on their benches:** CRIM 8/22, applications for passes to Christie's trial at The National Archives, London.

150 **A man sitting next to Cox:** Francis Iles, 'Trial Without Drama', *Sunday Times*, 28 June 1953.

151 **On the previous Thursday, a jury at the Old Bailey:** *Daily Mirror*, 19 June 1953.

152 **The 'white curves went up':** Jesse, *A Pin to See the Peepshow*.

152 **At 11 a.m., an usher rapped:** Account of trial from PCOM 9/1668; MEPO 2/9535; Jesse, *Trials*; Jesse papers, Lincoln; GB 275 Beaton, University of Cambridge; Duncan Webb, *Deadline for Crime*, Francis Mueller, London, 1955; Iles, 'Trial Without Drama';

photographs at Getty Images and Alamy; reports in *Manchester Guardian*, *Evening Standard*, *News Chronicle*, *Daily Express*, *Daily Mirror*, *Evening News*, *Daily Herald*, *Daily Telegraph*, *Daily Mail*, *Yorkshire Evening Post*, *Sunday Dispatch*, 22 to 28 June 1953.

155 **They were now married:** England & Wales, Civil Registration Index, 1916–2005.

156 **The foreign reporters:** Lunch arrangements from Sybille Bedford, *The Best We Can Do: the Trial of John Bodkin Adam*, Collins, London, 1958.

164 **Tottie was waiting:** Colenbrander, *A Portrait of Fryn*; Jesse papers, Lincoln.

CHAPTER TEN: THE ROPE DECKCHAIR

165 **Cecil Beaton, fresh from photographing:** Account of trial from PCOM 9/1668; MEPO 2/9535; Jesse, *Trials*; Jesse papers, Lincoln; GB 275 Beaton, University of Cambridge; Webb, *Deadline for Crime*; Iles, 'Trial Without Drama'; photographs at Getty Images and Alamy; reports in *Manchester Guardian*, *Evening Standard*, *News Chronicle*, *Daily Express*, *Daily Mirror*, *Evening News*, *Daily Herald*, *Daily Telegraph*, *Daily Mail*, *Yorkshire Evening Post*, *Sunday Dispatch*, 22 to 28 June 1953.

178 **Rosalind Wilkinson:** Rolph (ed), *Women of the Streets*.

179 **At Pentonville prison:** *Daily Sketch*, 29 June 1953; CAB 143/9.

CHAPTER ELEVEN: GASSINGS

181 **According to a *Pictorial* columnist:** *Sunday Pictorial*, 5 July 1953.

182 **Agnes sent her letter:** PCOM 9/1668; CAB 143/9.

182 **'He was anxious to try out his story':** *Sunday Pictorial*, 28 June 1953.

183 **In the foggy morning:** *Sunday Pictorial*, 28 June 1953; MEPO 2/9535; CAB 143/21.

185 **The *News of the World*:** 28 June 1953; MEPO 2/9535.

185 **When Christie was on the run:** MEPO 2/9535.

187 **In the run-up to the trial:** Judy Cameron-Wilson, 'I Once Met… John Christie', *The Oldie Annual 2004*, Oldie Publications Ltd, London, 2004.

188 **Faith Wallis had been in charge:** MEPO 2/9535.

190 **Perhaps Faith was also right:** MEPO 2/9535; PCOM 9/1668.

190 **Christie's injury:** Frederick Mott, *War Neuroses and Shell Shock*, Hodder & Stoughton, London, 1919; S. C. Linden & E. Jones, '"Shell shock" Revisited: an Examination of the Case Records of the National Hospital in London', *Medical History*, Vol 58, No 4, 2014; M. Satkin, M. Ghanei, A. Ebadi, S. Allahverdi, M. Elikaei, 'The Quality of Life of Mustard Gas Victims: a Systematic Review', *Tanaffos*, Vol 16, No 2, 2017.

191 **The most revealing:** *Sunday Dispatch*, 28 June 1953; MEPO 2/9535.

193 **The Australian newspaper *Truth*:** 3 July 1953.

194 **But the *News Chronicle*:** 26 June 1953.

194 ***The Daily Worker*:** 1 July 1953.

194 **On Sunday 28 June:** *Birmingham Daily Gazette*, 29 June 1953.

195 **As the last constable:** *Daily Herald*, 30 June 1953.

195 **Brown applied:** HO 287/196.

195 **Someone stole the black door knocker:** *Daily Mail* & *Daily Telegraph*, 4 July 1953.

196 **As Cecil Beaton was weeding:** GB 275 Beaton, University of Cambridge.

CHAPTER TWELVE: INTO THE FALL

197 **On Saturday 27 June:** Lawyers' dealings with Christie in PCOM 9/1668; CAB 143/9; CAB 143/45–46; HO 291/227; *Sunday Pictorial*, 28 June 1953.

197 **On Wednesday:** *News Chronicle*, 1 July 1953; PCOM 9/1668; CAB 143/9.

197 **Harry was frustrated:** Procter, *The Street of Disillusion.*

197 **Ross wrote to his MP:** PCOM 9/1668.

198 **'My Urge to Kill Ten Women':** *Sunday Pictorial*, 5 July 1953.

199 **He was not given an answer:** PCOM 9/1668.

199 **Scott Henderson called:** TS 58/843–864.

200 **In his cell:** PCOM 9/1668.

200 **Christie received a letter:** *Daily Telegraph*, 10 July 1953; PCOM 9/1668.

200 **In the second part:** *Sunday Pictorial*, 12 July 1953.

201 **The conclusions:** MEPO 2/9535.

201 **He was 'conceited, cool, cunning':** HO 291/227.

201 **Christie sent Harry:** Procter, *The Street of Disillusion.*

202 **Reg Christie made a will:** PCOM 9/1668.

202 **Shortly before 9 a.m.:** PCOM 9/1668; Albert Pierrepoint, *Executioner: Pierrepoint*, Harrap, London, 1974.

203 **Within an hour:** *Daily Mirror*, 16 July 1953.

203 **a week later:** *Daily Mirror*, 22 July 1953.

203 **They were interred:** MEPO 2/9535.

203 **Rita's mother:** MEPO 2/9535.

204 **Some of the psychiatrists:** PCOM 9/1668; MEPO 2/9535; Kennedy, *Ten Rillington Place*.

204 **the *Pictorial* had run a series:** 18 & 25 May, 1 & 8 June 1952.

205 **The final part:** *Sunday Pictorial*, 19 July 1953.

205 **Harry's last pieces:** Details of *Pictorial* office from Mangold, *Splashed!*

206 **In 1939:** Procter, *The Street of Disillusion*.

206 **Several prominent figures:** Richard Davenport-Hines, *An English Affair: Sex, Class and War in the Age of Profumo*, HarperPress, London, 2013; *Sunday Express*, 23 August 1953; *Daily Mirror*, 11 to 13 November 1953, quoted in Bingham, *Family Newspapers?*

207 **Harry begged his editors:** Procter, *The Street of Disillusion*.

207 **In a stormy session:** House of Commons: Evans Case (Report of Inquiry), Vol 518: debated on 29 July 1953.

209 **Jim Hodge told Fryn:** Jesse papers, Lincoln.

PART THREE

CHAPTER THIRTEEN: THE BACK ROOM

213 **Each morning:** Colenbrander, *A Portrait of Fryn*.

214 **Fryn thought that Reg Christie:** Jesse, *Trials*.

214 **A group of women:** Stephen Brooke, 'A New World for Women?' *American Historical Review*, Vol 106, No 2, 2001.

214 **The left-wing paper:** *Reynolds News*, 12 December 1952, quoted in Bingham, *Family Newspapers?*

214 **In her novel:** Jesse, *A Pin to See the Peepshow*.

215 **Even before the war:** Report of the Inter-Departmental Committee on Abortion, 1939: MH 71/30.

215 **A back-street abortionist:** Brooke, 'A New World for Women?'; Russell S. Fisher, 'Criminal Abortion', *The Journal of Criminal Law and Criminology*, Vol 42, No 2, 1952; Maggie Koerth, 'What the History of Back-Alley Abortions Can Teach Us

About a Future Without Roe', *FiveThirtyEight*, 2 June 2022; Emma Jones & Neil Pemberton, 'Ten Rillington Place and the Changing Politics of Abortion in Modern Britain', *The Historical Journal*, Vol 57, No 4, 2014.

215 **He 'assaults his subjects':** Jesse, *Trials*.

216 **it was widely rumoured:** Trevallion in MEPO 3/3147, CAB 143/39; Strait in CAB 143/43; Mackay & Endicott in CAB 143/46; Hide in CAB 143/39; customers at tobacconists in CAB 143/9.

216 **several neighbours assumed:** Procter, *The Street of Disillusion*.

216 **'Oh, I see':** Jesse, *Trials*.

216 **In 1949, the police:** MEPO 3/3147.

217 **'Such knowledge as she had':** Jesse, *Trials*.

217 **her doctor prescribed:** MEPO 2/9535.

217 **'bundle of nerves':** CAB 143/21.

217 **In April that year:** MEPO 2/9535.

218 **'My head was just splitting':** CAB 143/21.

218 **Ethel wrote to her elderly aunt:** CAB 143/21; MEPO 2/9535.

218 **'I wish we could get out of here':** MEPO 2/9535.

218 **a foul, claggy blanket:** Christine L. Corton, *London Fog: the Biography*, Belknap, London, 2015.

219 **'It was really dreadful':** MEPO 2/9535.

219 **Joanna drove:** Jesse papers, Lincoln; Jesse, *Trials*.

219 **At the end of 1953:** *The People*, 20 December 1953; Kensington North Electoral Register, 1951–1953.

219 **One day in the spring:** *Kensington Post*, 5 March 1954.

220 **Rosalind Wilkinson:** Rolph (ed), *Women of the Streets*.

221 **Sanchez and Brown had been arrested:** *Kensington Post*, 29 December 1950.

221 **Sanchez had since become:** *Sunday Dispatch*, 5 September 1954; *Daily Herald* & *News Chronicle*, 26 November 1954.

221 **Fryn and Joanna returned:** Jesse papers, Lincoln.

223 **She was so devoted:** Jesse, *Sabi Pas or, I Don't Know*, William Heinemann, London, 1935.

223 **Fryn and Tottie's poodle:** Jesse papers, Lincoln.

223 **Rosalind Wilkinson's survey:** Rolph (ed), *Women of the Streets*; *Truth*, 1 April 1955; Rolph, *Living Twice: an Autobiography*, Gollancz, London, 1974; *Marylebone Mercury*, 1 April 1955; *The Bookseller*, 2 April 1955; *Daily Mirror*, 17 September 1957.

CHAPTER FOURTEEN: A DEAR LITTLE BABY

225 **It had taken Jim Hodge:** Jesse's correspondence and research in Jesse papers, Lincoln.
229 **a strong defence of Evans:** *Observer*, 20 September 1953.
229 **'the risk of an innocent man':** Scott, *Scotland Yard*.
229 **But James Chuter Ede:** House of Commons: Capital Punishment (Royal Commission's Report), Vol 536: debated on 10 February 1955.
229 **Fryn laboured:** Jesse papers, Lincoln; Colenbrander, *A Portrait of Fryn*.
230 **'that space of some ten inches by five':** Jesse, *A Pin to See the Peepshow*.
230 **In April 1956:** Jesse papers, Lincoln; TS 58/851.
231 **Curtis-Bennett had sunk into dissipation:** Jesse papers, Lincoln; *Daily Herald*, 24 July 1956; *Liverpool Echo*, 1 March 1961.
232 **Joanna drove Fryn:** Jesse papers, Lincoln; TS 58/851.
236 **In her essay:** Jesse, *Trials*.
237 **Hodge told Fryn:** Jesse papers, Lincoln.

CHAPTER FIFTEEN: WITH THESE DIRTY HANDS

239 **Occasionally, in the years after the Christie case:** Procter, *The Street of Disillusion*.
240 **In the *Pictorial* conference:** Mangold, *Splashed!*; Mangold, 'Procter-Land Paradise'.
240 **Some of Harry's assignments:** Procter, *The Street of Disillusion*.
242 **In 1955 Harry's wife:** Lewis, *Come Fly With Me*.
242 **'If you get a job sweeping leaves':** Procter, *The Street of Disillusion*.
242 **In May 1956:** Procter, *The Street of Disillusion*; *Sunday Pictorial*, 27 May 1956.
243 **In the same month:** *Sunday Pictorial*, 20 & 27 May 1956.
244 **One night Harry was drinking:** Brian Hitchen, 'Drunk In Charge…', *Gentlemen Ranters*, No 155, https://www.gentlemenranters.com/16_july_2010_244/.
245 **In September 1956:** Jesse papers, Lincoln; Colenbrander, *A Portrait of Fryn*.
246 **Within weeks of leaving:** England & Wales, Civil Registration Marriage Index, 1916–2005.

247 **Fighting broke out:** Pearl Jephcott, *A Troubled Area: Notes on Notting Hill*, Faber & Faber, London, 1964; Fiona White, *Streets of Sin: a Dark Biography of Notting Hill*, The History Press, London, 2015; Ken Olende, 'The Notting Hill Riot and a Carnival of Defiance', *Socialist Worker*, 19 August 2008; Christopher Hilliard, 'Mapping the Notting Hill Riots: Racism and the Streets of Post-War Britain', *History Workshop Journal*, Vol 93, No 1, 2022.

247 **'They just stood by':** Colin MacInnes, *Absolute Beginners*, Allison & Busby, London, 1958.

247 **George Lawrence:** *Marylebone Mercury*, 12 September 1958.

248 **The Labour MP:** *News Chronicle*, 8 September 1958.

248 **The sociologist:** Ruth Glass, *London's Newcomers: the West Indian Migrants*, Harvard University Press, London, 1960.

248 **After being fired:** Procter, *The Street of Disillusion*; Lewis, *Come Fly With Me*; conversations and email exchanges with Val Lewis and Madeline Clark; *Gentlemen Ranters*, No 159, www.gentlemenranters.com/13_august_2010_249/; Revel Barker, introduction to Procter, *The Street of Disillusion*, Revel Barker Publishing, Brighton, 2010.

CHAPTER SIXTEEN: DUST AND RUBBLE

253 **In 1958 the *Daily Express*:** 7 February 1958.

254 **Later in 1958:** *Sunday Pictorial*, 1 June 1958; CAB 143/42; Duncan Campbell, 'Hacks in the Dock', *Guardian*, 31 July 2014; Roy Greenslade, 'How to Make an Excuse and Leave', *British Journalism Review*, 30 August 2018.

255 **In 1960, Harry Procter heard:** CAB 143/26.

256 **'the mind of a child':** Kennedy, *Ten Rillington Place*.

256 **Harry had another breakdown:** Lewis, *Come Fly With Me*; conversations and email exchanges with Val Lewis and Madeline Clark.

257 **In 1965 Ludovic Kennedy helped form:** Harold Evans, *My Paper Chase: True Stories of Vanished Times: an Autobiography*, Little, Brown, New York, NY, 2009.

257 **Charles Brown:** *Sunday Times*, 4 September 1966.

257 **a Jamaican-born former RAF corporal:** *Sunday Times*, 4 September 1966.

257 **'All these murders':** *Guardian*, 29 July 1965.
257 **Harry was diagnosed:** Information from Val Lewis.
258 **This one was held in public:** CAB 143/1–70; conversation with John Previte KC.
258 **Brabin had to consider:** *Sunday Times*, 23 January 1966.
259 **In May 1970:** *Guardian*, 18 May 1970.
259 **In October that year:** *Demolition Workers – Kensington* (1971) at www.britishpathe.com/asset/195116/.
260 **Maud Allen of No 19:** *Kensington Post*, 7 March 1969 & 9 October 1970.
260 **In November 1970:** *Birmingham Daily Post* and *Daily Mirror*, 30 November 1970; *Kensington Post*, 4 December 1970.
261 **Tom Ripley:** Patricia Highsmith, *The Talented Mr Ripley*, Coward-McCann, New York, NY, 1955.
261 **accepted that Evans was innocent:** *Mary Westlake v Criminal Cases Review Commission*, EWHC 2779 (Admin) (17 November 2004), High Court (England and Wales).
262 **On Sunday 28 June:** HO 291/227.
263 **Later that day:** House of Commons: Death Penalty (Suspension), Vol 518: debated on 1 July 1953.
264 **At the public inquiry:** CAB 143/38.
264 **Joseph Roberts, a medically trained warder:** PCOM 9/1668; CAB 143/9; CAB 143/38.
266 **He was as trapped:** Highsmith, *Strangers on a Train*, Harper & Bros, New York, NY, 1950.
268 **Beryl Evans's brother:** Thorley, *Inside 10 Rillington Place*.
268 **Kay left three daughters:** England & Wales Civil Registration Birth Index 1916–2007.

ACKNOWLEDGEMENTS

Huge thanks to my friends and my family for helping me to write this book, especially to those who read and commented on my drafts, and to Val Lewis and Madeline Clark, Harry Procter's daughters, for helping me to tell their father's story. I am very grateful to Thomas Grant KC and Colin Nicholls KC for advice on legal aspects of the case, to Anne Molyneux for showing me round the Old Bailey, to Craig Brown for pointing me to new material about Christie, and to John Previte KC for talking to me about the Brabin inquiry.

My thanks to the staff at the National Archives, the British Library, the London Library, St John's College, Cambridge, and the Tennyson Research Centre in Lincoln. Extracts from Cecil Beaton's diaries are © The Literary Executor of the late Sir Cecil Beaton, 2024, published by permission of the Master and Fellows of St John's College, Cambridge.

Thank you to my wonderful editors, Jasmine Horsey at Bloomsbury and Virginia Smith Younce at Penguin Press, and to all the others who helped to make this book, including Paul Baggaley, Anouska Levy, Rachel Wilkie, Jonny Coward, David Mann, Francisco Vilhena, Caroline Bovey and Kate Johnson. And thanks as ever to my excellent agents: Georgia Garrett, Laurence Laluyaux, Stephen Edwards and Julia Kreitman in London, and Melanie Jackson in New York.

INDEX

NOTE ON THE TYPE

The text of this book is set in Fournier. Fournier is derived from the *romain du roi*, which was created towards the end of the seventeenth century from designs made by a committee of the Académie of Sciences for the exclusive use of the Imprimerie Royale. The original Fournier types were cut by the famous Paris founder Pierre Simon Fournier in about 1742. These types were some of the most influential designs of the eight and are counted among the earliest examples of the 'transitional' style of typeface. This Monotype version dates from 1924. Fournier is a light, clear face whose distinctive features are capital letters that are quite tall and bold in relation to the lower-case letters, and *decorative italics, which show the influence of the calligraphy of Fournier's time.*

ALSO AVAILABLE

THE QUEEN OF WHALE CAY

The Eccentric Story of 'Joe' Carstairs, Fastest Woman on Water

THE BOOK OF PHOBIAS AND MANIAS

A History of Obsession

THE HAUNTING OF ALMA FIELDING

A True Ghost Story

THE WICKED BOY

An Infamous Murder in Victorian London